Soils, Land and Food
Managing the land during the twenty-first century

A major challenge of the twenty-first century will be to ensure sufficient global food production to cope with the burgeoning world population. *Soils, Land and Food* is a short text aimed at undergraduates, graduates, agricultural scientists and policy makers which describes how the use of technology in soil management can increase and sustain agricultural production. The book leads the reader through the development of techniques of land management and discusses reasons why some agricultural projects have succeeded while others have failed. It shows how surveying and protecting soils before new land is brought into cultivation, raising soil fertility, increasing inputs and improving economic conditions can all help to increase food production. Particular emphasis is placed on the need for both economic change and technological innovation in developing countries where, in many cases, food production will need to more than double in the next 50 years.

ALAN WILD is Emeritus Professor in the Department of Soil Science at the University of Reading.

Soils, Land and Food

Managing the land during the twenty-first century

ALAN WILD
University of Reading

PUBLISHED BY THE PRESS SYNDICATE OF THE UNIVERSITY OF CAMBRIDGE
The Pitt Building, Trumpington Street, Cambridge, United Kingdom

CAMBRIDGE UNIVERSITY PRESS
The Edinburgh Building, Cambridge CB2 2RU, UK
40 West 20th Street, New York, NY 10011-4211, USA
477 Williamstown Road, Port Melbourne, VIC 3207, Australia
Ruiz de Alarcón 13, 28014 Madrid, Spain
Dock House, The Waterfront, Cape Town 8001, South Africa

http://www.cambridge.org

First published 2003

Printed in the United Kingdom at the University Press, Cambridge

Typeface Swift 9/13pt   *System* LaTeX 2_ε [TB]

A catalogue record for this book is available from the British Library

Library of Congress Cataloguing in Publication data

Wild, Alan.
Soils, land, and food: managing the land during the 21st century / Alan Wild.
      p.   cm.
Includes bibliographical references (p.   ).
ISBN 0 521 82065 0 – ISBN 0 521 52759 7 (pb.)
1. Soil management.   2. Soil fertility.   3. Land use – Management.
4. Food supply.   I. Title.
S591.W723   2002
631.4 – dc21   2002067258

ISBN 0 521 82065 0 hardback
ISBN 0 521 52759 7 paperback

Contents

Preface

During the twenty-first century one of the greatest challenges for mankind will be to ensure that the production of food is sufficient to meet the demand of an extra two billion people by 2025 and three billion by 2050. Most of this increase in demand will be in countries of the developing world. If those living on the edge of starvation are to be better fed the increase will need to be bigger than the increase in population: a doubling of global food production may be required by the middle of the century.

From the early days of agriculture more land was brought into cultivation as populations increased (cause and effect are intertwined). Farming systems adapted to the local environment evolved from hunting and gathering economies. New crops and domesticated animals were introduced from other regions, more land was cultivated and new techniques were developed. There was success but also failure as some soils lost their fertility by nutrient mining and, more dramatically, by erosion. Although most people in the world have an adequate diet, whether we can meet the demand for food and still retain our prime ecosystems is a question for the future.

The underlying theme throughout this book is the standard of land and soil management, soil being essentially a non-renewable resource. The key player is the farmer, who will use good management skills if he has security of land tenure. He will increase output if he has incentive to make more profit, which depends on there being people with money to buy his produce. The required economic and social conditions are referred to in this book but are not discussed in detail. The other arm of development, which is more fully discussed here, is the use of technologies that can increase and sustain agricultural output.

It has been said that to understand ourselves we need to know our history. This applies with equal force to our understanding of land management. For this reason, following definitions of terms in Chapter 1 and a description of natural resources in Chapter 2, an overview of the development of land management since the start of agriculture is given (Chapter 3). This is followed by descriptions of soils, particularly as a source of nutrients (Chapter 4), a chapter on effects of land degradation (Chapter 5) and chapters on raising yields by fertilizer use (Chapter 6) and improved water supplies (Chapter 7). Readers whose interest is in agricultural development rather than in the technologies that help to make it possible may prefer to omit these four chapters. The three that follow deal with broader issues: examples of changing land use (Chapter 8) and the means of increasing agricultural production in developing countries (Chapters 9 and 10). These two latter chapters point to the probability that more land will be used for food production where land is available and cheap. However, raising crop yields by the means described in the earlier chapters will become increasingly necessary. As the populations of many developing countries are projected to increase for more than 50 years, and some for over 100 years, the land will need to remain productive, that is, agricultural output must be increased and this increase must be sustainable. Chapter 11 gives an overview of, and refers to uncertainties that may affect, food production in the future.

The great diversity worldwide of economic and social conditions, climates and soils makes it impossible for one book or one author to discuss the required agricultural development of individual countries. Further, decisions will be made within each country by farmers, the national government or both, ideally acting together. There are, however, general principles to be followed if agricultural development is to be successful. These principles emerge in the successive chapters.

Readers who are specialists will be aware that many references I have used are secondary sources of information. This could not be avoided, because I have tried to put the management of the land and its soils into the broad stream of agricultural development on which our supply of food depends. If specialists with more direct knowledge of the conditions in their own country or region put similar emphasis on the management of the land and its soils my broad treatment will have been justified.

Alan Wild
Reading

Acknowledgements

I am pleased to acknowledge my debt to the late Professor Hugh Bunting for early discussions that helped to develop ideas, for suggestions from his own extensive experience, particularly in Africa, and for his personal account of the East African groundnut scheme. Both he and Dr David Rowell drew my attention to errors in the manuscript; those that remain are my responsibility. I am also grateful to members of the Department of Soil Science at the University of Reading for references to material that I would otherwise have overlooked, and to the staff of the University Library for providing a wide range of books. It is also a pleasure to acknowledge the help of John Wild for calculating linear regressions and of the secretarial staff of the Department, particularly Sue Hawthorne, who typed several versions of the manuscript on top of her own programme of work. Finally, and most of all, I thank my wife Ann, whose sacrifices during the long period of writing this book I readily acknowledge. Without her this book could not, and would not, have been written.

I thank the following for permission to reproduce figures and tables: Applied Science Publishers (Figure 7.2); CAB International (Table 5.2); Cambridge University Press (Figures 3.1, 6.3, 8.1); Elsevier (Table 5.3); FAO (Tables 6.1, 9.5, 9.8); Intergovernmental Panel on Climate Change (Figure 2.1); John Wiley & Sons (Figures 5.1, 8.3 and Tables 9.5, 9.8); Longman (Table 7.1); Oxford University Press (Tables 2.2, 6.4); Routledge Publishers and the author J.N. Postgate (Figure 3.2); the Royal Society (Figure 7.1 and Table 4.5); Springer-Verlag (Table 2.1).

1

Managing land for food production in the twenty-first century: an outline

Agriculture is often seen as conservative in the sense that it changes only slowly. There are good reasons why this change is slow: agriculture is a complex activity that has to be adapted to particular environmental conditions, there must be no risk to food for the family, and the farmer has to perceive a material and usually financial benefit of any changes. It is nevertheless reasonable to assume that from the start of agriculture change has taken place in response to change in demand. The gradual change from hunting and gathering that supported limited, mobile populations to an increasing dependence on settled agriculture led to more and more people needing more productivity from the land.

Archaeological and historical records tell us about early innovations, for example the evolution and spread of the deliberate production of crops in different parts of the world aided by the introduction of such techniques as the animal-drawn plough, irrigation and terracing. Up until the last few centuries changes to agricultural practices occurred slowly. The changes became more rapid with the expansion of cultivation into new lands, with an increase in the human population and, especially from the sixteenth century, with the spread of crops between continents and countries and the development of more farm implements.

In the nineteenth and twentieth centuries the increase in demand for agricultural products was met by the use of more land, the introduction of higher-yielding crops and domesticated animals, and the use of fertilizers and pesticides. Of fundamental significance was the application of scientific methods. Farming no longer had to rely solely on experience and tradition. It could be made more secure by assessment of the natural resources, experimentation in the field and

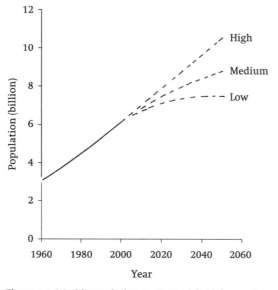

Figure 1.1. World population to 1995 with high, medium and low projections (variants) to 2050. Data from United Nations (1999).

laboratory, investigations of parts of the agricultural system and of the system as a whole, and monitoring the effects of the introduced changes. Although not always used, these methods have become more important as the increasing world population has resulted in the need for more productive and more efficient forms of agriculture in both rich and poor countries.

The upward trend in the world population since 1960 is shown in Figure 1.1. Depending on the assumptions made (the main one being by how much birth rates will change), the increase will continue until around 2040 or beyond 2050. In the medium variant the increase from 1995 is 2.15 billion people by 2025 and 3.24 billion by 2050 (United Nations, 1999). However, there is considerable uncertainty as projections are made further and further into the future: for example, the increases by 2050 are 1.67 billion and 5.0 billion in the low and high variants, respectively. Most of the growth will occur in Asia and Africa, as discussed in later chapters.

The demand for more food and other necessities of life will inevitably increase. If this increase is proportional to population, food production in the world as a whole, using the medium variant for the projection of population, will need to increase by 38 per cent between 1995 and 2025 and by 57 per cent by 2050. On the same basis the required increases in the less developed countries are 47 per cent and

72 per cent, respectively. These estimates do not take into account the clinically desirable need to raise calorie intake in poor countries or the trend, with urbanization, to greater consumption of animal products. If developing countries as a whole are to raise their nutritional levels and attain self-sufficiency in food production, the increase will have to be much higher. Imports by trade, or possibly as aid, from countries with surplus agricultural production will reduce the requirements, if the requisite foreign currency is available.

Food production can be raised by cultivating more land, increasing the yield of each crop, growing two or three crops per year on the same piece of land, or by a combination of these possibilities. Each can have problems. The best land, that is the land that is most productive, is usually already under cultivation. Most of the rest is forest or used for extensive grazing; further, conversion to agriculture results in loss of natural or semi-natural ecosystems. The other possibilities require more intensive methods of production, for example use of fertilizers and pesticides, irrigation, planting of higher-yielding crop varieties and mechanization. The conversion of land into agricultural use and intensification can cause both soil erosion and pollution of water supplies, although they need not, and deforestation to create more land for agricultural use adds to global warming.

Intensive agricultural practices have been subjected to public criticism in Europe, North America and elsewhere for several decades. To a large extent the criticism has been met by exercising greater control over the use of fertilizers and pesticides. More stringent regulations are now applied to the quality of water, food and air. Clear-felling and slash–burn of forests are criticized because of loss of plant and animal species and land degradation. Some of the important natural ecosystems are now protected. These are global issues that reached a wider audience with the publication of the Brundtland Report (World Commission on Environment and Development, 1987) and that will need more action as the demand for food increases.

The current trends in developing countries of rising crop yields and the use of more land for agriculture are expected to continue (Alexandratos, 1995). To cope with these continued increases successfully will require research, extension work, informed farmers and supportive policies from governments. Although this book deals mainly with the technologies required to support greater agricultural production, these are interwoven with several socio-economic requirements (Figure 1.2). Two examples of these requirements will suffice: firstly, fertilizers will not be used if the extra yield has less value in the market

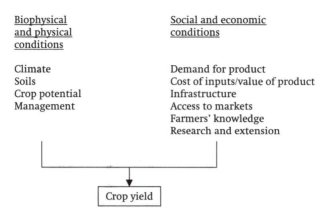

Figure 1.2. The conditions that determine crop yield.

than the cost of the fertilizer; secondly, a farmer with no land rights will move to new land, if there is any, rather than try to sustain production year by year. Two essentials for agricultural development, assuming suitable climate and soils, are that there is an incentive for the farmer and that the technological tools are available.

Returning to the population momentum, predictions indicate no significant decrease in the world population during the twenty-first century. Much greater agricultural production has therefore to be not only achieved but also sustained. Management must ensure that the land remains productive and, at the same time, that there is minimum damage to the environment. These are subjects for later chapters. First, some definitions are needed.

1.2 DEFINITION OF TERMS

The definitions given below are intended to prevent possible misunderstanding of the topics to be discussed, because not all authors attach the same meaning to the terms.

Land is the solid surface of the globe that usually supports biological production. Its components are soil, vegetation, animals and microorganisms; terrain (the physical features of land) is included in its description. When assessing land resources for agricultural development, the components also include climate, particularly rainfall and temperature, number and distribution of people, crops, domesticated animals, machinery, roads and markets.

Soil is the loose material composed of weathered rock and other minerals and also partly decayed organic matter and humus that covers

Table 1.1. *Examples of generalized farming systems, excluding intensive animal systems*

World farming systems (Grigg, 1974)	Farming systems of the tropics (Ruthenberg, 1980)
(1) Shifting agriculture	(1) Shifting cultivation
(2) Wet-rice cultivation	(2) Semi-permanent rainfed cultivation
(3) Pastoral nomadism	(3) Permanent rainfed cultivation
(4) Mediterranean agriculture	(4) Arable with irrigation
(5) Temperate mixed farming	(5) Perennial crops
(6) Dairying	(6) Grazing
(7) Plantations	(7) Regulated ley farming
(8) Ranching	
(9) Large-scale grain production	

large parts of the land surface of the Earth. In the context of arable farming it supports crop growth and can be tilled.

Agriculture includes all the economic production systems that depend on terrestrial plant biomass, that is, annual and perennial crops including herbage and pasture for human food and animal feed, livestock and animal products, timber and fuel wood, and materials for industrial and pharmaceutical use. The required resources are natural, human and economic.

Agricultural system (farming system) refers to a particular form of agriculture. Two lists of several systems, each of which has many variations, are shown in Table 1.1.

Agricultural development refers to increases in the output of the products from agriculture.

Land management is the management of land primarily for agriculture. Land on which commercial production is not profitable, or subsistence is not possible, is left for leisure activities, nature reserves or other purposes.

Environment, as used here, has four compartments: aerial (atmosphere, climate, weather), edaphic (soil), biotic (vegetation, animals, microorganisms), and aquatic (rivers, lakes, seas). Environmental conditions are all the chemical, physical and biological conditions that affect the growth, health and survival of plants, animals including man, and microorganisms.

Sustainable agriculture (reported by Harwood, 1990) is achieved by management of the land to produce, and to go on producing, outputs that meet human demands as these increase, at the same time conserving natural resources and not causing irreversible damage to the environment.

Farming communities, dependent as they are on the land for their survival, have usually, but not always, been careful to leave it in as good a condition as they received it. Concern over the last few decades is that intensification of land use and the cultivation of new land, both of which are expected to increase in the future, might result in forms of land use that cannot be sustained or could cause permanent damage to the environment. However, the term 'sustainability' is often used loosely, without reference to space or time (Bell and Morse, 1999).

Management for sustainable land use (derived from Smyth and Dumanski, 1993) will simultaneously (i) maintain or increase output, (ii) reduce the risk of output failing, (iii) avoid irreversible damage to the environment and degradation of the land, and (iv) be economically viable and socially acceptable to farmers and customers.

This definition takes into account the economic and social requirements of land management, important issues which will be referred to in later chapters when agricultural development is discussed. Because there is no time limit on sustainability (it implies forever, which cannot be known), it is more useful in practice to define management that *cannot* be sustained rather than management that is sustainable.

Unsustainable land management leads to irreversible biological and physical changes affecting the ability of land to produce equally as well in future cycles of land use, or where the costs of reversing the changes are prohibitive.

1.3   IMPORTANCE OF SUSTAINABLE LAND AND SOIL MANAGEMENT

The use of land for agriculture affects all the natural resources to a greater or lesser extent. Mineral nutrients are removed from the soil in harvested crops, but can be replaced by applying fertilizers. Loss of soil by severe erosion, by contrast, is almost impossible to reverse, because of the prohibitive cost. Loss of soil organic matter, which usually occurs when land is brought into cultivation, causes management problems, especially in soils of the tropics, and is difficult to reverse. Another advantage of defining unsustainable rather than sustainable land management is that it focuses on what can go wrong.

The various forms of degradation that occur can be recognized at an early stage by monitoring the system, and remedial action can then be taken.

With increasing populations it is necessary not only for agricultural output to be raised, but also for that output to be sustained by appropriate methods of land management. Developing countries will address the problem of large increases in population (a doubling in some countries during the next 30–40 years) by using more land and raising crop yields. Sustaining this increased agricultural output will not be easy, because many of the countries have little high-quality land to develop and there will be a high risk of soil degradation. As discussed in later chapters, to be successful these countries will need financial investment, research, extension services, a thorough understanding of the diverse environments of farming systems and direct support for farmers.

2

Natural resources for sustainable land management

To function successfully, terrestrial ecosystems require light, water, air, a supply of essential mineral nutrients and a suitable temperature. All agricultural systems also have these biological and physical requirements, but in addition depend on socio-economic conditions, referred to in later chapters.

Both natural and agricultural systems are adapted to local environmental conditions and they therefore vary greatly over the Earth's surface. Their nature depends on climate, including solar radiation, temperature and amount and seasonal distribution of rainfall, supply of soil water and type of soil. These are natural resources that determine the way the land is managed, the agricultural system used and the system's productivity, including crop yield. The total production from arable agriculture depends on both annual crop yield and the area of land that is cultivated; in turn, these are determined by the demand for products.

2.2 AREA OF LAND

Of the total land area of the Earth about 10 per cent (14.8 million km^2) is cropland, and in any year about two-thirds of this area grows a crop. Part of the rest is used for grazing by domesticated animals. The remainder supports natural vegetation (more usually, secondary or derived vegetation), is desert, is covered by snow or ice, or is too steep or too cold for any agricultural use. Although the total land area is not constant, the rate of change is very small over a time span of 100 years.

The biggest change resulting from natural processes since farming began has been the loss of land caused by the rise in sea level, counterbalanced to some extent by uplift of land masses. Since the Last Glacial Maximum around 18 000 years ago, global warming has raised the sea level by about 120 m (Fairbanks, 1989; various other estimates are in the range 60–180 m). Sea level reached about −25 m around 8000 years ago (Goudie, 1995) and may have risen between 2 m and 5 m during the last 2000 years. The causes of the rise in sea level were the melting of ice and the expansion of water caused by the rise in temperature.

Uplift occurred in northern latitudes when the load of ice melted. As the rate of ice melting slackened, other processes that caused uplift and subsidence of the land became important, for example uplift caused by plate tectonics. These effects can cause different local changes: for example, in the south and east of England the sea level is rising by up to 2 mm per year whereas in western Scotland there is uplift of the land at about the same rate (Goudie, 1995).

Earthquakes and volcanoes destroy land and create it, but more important is the land created by rivers, for example the deltas and valley alluvium of the Nile, Huang Ho, Yangtze, Ganges and Brahmaputra. The human influence has been to create new land from the sea, especially the polders in the Netherlands, and to lower the land surface by drainage and oxidation of organic matter, as in the Fens of eastern England (Richardson and Smith, 1977), and also the extraction of oil and water. The biggest human influence, however, has been to lessen the area fit for cultivation by urbanization and land degradation. The latter, some of which can be reversed, is discussed in Chapter 5.

2.3 CLIMATE AND VEGETATION

Vegetation zones of the Earth are determined primarily by climate, in particular by annual rainfall and its seasonal distribution, and by seasonal and day/night temperatures. The length of the growing season for rainfed agriculture is largely determined by the balance between evaporation of water from plants and soil and the rainfall during periods when the temperature is suitable for crop growth. Other factors are the presence of ground water, as in valley bottoms, and water storage in soil, the amount of which is affected by properties such as soil depth and particle size distribution.

For natural ecosystems the classification of Walter (1985) recognizes nine climate zones (zonobiomes), each with its characteristic vegetation (Table 2.1). Within each zonobiome there are orobiomes, at high altitudes, and pedobiomes, where soil properties have a greater effect

Table 2.1. *The nine zonobiomes of Walter (1985)*

	Climate	Vegetation
ZBI	Equatorial with diurnal climate, humid	Evergreen tropical rain forest
ZBII	Tropical with summer rains, humido-arid	Tropical deciduous forests or savannas
ZBIII	Subtropical-arid (desert climate), arid	Subtropical desert vegetation
ZBIV	Winter rain and summer drought, arido-humid	Sclerophyllous woody plants
ZBV	Warm-temperate (maritime), humid	Temperate evergreen forests
ZBVI	Typical temperate with a short period of frost (nemoral)	Nemoral broadleaf-deciduous forests (bare in winter)
ZBVII	Arid-temperate with a cold winter (continental)	Steppe to desert with cold winters
ZBVIII	Cold-temperate (boreal)	Boreal coniferous forests (taiga)
ZBIX	Arctic (including Antarctic), polar	Tundra vegetation (treeless)

on the vegetation than climate. For each biome Walter gives descriptions of the main types of vegetation and their associated climate on each of the continents. The area of each biome has become of increased importance because of the current loss of biodiversity. There is also concern that change of land use, especially deforestation, can change the rate of release of carbon dioxide into the atmosphere.

Changes in the past

Climate and changes in climate have largely determined the distribution of natural vegetation and soils, and agriculture has been similarly affected. However, there is little accurate information about the climate of any part of the world before the twentieth century. Although the first few measurements of temperature and atmospheric pressure were made in Europe in the seventeenth century, it is only during the last 100 years that climate measurements have been made over most of the land area and extended globally by observation from satellites.

Reconstruction of earlier climates and associated changes has instead depended on proxy data: movements of glaciers, the width of tree rings, records of pollen and insect remains, carbon-14 dating of peat bogs and a range of other methods. In addition, from more recent times, there are written records of extreme events such as very cold or

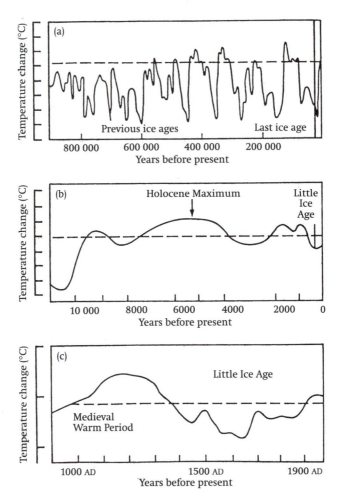

Figure 2.1. Schematic diagrams of global temperature variations since the Pleistocene on three time-scales: (a) the last million years, (b) the last 10 thousand years, and (c) the last thousand years. The dotted line nominally represents conditions near the beginning of the twentieth century. After Folland *et al.* (1990); © 1990, IPCC, reproduced with permission.

wet winters, dry summers and crop failures. The temperature sequence shown in Figure 2.1 is based on these proxy data. The climates of 18 000, 9000 and 6000 years ago have also been modelled using the Milankovich cycles and the effects of the retreating ice (Wright *et al.*, 1993). The account that follows is based on the reconstructions of the climate and vegetation during the Holocene (the past 10 000 years) assembled by Lamb (1977, 1995), Folland *et al.* (1990) and Roberts (1998).

In southwest Asia (the Fertile Crescent) domestication of crops and animals started around 10 000 BP (before the present), shortly after the end of the Younger Dryas (believed to have been an arid period with cold winters and probably hot summers) (Hole, 1996). Temperatures increased after about 8000 BP, because of larger receipts of solar radiation, and may have become 1 or 2 °C higher than at present between 6000 BP and 5000 BP. The greatest increase was at high latitudes. During this warm period, which is variously known as the Climatic Optimum, the Holocene Maximum or the Atlantic Climatic Period, ice sheets disappeared from most of Europe and North America. Forests of spruce, oak and other species spread across both continents and the tree line reached its highest level ever attained. Towards the equator it was wetter and temperatures were often lower than today. Savanna vegetation covered most of what is now the Sahara desert; Lake Chad and the lakes of East Africa were bigger and deeper. Warmer and moister conditions prevailed in China, and the monsoon rains are believed to have spread further north and northwest in the Indian subcontinent.

Temperatures decreased after around 4500 BP and remained below those of the present until around 2100 BP. Different regions were affected differently: bogs developed and grew in size in the temperate zones of the northern hemisphere and glaciers advanced in Norway, whereas river and lake levels became lower in Egypt, northern India and China. In the early part of this period the civilizations of Egypt, and of Mesopotamia (centred on Babylon), were strong; their later decline and that of the Indus valley civilizations may have been caused in part by a decrease in rainfall in the catchment areas.

There is more information on the short-term fluctuations of the climate during the last 2000 years. A warmer and generally dry period that started a little over 2000 years ago lasted until around AD 400 in Europe and as late as AD 1000 to AD 1200 in Iceland and Greenland. After spells of cold winters and some disastrously wet years in Europe, around AD 1000 it became warmer, with temperatures about 1 °C higher than at present. From around AD 1200 it became cool and wet in Europe. There were periods of severe storms, cold winters and wet summers that resulted in disastrous harvests; this was the period of the Little Ice Age, when glaciers advanced in central Europe and Scandinavia. Temperatures began to rise again during the eighteenth and nineteenth centuries (Figure 2.1), although with fluctuations. Cold and wet summers in the late 1870s led to crop failures and had a long-lasting effect on agriculture in England.

Table 2.2. *Global fresh-water resources*

Resource	Volume (10^3 km^3)	%
Ground water, deep	10 530	30.1
Ground water, soil	16	0.05
Glaciers and permanent snow	24 064	68.7
Ground ice/permafrost	300	0.86
Lakes	91	0.26
Swamps, river flows, biological water, atmospheric water	28	0.08
Total	35 029	100.00

Source: Gleick (1993).

In North America, east of the Rockies changes in climate were broadly similar to those in Europe; for example, farming extended into Minnesota and Wisconsin from about AD 700 until the area returned to drier conditions around AD 1200. Severe winters were reported in the seventeenth century. Measurements from during the middle of the nineteenth century indicate the Midwest to have been colder and with more precipitation than during the period 1931–1940.

There is still much to be learned about past climates and their effects, especially in the developing world. The upward trend of temperatures – the rise globally has been about 0.6 °C since the middle of the nineteenth century – is partly attributed to the accumulation in the atmosphere of greenhouse gases (H_2O, CO_2, CFCs, N_2O, CH_4). Theory predicts further rises during the twenty-first century which will affect agricultural productivity (see Chapter 11).

2.4 WATER

Estimates of global water resources are only approximate, good data being scarce (Gleick, 1993). The data collected by Shiklomanov (1993), summarized in Table 2.2, are probably as reliable as any. Of the total water on Earth about 96.5 per cent is in the oceans and another 1 per cent is saline, leaving about 2.5 per cent as fresh water. More than 69 per cent of this fresh water is locked up in glaciers, permanent snow, ground ice and permafrost, and of the rest about 30 per cent is present in ground water to a depth of 4–5 km.

Precipitation is the only important renewable resource. The total on land has been estimated to be in the range of from 99 000 to

Table 2.3. *Water resources in 12 countries*

Country	Population, 1990 (10^6 people)	Annual internal renewable resources, 1990 (10^3 m^3 a^{-1} person^{-1})	Annual river flows from outside country (km^3 a^{-1})
Australia	16.9	20.5	0
Bangladesh	115.6	11.7	1000
China	1139	2.47	0
Egypt	52.4	0.03	56.5
Ethiopia	49.2	2.35	0
France	56.1	3.03	15
India	853	2.17	235
Israel	4.6	0.37	0.45
Jordan	4.01	0.16	0.4
Somalia	7.5	1.52	–
United Kingdom	57.2	2.11	0
United States	249	9.94	0

Source: McCaffrey (1993).

119 000 km^3 a^{-1}, and the flow of rivers to the oceans as 27 000 to 45 000 km^3 a^{-1} (Gleick, 1993). Reducing these volumes to a size more readily grasped, a global river flow of 40 000 km^3 a^{-1} represents 5000 m^3 a^{-1} per person for a world population of eight billion. By comparison, Falkenmark (1997) estimates that 900 m^3 a^{-1} is the amount of water required per person for domestic use and to grow food crops under irrigation in a low-latitude country with a dry climate that is self-sufficient in food production.

Because of the variability in rainfall, which can result in floods one year and drought another, the stable water supply is only about one-third to one-half of the total supply (Falkenmark and Lindh, 1974). A severe limitation is the uneven distribution of rainfall: some regions have excess whereas over one-third of the land area is arid or semi-arid. An indication of the amounts of water in a selection of countries is shown in Table 2.3. Three of these – Egypt, Israel and Jordan – have internal resources well below their requirements, and depend on river water they receive from outside the country; potential and actual political problems arise from this dependence. The distribution is also often uneven within countries; for example, Australia has excess water in the north and northeast and large deserts in the centre.

The most serious water shortages during the next few years are expected to occur in parts of north, south and east Africa and south, west and central Asia, regions where the density of populations in many countries is growing rapidly, and in southern Europe and the western United States. The problems of supplying potable water to rural communities in the developing world are discussed by McDonald and Kay (1988).

The unequal distribution of water causes international controversies; abstraction of water from rivers puts downstream countries at a disadvantage. International agreements on water use either exist or are needed for the rivers Jordan, Nile, Tigris, Euphrates, Indus, Ganges, Rio Grande, Columbia and Paraná (McCaffrey, 1993). The controversies will increase as the demand for water becomes greater, and could lead to hostilities between affected countries. The problem is real: the issue of water supplies was a major factor leading to the war of June 1967 in the Middle East (Hillel, 1994).

The annual withdrawal of 3240 km³ of fresh water throughout the world is used in agriculture (69 per cent), industry (23 per cent) and households (8 per cent). To ensure a year-round supply a common solution has been to build large storage dams with the two-fold purpose of supplying water and generating hydroelectricity. Fewer large dams are now being constructed because most of the best sites have already been used. The environmental change they cause is a source of criticism, as is the evaporative loss of water from them. For example, it is estimated that the loss by evaporation from the Aswan High dam, probably the largest from any dam, is 3 m depth per year (Gleick, 1993). However, the Dam is essential to the Egyptian economy (Said, 1993).

All forms of agriculture depend on water, whether for rainfed or for irrigated crops and pasture. The more secure food supplies made possible by irrigation provided the foundation for the rise of civilizations. Irrigation reduces the effect of periods of low rainfall and allows crops to be grown and stocks of food to be kept in areas where habitation would otherwise be impossible. As domestic and industrial demands for water increase, it has become essential for it to be used more efficiently in agriculture (see Chapter 7).

2.5 SOILS

Soils cover a large part of the land surface of the Earth. They are three dimensional, often contain distinct horizons (layers), and vary with climate, parent material and topography. They also change over time. Soils largely determine the effective functioning of both natural and agricultural ecosystems. Together with climate, the properties

Table 2.4. *Functions of soil in terrestrial ecosystems*

(1) Recycles carbon (as CO_2 and CH_4) and plant nutrients from plant and microbial debris and animal faeces.
(2) Buffers temperature change.
(3) Buffers change of acidity and alkalinity.
(4) Provides a reservoir of water, air and nutrients.
(5) Regulates the rate of flow of rainfall into ground water and rivers.
(6) Absorbs nutrient cations and phosphate, and many organic substances including pesticides.
(7) Allows nitrate and to a lesser extent sulphate to pass into ground water and rivers.
(8) When acidified, releases aluminium into ground water and rivers.

of soils determine the potential agricultural production of land, but, more than those of climate, they can be manipulated to increase food production. Soil properties also affect the quality of surface water and the atmosphere (Table 2.4). Accounts of soils and their properties are given by Wild (1988), White (1997) and Brady and Weil (1999), and more comprehensively by Sumner (2000).

An outline of world soils

Description of world soils will be given only in very general terms; for further information the account by Nortcliff (1988) and the above references should be consulted. Detailed information is available in many countries from surveys that have been conducted either to assess land resources or with a more specific purpose, for example to establish the most appropriate sites for land development, or to assess the extent of soil salinization.

A general source of information is the *Soil Map of the World at* $1:5\,000\,000$ (FAO–UNESCO, 1971–1981), with 26 classes of soils in the higher category of the soil legend. This represented a giant leap forward in describing world soils and their distribution. It will become more useful as more information on the properties of the soils becomes available. A more detailed approach, developed in the United States, has been to classify soils according to their properties, including diagnostic horizons (layers within the soil profile), soil moisture regime and soil temperature (Soil Survey Staff, 1975; USDA, 1996; Buol *et al.*, 1997). At the highest level of classification there are now 11 orders of soils. Unfortunately, most of the names of the classes used in the legend of the FAO–UNESCO map differ from those in the United States system, although correlation between the two is generally possible.

An earlier concept was to describe soil properties in terms of five factors of soil formation (Jenny, 1941). Each soil property (s) was considered to be a function (f) of climate (cl), organisms (o) (including plants, animals, microorganisms and man), relief (r), parent material (p) and time (t). The relationship between s and the five factors is expressed as $s = f\ (cl,\ o,\ r,\ p,\ t)$. Although this notional relationship is not used to classify or map soils (some factors cannot be quantified, there are interactions between them, they are not constant, and time is often not known), it is useful in helping to focus on the conditions that affect soil properties.

Soils of the tropics and subtropics

The properties of soils in the tropics and subtropics cover a very wide range, and depend particularly on climate and topography. Because of the higher temperatures, weathering is more extreme than at higher latitudes, so that on a stable land surface in the humid tropics weathering of rock and of rock minerals can extend several metres below the surface. Tropical soils can also show well-developed profiles, but soil depth is often reduced by erosion caused by intensive rain storms. The result of intense weathering is that the soil minerals include oxides of iron, low-activity clay minerals such as kaolinite, and the more resistant minerals from the parent material. The oxides, which can also include those of aluminium and manganese, often form aggregates or a distinct horizon, as in Oxisols, which are common in the humid tropics. Other classes of soils in the humid and subhumid tropics include Ultisols, that have a horizon of clay in the lower part of the profile, and Alfisols, that also have a clay horizon but are less weathered than Ultisols and have a higher content of calcium and magnesium. An example of the characterization of the soils of the humid zone of southern Nigeria has been given by Greenland (1981).

In regions with a long dry season, surface soil can be lost by wind erosion or can receive wind-blown material. Intensity and depth of weathering are less, so that the soils contain more unweathered silicates and the clay fraction contains more active minerals (e.g. illite). The soils of deserts and their margins are Aridisols; under moister conditions in semi-arid regions there are Alfisols, widely used for agriculture.

Although generalizations can be misleading and should be regarded with caution, three that often apply to these soils are (i) the clays have low capacities to absorb nutrient cations and readily acidify (Vertisols are an exception), (ii) organic matter contents are low, particularly when the soils are cultivated, because of the high temperature and low inputs of organic residues, and (iii) the content of primary minerals is often low. For these reasons many soils of the tropics are low both in readily available nutrients and in a long-term supply of nutrients. Erosion is a common hazard.

Soils of higher latitudes

The soils of the temperate parts of North America, Europe and Asia are mainly the product of soil-forming processes that followed the Glacial Maximum around 18 000 years ago (Catt, 1986). Soils that had formed previously during an interstadial or an interglacial period were stripped away, buried or considerably modified. The new parent materials were the scoured rock surfaces, the unsorted debris from the glaciers, known as till or drift, coversands and loess that were size sorted, and deposits from the strongly flowing rivers, known as valley gravels. The soil-forming factors, which have varied greatly over time and between regions, determined the properties of the soils that formed. As would be expected from their origins, they have a very wide range of properties.

   Again, generalizations can be misleading, but three that generally apply here are (i) the soils carry a strong imprint of their parent material, (ii) their clay minerals have predominantly medium to high buffer properties (see p. 20), and (iii) their organic matter content is high because of the comparatively low rate of decomposition at low temperatures. Because of the last two points, many soils of higher latitudes are well buffered against changes in pH and contain a comparatively large supply of plant-available nutrients; exceptions are the class of Spodosols (mainly Podzols) that have an acidic, grey and often sandy layer overlying a dark brown or reddish horizon. Because the soils are relatively young and less strongly weathered than soils in the humid tropics, the mineral fractions contain a reserve of nutrients, except nitrogen, derived from the parent material.

Soil components and their properties

The main components of soil are mineral particles (stones, gravel, sand, silt and clay), organic materials (organisms, humus, remains of plant and other biological debris) and pore space (containing water and air). Other components that are present in some soils are calcium carbonate, magnesium carbonate, calcium sulphate and sodium salts. Soils are 'living' in the sense that most take in oxygen from the atmosphere and release carbon dioxide. There is a multiplicity of biochemical reactions in soils, that involve a vast array of microorganisms and animals. For accounts of soil fauna and microorganisms and their effects on soil properties, see Harris (1988a), Newman (1988), Killham (1994) and Edwards and Bohlen (1996).

Physical properties

Physical properties are related to the size distribution of the mineral particles and the extent to which these particles are held together by soil organic matter and iron oxides to form aggregates. The pore spaces between the particles and aggregates, and the spaces in cracks and channels (created by soil animals), are occupied by water or air depending on their size, recent additions of water and whether the soil is free draining. As a rough guide, water drains under gravity through pore spaces greater than about 0.05 mm diameter. After addition of excess water followed by drainage, small pores (less than 0.05 mm diameter) remain filled with water and the larger ones are occupied by air. In cultivated soils the pore space commonly occupies about half the volume of the soil.

Soil temperature is determined by the balance between incoming and back radiation at the soil surface and by soil water content. In cool seasons soil temperature is usually higher than air temperature, while the reverse is true in warm seasons; that is, soils buffer temperature changes. Wet soils are slow to warm up after a cool spell because they lose heat by evaporation of water; also, water has a high volumetric heat capacity, that is, it requires more heat than soil particles and air to raise its temperature.

Chemical properties

Chemical properties are determined mainly by the clay fraction and soil organic matter. The clay fraction of soils usually contains two types of minerals: aluminosilicates and oxides of iron, aluminium and manganese. The aluminosilicates can be broadly divided into three types: low activity (e.g. kaolinite), medium activity (e.g. illite) and high activity (e.g. smectite); other minerals may also be present. The level of activity refers specifically to pH buffering (amount of acid or alkali required to change a unit weight, or volume, of soil by one pH unit). Low-activity clays are weakly buffered and, further, become unbuffered at low pH values. Clays of medium and high activity are more strongly buffered and retain most of this capacity at low pH. Humus has the highest buffer capacity per unit weight, but this capacity is pH dependent; it decreases towards zero when soils acidify. Metal oxides have very little buffer capacity; they do, however, react chemically with phosphate and reduce its availability to plant roots.

Buffer capacity is important in two respects. Firstly, the higher it is, the smaller is the change in pH by natural acidification processes and by acidification from nitrogenous fertilizers containing NH_4^+ or urea (see Section 6.6). Secondly, cations that are plant nutrients (Ca^{2+}, Mg^{2+}, NH_4^+, K^+) are held at the sites that provide the buffer capacity. These cations are described as 'exchangeable' and are available for uptake by plant roots. They are not readily washed out of the soil by rain water.

Minerals present in the clay, silt and fine-sand fractions may slowly release nutrient ions by weathering processes. The amount and rate of supply depend on the particular minerals present and hence on the parent materials from which the fractions were derived.

The main source of nitrogen, phosphorus and sulphur in soils to which no fertilizer has been applied is soil organic matter. The mineralization (decomposition) of organic matter by a combination of soil fauna and microorganisms is a vital process in the circulation of nutrients in natural ecosystems. Soil organic matter is often the key to crop productivity because it supplies the required nutrients and buffer properties, and helps to create and stabilize soil aggregates (see Section 4.5).

Soils and crop growth

Although plants can be grown to maturity using various forms of solution culture, soil will continue to be the medium in which almost the whole of the world's crops will be grown. Soil provides crops with water, mineral nutrients, and air and anchorage for roots, all of which are essential for crop growth. It also buffers the crop roots against adverse changes in temperature and pH.

Farmers have always manipulated soil properties in order to grow arable crops. Before the nineteenth century the methods they used gave moderate to low crop yields. Together with the use of fertilizers, pesticides and improved varieties of crops and breeds of animals, good soil management has helped to produce the increased yields of recent decades. In the future the standard of land management will be a key issue if sustainable agriculture is to be achieved. This is especially important because cultivation of new land, and the more intensive use of existing land, will add to the threat of land degradation (see Chapter 5).

The next chapter provides a historical perspective on land management by describing the main techniques that have been introduced in the history of agriculture, and the long-term successes (and occasional failures) of most farming systems.

2.6 SUMMARY

This chapter has given an overview of the natural land resources on which agriculture depends. These include the global area of land, climate, vegetation, water and soil. During the next few decades the efficient use of these resources will be of paramount importance if agricultural systems are to be more productive and for this production to be sustainable. Climate is variable, water is distributed unequally, and soils are liable to degrade, all problems that will be discussed in relation to future agricultural production in later chapters.

3

The development of agriculture
and systems of land management

Starting about 10 000 years ago in western Asia a slow change began in the way people procured food. For many thousands of years they had relied wholly on hunting animals, fishing, and gathering plants, tubers and seeds. Now they began, in addition, to sow or plant a few species of plants and keep domestic and scavenging animals. Permanent settlements were established at watering-places and food was stored for times of shortage. At some centres urban civilizations developed. Hunting and gathering continued to provide food but to a progressively decreasing extent. This change from hunting and gathering to settled farming, which occurred at different times in different places, is known as the Neolithic or Agricultural Revolution because of the effects it had on human society.

From its very beginning farming has changed and evolved. From the work of archaeologists and historians we now know, though as yet imperfectly, something of the techniques that have been used during the last 10 000 years. We also know that some of the civilizations survived for very long periods while others failed or struggled to survive. Reasons for failure include climate change, as occurred in Iceland and Greenland around 800 years ago, and methods of land management that did not sustain food production, as probably occurred in Central America at the time of the Mayan civilization. Lessons for the future can be learned from the successes and failures of the past.

This chapter describes the development of agriculture, and particularly of techniques of land management, up to the middle of the nineteenth century. The empirical knowledge and skills of farmers, artisans and others provided the base from which later scientific applications could be developed. Much fuller information on the development of agriculture can be found in Slicher van Bath (1963), Grigg (1974, 1987), Redman (1978), Rindos (1984), Barker (1985), Simmons (1987) and Cowan and Watson (1992).

3.2   ORIGINS OF AGRICULTURE

Hunter-gatherers were often transhumant, moving to and from hunting grounds according to the season and with a principal place with permanent water where the old and very young could be based and food could be stored. The foods they collected depended on the biome in which they lived. Lakes, rivers and the sea provided fish, shellfish and molluscs; the land provided animals and birds, seeds in savanna and desert regions, and fruits, tubers and roots from forests.

Archaeological evidence is that hunting and gathering are as old as the human species itself, although the techniques became more efficient with the development of tools. Only a few societies now depend wholly on these means of acquiring food; more usually they are supplements for people who rely primarily on agriculture. Comprehensive accounts of hunter-gatherer societies have been given by Lee and Daly (1999).

Domestication of plants and animals

Although the term 'agriculture' has been defined in different ways, probably the most useful definition is that of Harris (1996 and earlier papers): 'a mode of deliberate biological production based largely or exclusively on the cultivation of domesticated plants and on the raising of domesticated animals'. An earlier stage, the manipulation of an ecosystem, including small-scale cultivation of wild plants for food, medicine or other uses, has been given the name 'plant husbandry' (Higgs and Jarman, 1972). Whereas plant husbandry has been practised by many societies, it has been developed into agriculture, as defined above, by comparatively few.

Although our knowledge of early farming has improved over the last few decades, some important questions remain. For example, why, when and where did settled farming start and what circumstances determined its development and spread? In the northern hemisphere the trigger for the start of settled farming is increasingly believed to be the dry conditions of the Younger Dryas phase around 11 000–10 000 BP (Blumler, 1996). The dry conditions may have reduced the supply of food for the hunter-gatherers and driven people to settle permanently close to a reliable year-round supply of water. Alternatively, summer drought may have favoured wild variants of the cereals with larger seeds, which were deemed to be worth cultivating.

The domesticated varieties of wheat, barley, rice and maize had four characteristics that favoured their cultivation: their seed heads did not shatter when ripe, the seeds germinated well when planted, they could be stored until required, and yields were probably larger and more reliable than those of wild varieties. These characteristics meant that food that was needed to support a larger population could be produced more easily. The evolution of crop plants has been described in detail by Smartt and Simmonds (1995).

3.3 THE SPREAD OF AGRICULTURE FROM ITS CENTRES OF ORIGIN

The number and location of the regions in which agriculture began, and hence of the first farmers, are still uncertain. Generally accepted as such regions are southwest Asia (the Fertile Crescent), north and central China, Central and South America, west and central Africa, southeast Asia and New Guinea. From these centres of origin agriculture spread throughout the world.

Southwest Asia

Around 10 000 BC, wild emmer wheat (*Triticum dicoccoides*) was harvested in Palestine and the grain was ground to flour. It is believed that by 9000 BC it was being cultivated outside its area of origin, in northern Syria. By 8000 BC domesticated emmer (*Triticum dicoccum*) and einkorn wheat (*Triticum monococcum*) and barley (*Hordeum vulgare*) were being grown in the Jordan valley at Jericho. As the cultivation of these cereals spread, others were domesticated, including flax (*Linum usitatissimum*), pea (*Pisum sativum*), chickpea (*Cicer arietinum*) and bitter vetch (*Vicia ervilia*). Their domestication in southwest Asia has been described by Zohary (1996 and earlier papers) and Ladizinsky (1989). By 7000 BC their cultivation had spread west through Turkey and, where ecological conditions were suitable, east to Iraq and Pakistan (Hillman, 1996). By 4000 BC they supported communities throughout much of Europe.

Goats and gazelle were herded in Palestine around 10 000 BC. By 6000 BC goats, sheep, pigs and cattle had become domesticated. As with the domesticated crops, animal husbandry then spread east and west.

China and southeast Asia

The earliest cereals were the native foxtail millet (*Setaria italica*) and common millet (*Panicum miliaceum*) that were cultivated in parts of northern China from around 6000 BC (An Zhimin, 1989). Wild rice (*Oryza sativa* L.), which grows in India, China and southeast Asia, was domesticated as wet rice around 5000 BC, probably first in the lower and central Yangtze valley (Chang, 1989; Glover and Higham, 1996). The domesticated species (*Oryza indica* and *Oryza japonica*) spread widely from their centres of origin (Greenland, 1997). They reached India, Thailand and Indonesia during the third millennium and may have reached Iraq and the Jordan valley in the first millennium AD, before the Islamic invasion. Pigs and dogs were early domesticates. Water buffalo were used in southern China from around 5000 BC.

Central and South America

A wide range of crops have their origins in Mesoamerica and the Andes. Remains of plants found in Peru and Bolivia and dated to the eighth millennium BC (dates are subject to change) include beans (*Phaseolus lunatus* and *P. vulgaris*), oca (*Oxalis tuberosa*), chilli pepper (*Capsicum* spp.) and potato (*Solanum tuberosum*). The domestication of maize (*Zea mays*) began some time before 5000 BC in Mexico and in the Andes. Cultivation of these and other plants supported the first civilizations on the Peruvian coast and in parts of Mesoamerica during the second millennium. Further details of plants that were domesticated in these two regions are given by Hawkes (1989), Pearsall (1992) and de Tapia (1992). The few species of animals that were domesticated included the llama, alpaca and guinea pig in the Andes, and the dog, dove and turkey in Central America.

Africa

Agriculture started in sub-Saharan Africa much later than in southwest Asia or the Nile valley. Because of the presence of few people and the richness of the biome there may have been less incentive to turn to agriculture, despite the occurrence of plant species that later became domesticated. It has been debated whether agriculture developed independently or was introduced (Stahl, 1984). It seems that sorghum (*Sorghum bicolor*) had its primary location of domestication in the Sudan–Chad area, possibly before 2000 BC; from there it spread through Africa and to India (Harlan, 1989a,b). Also referred to by Harlan are other crops that were domesticated, namely pearl millet (*Pennisetum typhoides*), finger millet (*Eleusine coracana*), African rice (*Oryza glaberrima*), teff (*Eragrostis tef*) and Bambara groundnut (*Voandzeia subterranea*). In the forested region people depended on the yam (*Dioscorea* spp.) and oil palm (*Elaeis guineensis*). The donkey was the only animal of African origin that is known to have been domesticated and used in agriculture, although there are claims that wild cattle of north Africa became domesticated.

New Guinea

The claim for New Guinea to be a centre of origin of agriculture rests on the discovery of drainage channels at an altitude of 1550 m and dated to around 7000 BC. The evidence for the claim has been reviewed by Bayliss-Smith (1996). The early crops are not known but later ones probably included taro (*Colocasia esculenta*) and yams (*Dioscorea esculenta* and *D. alata*). Remains of early root crops would not be expected because of their poor preservation.

Later spread of crops

The spread of domesticated crops to new areas depended on human contact or migration, on how well the crops were adapted, or were able to adapt, to conditions of climate and day-length, on the suitability of the soils, and on whether they were deemed useful in meeting human requirements. Over a long time span new varieties became better adapted to the new conditions. Amelioration of the climate in the northern hemisphere was also an important factor.

The cultivation of maize, that had first become domesticated in Mexico by 5000 BC, moved slowly northwards, reaching the Mississippi River about 2000 years ago and the more northern parts of America about 1000 years later (Cowan and Watson, 1992). Similarly, rice was cultivated in northern China about 2000 years after it was first domesticated in the Yangtze valley, and a further 800 years later there is evidence for it in Korea (Harris, 1996). It took about 4000 years for wheat and barley to reach northern Europe.

China provided a wealth of plant species to the West, including rice, soybean (*Glycine max*), tea (*Camellia sinensis*), apple (*Malus* spp.), pear (*Pyrus* spp.) and citrus fruits.

During the early centuries of Islam, new crops that were taken westward across North Africa and into Spain included rice, sorghum, hard wheat, sugar-cane and cotton; fruits and vegetables included sour oranges, lemons, limes, bananas, watermelons, spinach, artichokes, colocasia and eggplants (Watson, 1995). These crops, and the associated techniques of irrigation and rotations, were only slowly adopted across the political and cultural borders, even where the climate was suitable. As Watson observed: 'What seems to be a superior technology may, as it attempts to move into a new context, encounter economic, social, cultural, and even environmental obstacles that make it inappropriate and, to all intents and purposes, inferior'.

The Romans introduced the grape-vine to Britain and the Greeks took some of their favourite herbs to Egypt. The greatest impact, however, especially in Africa, was made after the settlement of Central and South America by Europeans in the sixteenth century and later. Among the many crop plants that were subsequently grown elsewhere were maize, groundnuts (*Arachis hypogaea*), sweet potato (*Ipomoea batatas*), potato (*Solanum tuberosum*), cassava (*Manihot* spp.), tomato (*Lycopersicon esculentum*), *Phaseolus* beans, chillies (*Capsicum* spp.) and tobacco (*Nicotiana tabacum*). These crops came to be grown throughout the world in suitable ecological niches. New crops in the Americas included wheat, rice, soybean and sorghum. Sheep, cattle, pigs and the horse were the main species of animal taken to the Americas.

3.4 DEVELOPMENT OF TECHNIQUES

An important feature from the earliest days of agriculture in the Fertile Crescent, and later in Europe, was that it included both crop husbandry and animal husbandry. Barley, wheat, flax and pulses originated in the same area as sheep, goats, cattle and pigs, and from the regions nearby came the donkey, horse and camel. China had its own crops (rice, millets) and animals (buffalo, pigs) whereas the early civilizations of Central and South America had crops but very few kinds of domesticated animals. In central Africa there were no animals that could be domesticated, with the possible exception of the dog, and in New Guinea there was only the pig.

The advantages of the wide range of crops and animals in the Fertile Crescent and its environs would have been (i) the flexibility that enabled farmers to adapt to different soils and climates, (ii) the value of animals as an additional source of food and in providing secondary products such as wool, leather and milk for making cheese, (iii) as techniques developed, animals could be used to pull the plough, the cart and the chariot, and (iv) dung from animals penned at night could be used to return nutrients to the soils used for cereal crops. The long-term success of the farming techniques that were developed in the Fertile Crescent were due at least in part to the close link between crop and animal husbandry.

All the techniques to be described in this section helped to increase crop yields and allowed agriculture to extend into new regions. The technique that probably had the greatest impact, certainly on the development of civilizations, was irrigation. It is described later in this chapter, more fully than other techniques, because much is known about it from archaeological digs and historical records, and it shows how one form of farming evolved.

Agricultural implements

When wild varieties of plants and, later, domesticates were first cultivated, digging sticks, spades and hoes were used for planting and weeding. Several examples are known of the use of these tools in southwest Asia (Harris, 1996) and in China (Bray, 1984). In the Fertile Crescent, flint-bladed sickles which had been used to harvest wild grasses continued to be used to harvest planted crops. In China harvesting knives were made of stone, shell and perhaps pottery; sickles made of stone or shell and later of iron were used when wheat and barley were introduced.

Early hand tools in America, Europe and Asia were made of wood and other materials available locally; for example, in eastern North America prehistoric farmers used hoes made of chert, elk scapula and shell (Smith, 1992). In Mesopotamia during the third millennium, sickles, hoes and spades were made of copper (Postgate, 1994). Iron was used to an increasing extent during the first millennium BC in Europe (Barker, 1985) and in China (Te-Tzu-Chang, 1976). The Chinese in particular had a wide range of hand tools.

An important development was the innovation of the animal-drawn ard plough (Figure 3.1). This originated in the Fertile Crescent during the fifth millennium BC, probably in Mesopotamia. It was suitable for 'light', that is, generally coarse-textured, soils, giving shallow tillage and stirring the soil to create a seedbed. It may also have been used to cover seeds that had been broadcast. Over the next 2000 years it was used across Europe, North Africa, the Indian subcontinent and China.

The ard plough was originally made of wood or stone and later became successively made of copper, bronze and iron. Depending on the region, it was drawn by cattle, buffalo or donkeys. A variant of the

Figure 3.1. Example of an ard plough. The curved beam on the right is attached to a draught animal. The pole to the left has a handle for steering the plough. From White (1967).

design was the seeder plough in Mesopotamia, which distributed seed at regularly spaced intervals in the furrows left by the ard (Postgate, 1994). It has been suggested that the use of the seeder plough for sowing wheat and barley spread to Iran, the Indian subcontinent and China (Bray, 1984). Some of the early designs of the ard plough are described by Partridge (1973).

The ard was used by the Romans, who also knew of the mould-board and the coulter (cutting blade) (White, 1967). Strong mouldboard ploughs drawn by four or more oxen came into use in Europe on heavy (fine-textured) land towards the end of the first millennium BC. They made it possible to extend the area of cultivation into woodland that had been cleared by felling trees with axes (Barker, 1985). Ploughs drawn by water buffalo in China are believed to date from the fifth century BC, and ploughshares were made of iron around the same time (Bray, 1984).

Other tools are known from the ancient world. Referred to in *The Farmers' Instructions* from Mesopotamia, probably from the late third millennium, is the mattock, to crush clods, and the harrow (Civil, 1994). In Egypt a bush harrow, referred to by Partridge (1973), was a bush that was drawn by hand over the soil to cover the seeds. In Roman times a variety of hand tools were introduced to suit local soils and cropping conditions; in addition to the traditional tools there were scythes, forks, saws and shears (White, 1967). Also described by White were primitive reaping and threshing machines and harrows that depended on animal power.

There was little improvement in farming tools in Europe for several centuries after Roman times. Various designs of the mouldboard plough, to meet local conditions and requirements, were in use during the Middle Ages (Partridge, 1973). Revived interest in farming during the eighteenth and nineteenth centuries resulted in the development of a wider range of machinery, including the drainage plough, the mole plough, the subsoil plough, harrows, cultivators, the horse-drawn hoe, the seed drill, the reaping machine and the threshing machine. These important developments in Britain, continental Europe and the United States allowed larger areas to be cultivated with less labour and helped to provide the higher crop yields of the last two centuries. General accounts of the development of agricultural implements are given by Fussell (1965).

Manures

In southwest Asia and Europe the cultivation of crops and animal husbandry formed an integrated system. As summarized by Dennell (1992), 'it is difficult to treat early European plant domestication in isolation from animal husbandry, because crop yields depended heavily on animal manure as fertilizer, while livestock – including oxen for ploughing – often relied on crops for much of their winter feed'.

In southern Mesopotamia cattle were kept from the third millennium BC for traction and for milking. To be provided with an adequate diet they were often kept in stalls, in which manure accumulated. Although there appears to be no evidence for or against the use of animal manure, it seems safe to assume that when the stall was cleared it was applied to soil where field and garden crops were to be grown. Flocks of sheep that were allowed to graze marginal and fallow lands during the day would have transferred nutrients to cropland when they were corralled at night (Postgate, 1994). Pigs and, later, donkeys and horses would also have provided manure.

Animal manures were also available for use in Egypt, as was guano from dovecotes. Records show that late in the second millennium BC, night soil was collected in China and used as manure after being composted with manure from farm animals (pig, ox, sheep, chicken), chopped straw, leaves and domestic waste (Bray, 1984). The use of night soil as manure by other early societies is probable, not only because it would have had to be collected and disposed of, but also because increased crop yields from its use would have been observed.

Throughout most of Europe, cattle, sheep, goats and pigs formed part of the agricultural system and provided manure (Barker, 1985). The practice of using manures was well established by Roman times, when authors described the best ways for them to be used. White (1970) refers to Pliny's comment that 'everyone is aware that sowing must not take place except on ground that has been manured'. The wide range of materials that was spread on land used for growing field, garden and orchard crops included night soil, pig manure, human urine, olive waste, wood ash, seaweed, lime and marl. Some of the manure was composted with vegetable waste, as in China. The use of green manures by the Greeks is referred to by the Roman writers.

Manure from farm animals continued to be used in Europe as the main means of maintaining soil fertility, supplemented in some places by seaweed, marl and lime. As the size of cities in the Netherlands and Flanders grew in the sixteenth and seventeenth centuries, refuse, including night soil, was spread on the land. Crushed bone and Peruvian guano came into use in England during the first half of the nineteenth century.

Fallows and rotations

Early hunter-gatherers probably used systematic burning as an aid in hunting and to maintain or increase the diversity of food plants (Hillman, 1996). Together with felling and ring-barking of trees, burning was used across Europe, Asia and probably Central and South America to clear land for cultivation. From the early days of farming it is probable that new land was cleared when crop yields fell, the abandoned land being cultivated again after several years of regrowth of trees or bush. This type of fallow rotation is known nowadays as swidden or slash–burn cultivation. It controls weeds, and the ash from the burn corrects acidity and supplies nutrients (other than nitrogen) to the cultivated crops.

On the scrubland and grassland of the Fertile Crescent where rainfed crops were grown it is not known whether fallows were used. A one-year weed fallow was used in Mesopotamia from the third millennium on irrigated land, the effect being to lower the water table. During Roman times, in the winter rainfall region around the Mediterranean a one-year bare fallow was the norm (White, 1970). It would have provided weed control, increased water storage in the soil, and plant nutrients from the mineralization of soil organic matter. Bare fallows were also common elsewhere in Europe.

One of the earliest reports of crop rotations is from late in the first millennium BC, when there were two-year (cereal/grass) and three-year (cereal/cereal/legume) rotations with irrigation in the Fayum depression of Egypt (Crawford, 1971). Writers in Roman times advocated rotations (White, 1970). The typical rotation in regions with adequate rainfall was the two-year legume/cereal rotation, where the legume was peas, beans, vetches or lupins. Lucerne (alfalfa) was grown as a long-term break crop (up to 10 years) where there was sufficient rainfall or irrigation could be used.

In northern Europe the fallow was gradually replaced by rotations, first using turnips in the Netherlands in the fourteenth century, then with clover and a variety of rotations that usually combined crop and animal husbandry (Slicher van Bath, 1963). Cash crops included flax and cole seed for oil. By the eighteenth century the growth of towns and cities in Europe had led to an increasing demand for cereals, dairy products and meat that was met by new rotations that varied with place and time. They often included winter- and spring-sown cereals and a root crop or legume.

Drainage and land reclamation

The earliest artificial drainage system is probably that employed in the Nile valley from the fourth millennium or earlier, to remove flood water and lower the water table. It consisted of natural channels that were unblocked after the flood to allow the water in the irrigation basins to drain under gravity when the level of water in the river had fallen. No (artificial) drainage system was used in early Mesopotamia.

By Roman times the principles of field drainage seem to have been understood (White, 1970). Transverse ditches diverted water flowing down hillsides; open ditches were used to drain clay soils and closed ditches for lighter soils. The lower half of a closed ditch was filled with small stones, gravel or brushwood which was topped with excavated soil. Also referred to is the ridging of land for growing cereals, with the furrows providing drainage.

Land was brought into cultivation in Europe in the eleventh century as the population increased. In the Netherlands ditches and canals were dug to drain marshes, and reclamation of land from the sea (poldering) was started. Reclamation lapsed until the rise of cereal prices led to renewed activity between the middle of the sixteenth and seventeenth centuries and again towards the end of the eighteenth century. Drainage of marshes took place across Europe at this time. In each period agricultural activity increased with the rise in agricultural prices (Slicher van Bath, 1963).

Poldering of marshes along the lower Yangtze is referred to during the first century BC (Bray, 1984). The method seems to have been the same as in Europe, that is, banks were constructed on a piece of marshy land, flood waters deposited silt to raise the land surface, and flumes controlled the water flow in and out of the polder.

In Mexico the Maya converted marshes into raised fields to support a variety of crops. The soil dug from narrow channels was used to form raised beds that were maintained by regular additions of soil and debris that had fallen into the channels. The channels may also have supported fish and molluscs that could be harvested (Sharer, 1994). In the Andes around Lake Titicaca on the Bolivia–Peru border, raised beds 5–10 m wide and up to 200 m long were made during the first millennium AD over an area of at least 70 km² (Kolata, 1986).

Planting crops on ridged land that provided drainage in the furrows was described in China during the third century BC (Bray, 1984). On pasture land with slow natural drainage in Europe, a ridge and furrow system provided grazing during wet periods.

Terracing

The construction of terraces to grow crops on hillslopes is known from several regions of the world including the Philippines (northern Luzon), Indonesia (Bali), the Andes, northern and southern China, and the Himalayan kingdoms, and in part of the Mediterranean region, south and southeast Asia, Japan and Africa.

It is not known when terracing began or where it was first developed. There is evidence for it in the eastern Mediterranean region in the first millennium BC. Late in the same millennium in the Yangtze valley of China, the bunded fields used for wet-rice cultivation were constructed up hillslopes effectively to create terraces that could be irrigated by the diversion of streams; they were developed into ladder fields around AD 900. Further north, in the loess region, dry terraces were constructed on the contour (Bray, 1984).

In the Andes, extensive terraces were built by the Huarpo people who lived in the Ayacucho valley of Peru around AD 200–600. The terraces were used for both irrigated and dryland farming. Later, they were built throughout the highlands and continued to be used through the Inca period to the present day (Moseley, 1992). Those in Luzon are known from the time of the Spanish occupation in the sixteenth century, but might be older.

Terracing provided a means of cultivating hillslopes with a minimum of erosion. The stone walls of the terraces used in the Andes, Ethiopia, western Uganda and elsewhere required a huge communal effort that was possible only with direction from a strong central authority. The walls also required regular maintenance to repair breakages that would otherwise result in uncontrolled runoff and soil erosion.

Irrigation

Irrigation made crop production possible in dry regions, and elsewhere overcame the problem of erratic rainfall. Its effects were, however, greater than this for two main reasons. Firstly, the surplus of agricultural produce that irrigation made possible could be used for trade. Secondly, control of the water supplies required the development of skills, co-operation between farmers, the establishment of local and regional government, and methods of survey and measurement. Mathematics and technology were required to design and construct dams, canals, aqueducts, qanats and various water-lifting devices (Drower, 1954).

Aside from its importance in the development of civilizations, irrigated agriculture deserves special attention here for three reasons: (i) it represented a major change in land management; (ii) during the 6000–7000 years that it has been practised the record of successes and failures provides a guide to its future use; and (iii) it continues to be responsible for providing a large part of the world's food supply.

Irrigation in Mesopotamia

Management of irrigated agriculture in the Mesopotamian plain using water from the rivers Euphrates and Tigris is known from the results of archaeological digs and a number of written records (Adams, 1981; Jacobsen, 1982; Postgate, 1994). It is relevant to the present day in that it demonstrates the effect of natural, as well as man-made, problems.

Three stages in the development of irrigation, starting around 8000 years ago, have been recognized by Adams (1981): (i) during the sixth, fifth and fourth millennia the bifurcating and rejoining branches of the river Euphrates in the south were used as the source of water; (ii) during the next three millennia canals were dug to extend the area of irrigation, branch canals supplying water up to 15 km from the main water course; and (iii) towards the end of the first millennium BC or early in the first millennium AD the Sassanians from Persia constructed a system of canals that covered most of the alluvium, even to the far south. Branch canals divided the land into polygons of between 20 ha and more than 1000 ha. The water-lifting device, the shaduf, is known from the third millennium, and there is evidence for the saqiya, the waterwheel driven by animals, from the sixth century BC. They were

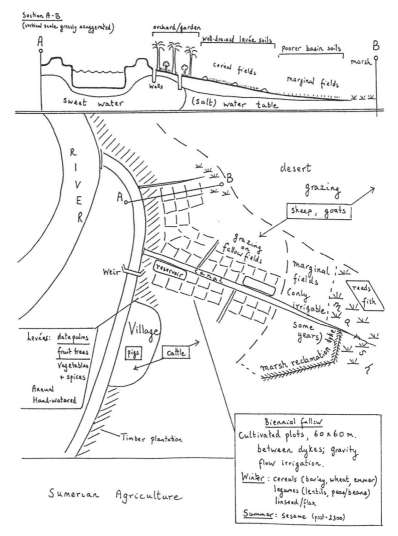

Figure 3.2. Hypothetical sketch of an agricultural cell in South Mesopotamia. From Postgate (1994).

used to irrigate crops, but there is no evidence that they were used as part of a drainage scheme.

Winter cereals were grown on the main part of the river levees for a distance of 2 km or more from the main water channels (Figure 3.2). The earliest crops were barley, emmer wheat and flax; later, bread wheat (*Triticum aestivum*) was included. The cereal crops may have been grown mixed with pulses such as vetches. Less widely grown were millet and sesame as summer crops. A wide range of vegetable and fruit crops were grown on the higher parts of the levees. Domesticated animals included sheep in large numbers, goats, cattle and pigs. Records show that a rotation of one year of cropping followed by one year of weed fallow was in use before 2000 BC. It was still being used in part of the Tigris valley in the 1950s (Postgate, 1990).

The winter cereals were planted in September and October and harvested the following April and May. Before planting the field was flooded and weeded. When sufficiently dry it was ploughed and harrowed; clods were broken with mattocks and hoes. Seed was planted in a furrow at regularly spaced intervals from a funnel placed at the back of the plough. Furrows were 50–75 cm apart and the seed rate was probably about 30–50 kg ha^{-1}. The crop received at least four irrigations, the last during crop ripening. The total amount of water used is not known and may have depended on the winter rainfall and on how much was available from the rivers. The required amount from the two sources was probably about 400 mm. Assuming that the pattern of flow of the rivers was the same as at present, the peak flow (and floods) may have occurred before the cereal harvest, with low flow (August to December) when water was required for irrigation. The care taken over irrigation is shown in *The Farmers' Instructions* dated to the eighteenth century BC (Civil, 1994).

Successes and problems

Three elements helped to make the farming system a success.

(1)   A rotation of one year of cropping and one year of weed fallow was used. Weeds in the fallow included shok (*Prosopis* spp.) and agul (*Alhagi*), which are deep rooted and dry the soil seasonally to a depth of about 2 m, thus keeping the water table low and helping to prevent an increase in salt concentration in the surface soil. They would also protect the soil from wind erosion in the hot, dry summer. Land that had become salty may have been abandoned for several years to allow the water table to fall through natural drainage.

(2)   The irrigation schedule included a pre-planting wetting of the soil that would wash salts down the soil profile.

(3)   Nutrients for the crop were provided by deposits of river silt, the leguminous weeds of the fallow, and dung from cattle, pigs and the flocks of sheep that grazed the fringes of cultivation. Night soil was probably also used.

Evidence for the success of the system is that cereal yields from nine fields in the south of the plain during the third millennium ranged from 790 to 2990 kg ha^{-1} (Powell, 1985), although probably more typical is a yield of around 1000 kg ha^{-1} suggested by Halstead (1990). The survival of the great city-states of the south, for example Ur and Lagas, for 2000 years or more is also evidence of a sound agricultural base. There were nevertheless shortages of food in some years, caused by shortage of water for irrigation, floods before the crop was harvested, or destruction of the crop by locusts. There was also soil salinization.

Jacobsen and Adams (1958) and Jacobsen (1982) reported records of soil salinity in the southern alluvium from the third millennium. These authors also gave indirect evidence of salinization: a change from wheat to barley and the use of a higher seeding rate were interpreted as attempts to overcome the problem. Jacobsen and Adams attributed the decline in prosperity and abandonment of several cities in the south around 1700 BC to soil salinization. While accepting that salinization had occurred, Adams (1981) later wrote that it 'seems inadequate as the immediately precipitating agent for an event so abrupt and general'.

Irrigation fell into decline in southern Mesopotamia during the second millennium BC, after being successful for about 3000 years. It was revived by the Persians when Baghdad had become the principal city, but then once again declined. There may have been both natural and man-made causes of this failure.

The natural problems of the Mesopotamian plain are (i) it is a subsiding basin (Lees and Falcon, 1952) with a low gradient of about 10 cm km^{-1} that decreases to about 3 cm km^{-1} in the south, and (ii) there were periods when the sea level rose relative to the land surface (Sanlaville, 1992). The effects of these include slow subsurface drainage and change of the courses of the rivers, isolating cities from their supply of water. The slow subsurface drainage and the rise in the level of ground water as a result of subsidence led to soil salinization, and the low gradient led to large deposits of silt in the river beds. Jacobsen and Adams (1958) report silt deposition of 10 m depth during 5000 years at archaeological sites, and Buringh (1960) reports 0.5–5 m more generally.

The problem of soil salinization is generally attributed to irrigation. The hazard posed by the salt concentration in the river water is now low to medium, depending on the classification used, and the sodium hazard is classified as low. The hazard in the ancient past is not known, but salinization was probably inevitable even with a small input of salt because of the very slow drainage (Artzy and Hillel, 1988).

There were other problems relevant to the present day. Upstream cities controlled the supply of water and in years of shortage probably used all that was available. Water supplies may have been reduced by the arid phase in the river catchments between 1900 BC and 1200 BC (Weiss *et al.*, 1993). Adams (1981) has suggested other reasons for the decline of irrigation, including the neglect of canals and ditches during periods of war and political instability, reasons that apply particularly to the second period of decline from about 1000 years ago.

Irrigation in Egypt

Residual moisture from the Nile river flood may have been used to grow crops during the sixth millennium. During the rule of the Pharaohs over about 2800 years, the area under basin irrigation extended over much of the valley of and parts of the Fayum depression and the delta. The main channels for carrying water from the river were either natural overflow channels or were cut into the river bank. When the main channels were full, water was allowed to flow into the basin channels from which it was admitted to the basin to a controlled depth. After a period of 4–6 weeks during which the water depth was about 1–3 m, the river level had fallen and ditches were opened to allow the water to drain back into the river. Winter crops were sown when drainage was complete. Before the next flood the water table had fallen to at least 3 or 4 m below the soil surface. The system was simple and effective. Village communities were responsible for the clearing of silt from the channels. Direction from a central authority was needed when levees had to be raised or strengthened and when canals were to be dug to extend the area under irrigation.

The Fayum depression is known to have been irrigated during the second millennium using water carried from the Nile in the Bahr Josef channel. There was further development in the third century BC under the Ptolemies: land was reclaimed, radiating canals and drainage channels were dug, and there were storage reservoirs (Crawford, 1971). The delta was developed more gradually, proceeding during the Pharaonic period from the south and central areas, and continuing during the Ptolemaic and later Roman occupations. Summer irrigation in the delta took place after the construction of barrages near Cairo that began in the nineteenth century AD.

From early times buckets were used to raise water manually for domestic purposes and to irrigate vegetable plots and fruit trees. According to Butzer (1976), the shaduf (pole and bucket lever), which could lift water up to 1.5 m, can be dated to the fourteenth century BC. The saqiya (sakia), the animal-drawn waterwheel also known as the Persian waterwheel, lifted water up to 6 m and is known from the sixth century BC. The hand-operated Archimedes screw may have been introduced during the Ptolemaic period but became more common during Roman times. The device made possible the cultivation of summer crops.

Throughout early Egyptian history the main crops – emmer wheat, barley and flax – were grown in the winter. Seed was broadcast when the land had drained, and pigs were let loose to trample it in or a brush (bush) harrow was used. Harvest was in April or May. Grain yields are not known and must have varied greatly between years and also spatially. Crawford (1971) described as scanty the evidence for a yield of about 1100 kg ha^{-1} in the Fayum during the Ptolemaic period. An estimate for the end of the first millennium AD is 600–900 kg ha^{-1} (Hassan, 1983). Date palms, olives, grape-vines and vegetables were grown on the levees.

Summer crops included sesame, the castor oil plant, and such legumes as faba beans, lentils and berseem (*Trifolium alexandrinum*, also known as Egyptian clover) that was used as a fodder crop. Cotton, sugarcane and rice were probably introduced in the seventh century AD or later by the Moslems. Cattle, sheep, pigs, donkey, geese and pigeons were kept. These early developments have been described by Butzer (1976), Trigger *et al.* (1983), Kemp (1989) and Bowman and Rogan (1999).

Successes and problems

Although cereal yields were low by present standards, the basin system of irrigation and drainage was a successful form of agriculture for perhaps 7000 years. Whereas the population in the fourth millennium is estimated as 0.25 million, it had increased to about 2.9 million by 1250 BC and to about 5 million by early Roman times (Butzer, 1976), when an average of some 135 000 tons of grain were exported annually to Rome (Lewis, 1983). The subsequent decline in the population, estimated by French savants to be 2.5 million by AD 1800 (Stanhill, 1986), may have been the result of unusually high floods, famine and outbreaks of plague (Said, 1993).

The hydrological cycle of the river that provided irrigation water during the flood and drainage at low water was an essential condition for success. Because of the effective drainage, soil salinization was not a problem, except in the northern part of the delta where there was incursion of the sea. In the valley itself salinization was confined to the outer limits of the irrigated area, probably during periods when the water supply was insufficient to flush out all the salt.

Another condition that made irrigated farming a long-term success was the silt, derived in part from the basalt rocks of the Ethiopian highlands, which supplied mineral nutrients. Jenny (1962) calculated that $15\,\text{kg N ha}^{-1}\,\text{a}^{-1}$ would be mineralized from the organic matter in deposited silt, which would produce a grain yield of about $540\,\text{kg ha}^{-1}$. There may also have been addition of nitrogen to the soil by nitrogen-fixing organisms such as cyanobacteria (blue-green algae). A rotation of two years of cereal crops followed by grass fallow or a leguminous crop appears to have been used in the Fayum during the Ptolemaic period. The highest rent was charged after grass or legume (Crawford, 1971), suggesting a benefit from residual nitrogen. Fallows or rotations may have been used elsewhere in Egypt during the Pharaonic period. Animal manure would have been available and would probably have been used primarily on vegetable plots and fruit trees.

The well-known problem that most seriously affected the farmers and the Egyptian economy was a low flood or a very high flood. The historical record has been described by several authors including Bell (1971, 1975), Butzer (1976, 1983) and Said (1993).

One problem is that the river in middle and northern Egypt has shifted its course eastwards, although to nothing like the extent of the shift of the Euphrates in Mesopotamia. In historic times the Nile has moved by as much as 3 km, so that ancient sites such as Memphis are no longer on the river bank (Said, 1993). There has also been change in the delta, the sea level having risen about 2 m during the last 2000 years, with an even greater rate of rise in earlier millennia (Stanley and Warne, 1993a,b). Subsidence caused by compaction of sediments and a tilting of the delta to the northeast have also occurred. Marine incursions during the first millennium AD led to abandonment of settlements in the northern fringe (Butzer, 1976).

Irrigation in China

The cultivation of rice (*Oryza sativa*) in China began on the swampy plains of the middle and lower Yangtze River around 5000 BC (Glover and Higham, 1996). Much more needs to be found out about this early form of agriculture, but it seems likely that it was similar to the long phase of agriculture in Egypt using the natural irrigation described by

Butzer (1976). It differed markedly from irrigation in the dry areas of Egypt and Mesopotamia in there being much higher rainfall. Historical documents from the first millennium BC up to recent times were used by Bray (1984) to describe the development of agriculture in China, and by Needham (1971) to describe the construction of canals used for transport and to supply water for irrigation. The account that follows draws largely from these two sources.

The main river systems of China are the Huang Ho (Yellow River), Chang Jiang (referred to as the Yangtze), the Huai, which now flows into the Yangtze, and the Canton. The cradle of Chinese civilization lay in the basin of the Huang Ho in northern China. The Huang Ho is well known for carrying a huge amount of silt (about $10^9 \, t \, a^{-1}$) originating in the loess plain. By raising the river bed, by an estimated 1 m per century, deposits of silt have created devastating floods in the alluvial plain. The river has changed its course both north and south of its present position during the last two and a half millennia. The concentration of suspended silt in the river Yangtze is less than that of the Huang Ho but its average flow rate is much higher (Allen, 1997).

Nine agricultural regions are recognized by Bray (1984), and farming systems have been described by Wenhua (2000). For the present purpose two distinct types of irrigated farming will be described: (i) in the southern half of the country, wetland rice grown in river valleys has been the staple food for about six millennia; (ii) in the northern half, which has cold winters, irrigation is known from the first millennium BC.

Central and southern regions

In the wetland-rice region of the Yangtze valley, schemes to supply irrigation water were begun in the middle of the sixth century BC (Te-Tzu-Chang, 1976). Around 500 years later small fields had been embanked over a wide area to receive water either from small reservoirs (tanks) or, on low-lying fields, from flood water. The tanks were dug by individual farmers or by small groups to provide their own water supply (Bray, 1984, 1986). As the population increased during the first millennium AD, more fields were embanked upslope.

Wetland rice was grown over a range of conditions of rainfall, temperature and day-length, and depth of water, requiring many varieties to suit the varied conditions (Greenland, 1997). The usual method of preparing the land for planting was to plough with water buffalo, turning the wet soil into mud, and at the same time creating an almost impermeable ploughpan to retain irrigation water. Until about 2000 years ago, seed was sown directly in the field where the crop was to be grown. Transplanting gradually replaced this method of direct seeding. The seedlings were raised in nursery beds and transplanted when they were between two and eight weeks old, depending on variety (Bray, 1984). The advantages of transplanting included better control of weeds, the possibility of double-cropping as populations increased, and less seed and less water were needed; that is, it made better use of space, time and labour.

Before the seedlings were planted, manures were applied that might have included composted night soil, river mud, hemp and oil seed waste and green manures. The crop was irrigated during its growth, but a dry period was allowed during mid-growth in some places. Drying the soil and then rewetting it would have stimulated the mineralization of organic matter, releasing nutrients to the crop.

Rice yields in early times are uncertain, and would have varied between sites and between years. According to data summarized by Greenland (1997), average yields at the beginning of the first millennium AD were about 500 kg ha^{-1}; they rose to about 1000 kg ha^{-1} by the end of the millennium and increased above 2000 kg ha^{-1} from the middle of the nineteenth century. Yields have also been estimated by Bray (1984, 1986) and Perkins (1969). Among the factors that determined the high and sustained yield of wetland rice must have been the maintenance of nutrient supplies from river silt, the use of composts and the biological fixation of nitrogen by the alga *Anabaena azollae* in association with the water-fern *Azolla*.

Between the tenth and thirteenth centuries AD (the period of the Sung Dynasties) changes were made to rice cultivation that have been compared with the Green Revolution of recent decades (Bray, 1984). Increased production was needed to feed an increased population that had resulted from emigration from the north. The measures that were taken included (i) the cultivation of short-season varieties of rice from Champa in Vietnam, (ii) a taxation system that promoted agricultural productivity, (iii) land reclamation with improved irrigation, and (iv) the appointment of local, skilled farmers to ensure that improvements were implemented.

Northern regions

In the north, the hydraulic engineers faced problems greater than those in Egypt and Mesopotamia in trying to control the Huang Ho River.

The floods created by the deposition of silt led them to build increasingly strong embankments and to deepen the river bed. The engineers also built diversion canals to control the river and for irrigation and water transport. The longest and most famous was the Grand Canal, that facilitated transport of grain from the Yangtze valley to the north. Where the canals were primarily for irrigation they ran close to the contour, distributing water downstream by gravity. According to Needham (1971), the Chinese stand with the greatest engineers of ancient times.

The development of schemes to control flooding and supply water for irrigation has continued to the present day, much work being done in particular, according to Perkins (1969), during the sixteenth and seventeenth centuries. Part of this was to repair damage caused by incursions from outside China, and Perkins suggests that several factors determined the development of new schemes: the settlement of new areas as a result of population growth, the occurrence of severe droughts, and the vigour of the Emperor and his bureaucracy.

Although dryland cropping has always predominated in the north, supplementary irrigation has been used from the first millennium BC and possibly before. The main summer crops in early times were millets and, later, soybean, sorghum and maize. Wetland rice was grown in the first millennium BC during a warm period and also more recently. Wheat and barley were grown as winter crops on residual water. Manuring was probably similar to that described above for the Yangtze valley.

Successes and problems

There seem to be no early reports of soil salinity in irrigated areas, although it is estimated that 15 per cent of irrigated cropland is now affected (Gleick, 1993). Where salty land occurred in the past, for example in coastal areas, it was reclaimed. Soil described as alkaline occurred in the area to which the Chêngkuo irrigation canal brought water (Needham, 1971), an area that was presumably reclaimed.

The two main physical problems the farmers faced were in the north. Here soil erosion of the loess regions caused loss of land and, probably with a much greater effect, the deposition of silt in the Huang Ho increased the severity of floods. Some of the silt came from natural erosion and some was caused by deforestation; the proportion of each is unknown. Estimates of deforestation during the first millennium AD have been given by Wen Dazhong (1993), who also reported the earliest records of the need for soil conservation, from 950 BC, and of terraced fields, from AD 760.

There may have been neglect and possibly some destruction of irrigation works at various times, for example during the first half of the first millennium AD (the period of the Three Kingdoms), when there were internal wars and foreign invasions from the north and west. As farming survived these difficult periods any damage must soon have been repaired. A recurring problem was the increasing population, which needed more land to cultivate and more wood as fuel.

Irrigation in the Andes and Mesoamerica

Agricultural development, including irrigation, occurred later in this region than in the Fertile Crescent. During the early years (300–50 BC) of the Maya civilization in Mesoamerica, a small, radiating canal system was built in a low-rainfall area of the Yucatan peninsula of Mexico which is assumed to have been used to irrigate crops (Sharer, 1994).

Irrigation was much more important in the Andean region. According to Moseley (1992), more than 85 per cent of all farming along the arid Pacific watershed of the Andes and in the terraced highlands depended on canal irrigation. The construction of canals is thought to have started around 1500 BC (Zimmerer, 1995). The system that developed on the coastal plain and much later in the mountains was in contrast to that of Mesopotamia and Egypt where the people were united by the rivers. Here, as irrigation developed on the western side of the Andes, multiple canals fed off each of 60 or more rivers, each canal being capable of operating independently. Each river or canal could support a small, economically independent group of people.

Among the first people to build terraces in the mountains for irrigated and dryland farming were the Huarpo, who lived on the eastern side of the Andean divide around AD 200–600. Moseley (1992) describes these thus: 'Contour terraces were laid out and erected as integrated flights of farmland, each narrow but long step being of equal length and some flights had as many as 100 terraces from the top of a hill to the valley below. Some terraces may have been irrigated from cisterns that caught runoff from rainfall. In other cases springs fed chains of small reservoirs situated at different levels supplying different terraces'. The same people also constructed a canal several kilometres long that fed water into the terraces. The construction of terracing spread to other areas during succeeding centuries when the required labour force could be mustered. By the sixteenth century the terraces and canal networks covered millions of hectares. The terraces of the Andes have been described as the largest archaeological phenomenon of the western hemisphere (Moseley, 1992).

Irrigation in the Indus valley and southeast Asia

Civilization in the Indus valley, which dates from around 2500 BC to 1800 BC, depended on agriculture. The main food crops were wheat and barley, which were probably sown in spring on residual soil moisture after the annual flood. Cotton, rice, vegetables and fruit were also grown; sheep, cattle, buffalo and pigs were kept (Cotterell, 1980). Little is known about the irrigation system. There were probably canals to extend the area of cultivation and dams for the storage of water. The river caused catastrophic floods on several occasions, which may have been exacerbated by the felling of trees in the upper catchment for fuel. In view of recent experience of irrigation in the Indus valley, salinization of the soil is likely to have occurred. After the decline of the civilization, canals were dug elsewhere in India from the first millennium BC onwards, as outlined by Needham (1971).

In Sri Lanka an elaborate irrigation scheme is known to have been developed on the arid plains around 300 BC (Needham, 1971). Rivers flowing from the hills were dammed to form reservoirs (tanks) and canals were dug across the plain. Rice and vegetables were probably the main crops. The system is still in use at the present day. Small reservoirs are also known to have been constructed in Cambodia and Vietnam during the first millennium AD.

3.5 LAND TENURE, TAXATION AND TRADE

In his village community the farmer aimed to provide enough food for his family, including some for storage for use during lean times, and a small surplus to trade for essentials such as salt. The community acted as a unit in the same way as in much of Africa today, regulating how the village land was used. With the growth of communities in most regions of the world, the land became owned or controlled by a more distant authority, king or temple, that required the payment of rent and tax in the form of produce or labour, or both, and later as money. As a result a bigger surplus of produce was needed by the farmer. Markets in towns and cities provided the means to exchange surplus produce; internal and external trade developed. Although economic and social changes are not a central theme in this account, they will be described a little more fully because they will continue to be important in future developments.

Land ownership and taxes

It is possible that the hunter-gatherers had some form of social organization that continued with the early farmers. Price (1996) reviews various hypotheses based on the idea that leaders or individuals 'may have directed their followers to adopt agriculture as a means of producing food surpluses and increasing exchange'.

By the third millennium BC at latest, and almost certainly much earlier, society in Mesopotamia was stratified: land was owned by the temple, the palace and privately. For work on the palace and temple lands there was a three-way division between tenants, institutional staff who produced supplies for the palace or temple, and institutional staff who cultivated land for their own benefit. Private landowners rented land to tenants, who usually owed the landlord one-third of the crop (Postgate, 1994). Larger institutions had many advantages over the small farmer. Firstly, in times of need they could supply tenants whose labour they needed with food from their granaries; secondly, they could use marginal land that would be too risky for the small farmer; and thirdly, they could afford new implements, crops and breeds of animals that could then be made available to tenants. Only the large institutions could construct and maintain large canals (Postgate, 1994).

There is less information on land ownership in early Egypt. During the third millennium most of the land belonged to the state in the person of the king and his administration; some was also in private ownership. Stores of food for distribution in lean years were kept by the king, local governors, the temple and in private ownership. By the end of the second millennium most land was effectively owned privately and by the temple (Trigger *et al.*, 1983). Small farms of about 1.25 ha were for the subsistence of a family of about eight persons. Rent was paid in kind to the owning institutions. Small farms were allocated to soldiers of the Egyptian army and later to those from Greece and Rome.

In Greece the norm was the small farm owned by a family. During the period of Classical Athens (fifth century BC) there was no major difference in the size of farms, whereas in Sparta the land was much less evenly distributed (Isager and Skydsgaard, 1992). Small farms were also the norm in early Rome, but towards the end of the first millennium BC large estates were created near Rome and in the overseas territories. The owners of these large agricultural estates (latifundia) of the Roman

Empire became more powerful as the Empire declined, the farmer becoming a serf.

The manorial system developed in Europe during the ninth and tenth centuries; most farmers were tenants but a few may have been independent. Tenants cultivated strips of land in a three-field system allocated to winter cereal, spring cereal and fallow. From the beginning of the thirteenth century in England and later in continental Europe the common land was gradually enclosed and the dispersed strips of land were consolidated. By the early nineteenth century the medieval structure of agriculture in Europe had been dismantled but agriculture was still backward (Grigg, 1974).

In the north of China during the Han Dynasty (around 2000 years ago), peasant households paid poll and land taxes direct to the state. Each had been provided with a plot of irrigated land, chiefly in the Wei river valley and the lower Huang Ho, of a size that, depending on its fertility, was probably about 2 ha (Bray, 1984). Peasant families also worked for large landowners and paid them a proportion of their crop, to be passed on to the government, and also a small cash sum. The government of the time provided farmers with tools such as the mouldboard plough and the seed drill and encouraged use of the ridge and furrow system. Although these improvements were aimed at the peasant farmer, the large landowners benefited most by being able to grow a wide range of crops including indigo, soya, broad beans, sesame and alfalfa that could be marketed. This commercial production 'brought Northern Chinese agriculture to its technological apogee' (Bray, 1984).

In the Yangtze valley, where rice production had been predominant for 2000 years or more, the farms were worked by a single family. Depending on the quality of the land, the area of each farm was commonly between 0.5 and 2 ha. The landowners paid a land tax to the state, and farmers paid feudal and state taxes, principally in grain and textiles and as labour. Grain collected by the state was stored in granaries and was available for sale and for famine relief. Because the rice farms were small family units the landowners had little or no involvement in their management. There were many different forms of contract between landowner and tenant, fixed rents becoming more common by the middle of the second millennium AD, which provided the tenant with the incentive to increase production.

Taxation was different in the Andes during the Inca Empire, being based mainly on labour. The land belonged to communities of people who co-operated in the management of the land and herds (Moseley, 1992). They were required to cultivate land to support the gods and the Emperor. When an individual was called away as a labourer other members of the community did his work. The system provided labour for building monuments and the terracing of hillslopes.

Trade

Internal and external trade have long been the driving force for agricultural development. In Mesopotamia and Egypt imports of precious stones, metals, timber, grindstones and salt were exchanged for food surpluses and, especially in Mesopotamia, for textiles and leather goods. The peasant farmer and the wealthier members of society depended on this trade, which extended over the eastern part of the Mediterranean, the Arabian peninsula and eastwards to Afghanistan and the Indus valley. It was in the interests of all strata of society that trade should flourish and hence that agriculture should be productive.

Similarly, in China there was local, internal trade in grain and vegetables from an early date. Tea, silk, bronze goods, lacquer, ramie cloth and sugar were exported during the first millennium BC; hoe blades, amber, ivory, precious stones, and gold and silver coins were imported.

Trade was especially important in the Andean civilizations: the wide range of ecological conditions, from the sea coast to the high mountains and eastwards into the forest zone, allowed the exchange of many different agricultural products. Gold, precious stones and shells were used in external trade. Trade was also very important to the Maya: the highlands provided jade and obsidian, coastal regions produced cacao for export, and each centre of population had its market for the sale of agricultural products.

External trade expanded considerably in the twelfth and thirteenth centuries AD. Spices reached north and east Africa and the Mediterranean region from the Moluccas (Spice Islands) in southeast Asia. Voyages by Europeans during the fifteenth to eighteenth centuries led to settlements and trading posts in the Americas, southeast Asia, Africa, Australia and New Zealand. During this period the big increase in trade was largely in the form of agricultural produce from these territories. Thus trade and agriculture have always been closely linked.

3.6 SUMMARY

Successful agricultural systems developed by adapting to the prevailing environmental, social and economic conditions. For example, irrigation was essential in the climatically dry valleys of the Tigris/Euphrates, Nile and Indus, and in the coastal region of Pacific South America. Rice was grown in the warm, wet conditions of southern China and southwest Asia, and dryland cereals were grown in northern China. Probably because of the shortage of land caused by an increase in population, paddy fields were constructed on hillslopes and developed as terracing. In the Mediterranean (winter rainfall) region, dry summers led to summer fallows that allowed weeds to be controlled, and more water to be held in the soil after winter fallows. Fallows were also used for weed control in northern Europe until turnips were introduced as a row crop that could be hoed to kill weeds.

Manure from animals and humans was collected in China, southwest Asia, Central and South America and Europe and used for vegetables, fruit crops and cereals. The value of leguminous crops was recognized in Ptolemaic Egypt. Of great importance was the spread of crops between regions of the world.

Techniques of farming changed. Of all the farm implements that came to be used, the plough is generally regarded as the most significant. Wet soils were drained by ditching and tile drains had started to be used by the middle of the nineteenth century. For harvesting, knives and sickles were replaced by scythes and, again by the middle of the nineteenth century, a further change took place with the introduction of mechanical harvesters.

The changes before the middle of the nineteenth century had taken place slowly as farming systems and their associated methods of land management evolved. By this time in northern Europe (Britain and Scandinavia) most of the land had become enclosed and was farmed by the landowner and his tenants, who had a personal interest in making long-term improvements. Industrialization took labour into the growing cities, populations were increasing rapidly and science was being applied to agriculture. Of comparable importance to all these changes was the expansion of farming in the Americas, Australia and New Zealand.

What has happened to farming systems and land management since the middle of the nineteenth century reflects the experience gained during the long period since farming began. Some of the techniques that were developed during that long period are still relevant today, especially where intensification is not needed or is inappropriate. Finally, the success of early farmers depended on having a peaceful and stable society, a fair rate of taxation, and secure trading facilities, conditions that still apply today.

4

Maintaining and improving soil fertility

By the middle of the nineteenth century a world population of about 1.2 billion cultivated an area estimated at 0.4×10^9 ha. Based on data reported by Evans (1997) and Greenland (1997), the average yields of wheat were probably about $1\,t\,ha^{-1}$ and rice about $1.5–2\,t\,ha^{-1}$. Cultivations were by hand or by animal-drawn implements and crop harvesting was by sickle or scythe. The small increases in crop yield during preceding centuries had been by selection of varieties. Nutrients were recycled, with the only additional inputs being from river silt, the weathering of minerals derived from rocks, and biological nitrogen fixation. Pest control depended on the use of fallows and rotations, and the area of irrigation had increased little during the previous 2000 years. All this changed as an increased population demanded more food.

Later chapters describe how food production has increased in the last 150 years, and will continue to do so in the future, through the use of manufactured fertilizers, water conservation and irrigation, pesticides, and increases in crop yield potential. However, success in obtaining the required output of food ultimately depends on soil fertility, defined as the capacity of the soil to produce the required crop yield.

Soil properties and processes can be physical, chemical or biological (see Chapter 2). Each of these affects soil fertility either independently or, more usually, by interaction to produce a synergistic effect. A soil that is fertile has to provide adequate rooting depth, nutrients, oxygen (not required by wetland rice), water, a suitable temperature and no toxicities if the required crop yield is to be produced. However, crop yield is often determined by climate, especially rainfall. In addition, the soil conditions required also depend on the particular crop that is being grown. For example, tea requires an acid soil whereas alfalfa (lucerne) requires a soil that is at about pH 7; the date palm can tolerate salinity at concentrations that are toxic to wheat; some legumes require a specific form of rhizobium if they are to fix nitrogen and some trees require specific fungi to form a mycorrhiza, as described later in this chapter.

A further consideration is the effects of economics (cost/benefit of inputs) and level of management. Thus instead of some general index of soil fertility, a soil is considered fertile if it does not limit growth and yield of a particular crop under the prevailing climatic, economic and management conditions.

Soil fertility has usually been maintained by the skill and experience of the farmer. Not all management has been good, however; witness the extensive degradation or loss of soils in the past and which is still occurring (see Chapter 5). If the food requirement in this century is to be met it is therefore essential for soil fertility to be maintained and, where possible, improved.

This chapter deals with the effect of soil conditions, particularly soil nutrients, on crop growth and yield. Fertilizer can be applied to soils with low supplies of nutrients (see Chapter 6), and where water is limiting, water conservation or irrigation can be implemented (see Chapter 7). Increased crop yields followed the introduction of modern crop varieties (having a larger yield potential) that made more profitable the package of inputs; together they came to be known as the Green Revolution. Soil fertility is important if the larger yield potentials are to be converted into actual yields.

4.2   SOIL PROPERTIES THAT AFFECT CROP GROWTH

The properties of the soil affect the success of all stages of the growth of a crop. For germination the seed requires water, oxygen and a suitable temperature. The emerging root needs to push through the soil and the shoot needs to emerge above the soil surface so that the seedling can become independent of the organic compounds and minerals stored in the seed. Successful germination, emergence and early growth of the seedlings ('crop establishment') depend in particular on (i) a suitable soil temperature to encourage rapid germination and emergence, (ii) water in the top 10–20 cm of soil to provide water for the leaves to transpire and to remain turgid, (iii) nutrients in the topsoil to meet the requirements for growth, (iv) air-filled pores to provide oxygen and for the roots to grow through, and (v) a non-crusted soil surface to allow the shoots to emerge. The first four of these requirements need to be met throughout the period of growth. The most

Table 4.1. *Approximate amounts of nitrogen (N),*
phosphorus (P) and potassium (K) in the main
cereal crops of the world, expressed in kg per tonne
of crop dry matter

Crop		N	P	K
Wheat	Grain	20	4	5–5.5
	Straw	3–7	0.8	8–14
Maize	Grain	20–25	4–6	10–15
	Straw	10	2	12
Rice	Grain	18–23	4–5	5–7
	Straw	4–5	1	10–12
Sorghum	Grain	20	0.9	4
	Straw	5	0.3	2

Source: Data are from Sanchez (1976) and Wild and
Jones (1988), who also give analyses for other crops
and other nutrients.

common limitations to crop growth are the supplies of water and
nutrients.

When the crop canopy is fully formed, transpiration under good
growing conditions is usually in the range of 30 mm to 100 mm per
week, depending on the atmospheric conditions (see Chapter 7). The
total amount of water used by a crop during a 12-week growing
period will be approximately 300–900 mm. This amount exceeds the
plant-available water stored in soil (usually 30–250 mm per metre depth
of soil); further, growth rate is reduced before the available water has
been used (see Section 7.3). For large yields of arable crops, rainfall or
irrigation during the growing season is therefore usually essential.

Nutrient uptake is most rapid during and a little before the period
of most rapid vegetative growth. The highest rates of uptake of nitrogen
(N), phosphorus (P) and potassium (K) for maize, winter wheat, potatoes
and ryegrass over periods of 7–14 days average 6.2, 0.9 and 9.4 kg ha^{-1}
day^{-1}, respectively (from a review by Wild and Jones, 1988). For a cereal
crop yielding 5 t ha^{-1} of grain, the total uptake (kg ha^{-1}) of N, P and K
by the time of harvest is about 100–200, 20–30 and 50–100, respectively,
amounts that vary with the crop (see also Table 4.1). For high crop yields
no soil can continue to supply nutrients over a succession of years in
the amounts required unless fertilizers or manures are applied.

Soil organic matter is not itself required by plants, as is evident
from the commercial use of hydroponics, but it is of vital importance

Table 4.2. *Elements required by higher plants*

From the atmosphere and water:	Carbon, hydrogen, oxygen
From the soil:	
Macronutrients	Nitrogen, phosphorus, potassium, calcium, magnesium, sulphur
Micronutrients	Iron, manganese, copper, zinc, boron, molybdenum, chlorine, nickel
Beneficial elements	Cobalt, sodium, silicon

in managing soil properties. It is one of the key components measured when assessing changes in soil fertility over a period of cropping (see Section 4.5).

4.3 NUTRIENTS IN SOIL

The nutrients required by crops are listed in Table 4.2. When animal, and particularly human, health is considered an additional list of mineral nutrients is required, including cobalt, chromium, fluorine, iodine, selenium, tin and vanadium (McDowell, 1992; Oliver, 1997). Of the elements listed in Table 4.2 boron seems not to be required by animals or microorganisms. The chemical forms of soil nutrients and their uptake by plants have been discussed by Gregory (1988a), Wild and Jones (1988), Barber (1995) and Marschner (1995).

The stock of plant-available nutrients held in a soil that has never received fertilizer or manure depends on (i) the chemical composition of the minerals from which the soil was formed and their degree of weathering, (ii) the soil's content and rate of mineralization of organic matter, (iii) nutrient additions from the atmosphere and in river sediments, and losses in drainage water and by erosion, and (iv) removal of nutrients in agricultural products.

Because of different parent materials and history, the nutrient content of soils varies greatly between regions of the world and also locally. For example, average total phosphorus content of topsoils in the United Kingdom (700 μg g^{-1}) is twice that in Australia (350 μg g^{-1}) and five times that in the West African savanna (140 μg g^{-1}) (Wild, 1988, pp. 695–742). These differences are due partly to differences in parent materials and soil history and partly to the use of manures and fertilizers containing phosphate (as in the UK). Another difference is the total nitrogen content of topsoils: in temperate regions nitrogen content is usually 1000–3000 μg g^{-1} (Parsons and Tinsley, 1975), whereas in the West African savanna the average nitrogen content of 295 soils was 510 μg g^{-1} (range 80–2900 μg g^{-1}; Jones, 1973).

A useful distinction is between the 'volatile' nutrients (nitrogen, sulphur, chlorine), which reach the soils at least partly from precipitation, gases and aerosols, and the 'non-volatile' nutrients (phosphorus, potassium, calcium, magnesium, micronutrients), which are mainly the products of weathering of parent materials and are therefore more site specific (Likens *et al.*, 1977). The distinction is not absolute, because 'non-volatile' nutrients are deposited in small amounts from the atmosphere and sodium and sulphur are added to the soil from both sources. Likens *et al.* illustrated the difference between the two groups of nutrients from their study of the Hubbard Brook Experimental Forest in New Hampshire, USA. A comparison using published data on forest soils in Venezuela, Ghana and Sarawak supports their conclusion that, at least under some conditions, soils that had never received manures or fertilizers differed more in their content of 'non-volatile' nutrients than in that of 'volatile' ones (Wild, 1993).

4.4   NUTRIENT SUPPLY TO PLANT ROOTS

Plant roots and root hairs absorb nutrients from the soil solution through their surfaces. The rate of absorption depends on several factors, including (i) the plant demand, which is largely determined by the rate of plant growth, (ii) the area of root surface and its distribution through the soil, (iii) the concentration of nutrients in the soil solution at the root surface, (iv) the rate of replenishment of nutrients in the soil solution, (v) biological conditions in the vicinity of the root (the rhizosphere), and (vi) effects of mycorrhizal fungi.

Effects of plant growth rate

Several experiments have shown that nutrient uptake is closely related to plant demand, especially during vegetative growth (Gregory, 1988a). For a high growth rate of 280 kg ha^{-1} day^{-1} of dry matter, the nutrient requirements (kg ha^{-1} day^{-1}) are 5.6, 1.1 and 5.6 of N, P and K, respectively, to meet the critical concentrations in the new tissues of about 2, 0.4 and 2 per cent of N, P and K, respectively, of the dry matter. The rates of uptake are a little higher than plant growth rates during early vegetative growth, but subsequently the two rates are about in synchrony.

Absorption by plant roots

The greater the distribution of roots through the soil profile the greater is their access to nutrients. This applies particularly to nutrient ions of low mobility in the soil, such as phosphate. Soil physical and chemical properties that affect the growth and proliferation of roots are therefore important. Absorption of nutrients is an active process requiring energy, it is selective and it has to maintain electrical neutrality, all of which affect the rhizosphere (see below).

Nutrients in the soil solution

Nutrients are present in the soil solution in ionic form, the major nutrients as NO_3^-, NH_4^+, $H_2PO_4^-$, HPO_4^{2-}, K^+, Ca^{2+}, Mg^{2+} and SO_4^{2-}. In the top 30 cm of moderately fertile arable soils to which a complete fertilizer has been applied, the concentrations of nitrate, potassium and phosphate in solution are about 10^{-2} M, 10^{-3} M and 10^{-5} M, respectively. In soil containing 6 cm of water to this depth the amounts from these concentrations are 84 kg N, 23 kg K and 0.2 kg P per hectare.

Replenishment of the soil solution

Because the requirement of crop plants for nutrients usually exceeds the amount in solution at any one time, replenishment close to the root surface is needed if plant growth rate is not to be limited. This replenishment happens by two processes: firstly, by release of nutrients from the inorganic and organic components of the soil; and secondly, by the transport of nutrients to the root surface.

Exchangeable cations (Ca^{2+}, Mg^{2+}, K^+, Na^+) held by clay and humus pass into solution when their concentration is reduced by plant uptake. In most cultivated soils Ca^{2+} is the dominant cation, and because more K^+ than Ca^{2+} is taken up by roots, K^+ is released into solution by exchange with Ca^{2+}. Phosphate can also pass into solution by desorption from clays. Mineralization of soil organic matter releases the nutrients nitrogen, phosphorus and sulphur into solution, as discussed in Section 4.5.

Transfer to the root surface is by diffusion down a concentration gradient created by uptake of nutrients by the root, and by mass flow, that is, the flow of solution towards the root to replace water lost by transpiration. Nitrate, which is present in the soil solution in relatively high concentrations, is transported to the root surface mainly by mass

Table 4.3. *Processes in the rhizosphere that may affect the supply of nutrients to plant roots*

(1) Cation/anion uptake ratio	H^+ is excreted when uptake of cations by the root exceeds uptake of anions; HCO_3^- is excreted when the uptake of anions exceeds uptake of cations (strictly each process depends on the electrical charge on the ions). The effect is to change the pH, which may affect the availability of nutrients.
(2) Exudation of organic compounds	Organic compounds form soluble complexes with iron, may solubilize phosphate and may hydrolyse organic phosphate esters.
(3) Release of oxygen	In anaerobic soils oxygen that has diffused down the aerenchyma of plants such as rice passes into soil, oxidizing Fe^{2+} to Fe^{3+} and producing H^+.
(4) Nitrogen fixation	There is evidence for associative nitrogen fixation in the rhizosphere of some grasses and other plants by bacteria using exuded carbon compounds as a source of energy.

flow, whereas phosphate, which is usually present at comparatively low concentrations, depends on diffusion, which is a relatively slow process.

The rhizosphere

The term 'rhizosphere' is applied to the volume of soil close to a living root in which the physical, chemical and biological properties are significantly perturbed by its presence. The properties of the rhizosphere differ from those of bulk soil because of processes at the root surface and the activities of the large numbers of microorganisms that are stimulated by the release of mucigel from root tips and the exudation of organic compounds. The properties that are affected have been reviewed by Marschner (1995, 1998), McLaughlin *et al.* (1998), Crowley and Rengel (1999) and Tinker and Nye (2000), and are summarized in Table 4.3.

Plants grown with nitrogen supplied as NO_3^- normally raise the pH of the soil close to the root surface by excreting HCO_3^-; if the nitrogen is supplied as NH_4^+ the roots excrete H^+ and the pH falls. These effects must occur if the plant is to maintain a cation–anion balance.

The pH change occurs in the rhizosphere, where it affects the availability of nutrients; for example, the solubility of iron, manganese and zinc increase at lower pH and that of molybdenum increases at higher pH. Acidification also occurs from nitrogen-fixing plants, because they use N_2 as their source of nitrogen and take up an excess of cations.

Acidification can also occur in the rhizosphere of plants growing in anaerobic soil. Here the effect is due to oxygen that has diffused down the aerenchyma (air-filled pores) in plants and passed into the soil. Oxidation of ferrous to ferric iron (which stains the roots brown) releases H^+.

Organic substances released from the roots may have several effects. Iron is made more soluble by some plant species by a combination of reduction, acidification and chelation, and by others by complex formation of ferric iron with specific amino acids called siderophores (Marschner, 1995). Carboxylic acids that combine with aluminium and iron increase the solubility of phosphate; an example of this effect is seen in the citric acid excreted by the roots of lupin (Gardner *et al.*, 1983).

The deposition of organic substances in the rhizosphere (rhizodeposition) allows it to support a microbial population that is much larger than in bulk soil by a factor of commonly between 5 and 20. The ratio differs between plant species; it increases with the stage of plant growth, is greatest in plants growing in unfavourable conditions, and is particularly large in droughty, saline and acid soils. The microorganisms in the rhizosphere probably release inorganic phosphate by hydrolysis of organic phosphates, but most attention has been directed towards nitrogen fixation by the bacteria *Azotobacter* and *Azospirillum* in the rhizospheres of grasses, rice, sugar-cane and other plant species (Boddey *et al.*, 1995). The amounts of nitrogen fixed by this mechanism in the rhizospheres of annual crops may be around 20–40 kg N ha^{-1} a^{-1}, and may be greater with perennials. The rhizosphere microorganisms may have other effects on plants, including some due to hormones; much has yet to be learned about their activities in the root systems of crop plants, and even more about their activities in root systems of plants in the wild.

Mycorrhizas

The roots of many plant species have a symbiotic association with a specialized fungus, called a mycorrhiza (meaning 'fungus root'). There are two common forms, ectomycorrhizas and vesicular–arbuscular mycorrhizas. Ectomycorrhizas can be seen with the aid of a magnifying glass, as they give a stubby appearance on the roots of some trees. Vesicular–arbuscular mycorrhizas (VAM; now known as arbuscular mycorrhizas, AM), in which specialized fungi infect the roots, can be observed only under a microscope. VAM occur in many plant species (exceptions are members of the Cruciferae and Chenopodiacae), including many tropical tree species. Plants, including trees, benefit from the mycorrhizal association by receiving nutrients from the soil via the fungal hyphae, and the plant provides the fungus with carbon compounds.

The association is particularly important in providing plants with nutrients of low mobility, such as phosphate, and metals with low solution concentrations in soils such as copper and zinc. By growing out from the root the fungal hyphae take up nutrients from a greater volume of soil than would otherwise be the case, and transfer them to the root. Inoculations of crop plants by the required AM fungus has not yet had commercial success, however. It is often different with trees introduced into a new area, which respond to inoculation with the required fungus or the transfer of soil in which the same tree species has previously grown. Detailed accounts of mycorrhizas are given by Harley and Smith (1983), Smith and Read (1997) and Tinker and Nye (2000).

4.5 IMPORTANCE OF SOIL ORGANIC MATTER

Although organic matter in the root environment is not required by crop plants, it is of very great importance because of its effects on the physical, chemical and biological properties of soils (Table 4.4). The importance of these effects differs between soils and treatment regimes. For example, under a no-fertilizer, no-manure regime, soil organic matter is the source of almost all the nitrogen and sulphur and a proportion of the phosphorus available to crop plants, but it is less important in this respect in regimes where fertilizers are used. Similarly, cultivations can produce some of the physical effects of organic matter. Organic matter plays a key role not only in maintaining soil fertility but also in minimizing the risk of various forms of soil degradation and in maintaining the quality of the environment.

In the top 10 cm of soil the organic matter contains about 50 per cent carbon and has a nutrient composition, expressed as percentage ratios by weight, of about 10 (C/N), 100 (C/P) and 80 (C/S). In this depth, in a soil containing 2 per cent organically combined carbon by weight (the usual range is from less than 1 per cent to over 5 per cent) these ratios represent 2600 kg ha^{-1} of N, 260 kg ha^{-1} of P and 325 kg ha^{-1} of S.

Table 4.4. *Beneficial effects of soil organic matter*

Physical	• increases aggregation of soil particles, which improves infiltration of water and reduces surface sealing and crusting
	• increases supply of water to crops
	• fine roots and root hairs can grow more readily
	• may increase drainage and hence early growth of crops
	• gives greater flexibility for timing of cultivations
Chemical	• releases N, P and S on mineralization
	• protects nutrient cations against loss by leaching
	• chelates micronutrient metals, generally increasing uptake by plants
	• acts as a pH buffer
	• reduces the environmental hazard of some metals, e.g. aluminium
	• adsorbs pesticides and other organic compounds
Biological	• soil fauna create channels that increase infiltration and drainage of water and through which roots can grow
	• fauna and microorganisms decompose leaf litter and other debris, an essential function in nutrient cycling
	• is a source of *Rhizobium* for legumes and of fungi that form mycorrhizas
	• supports fauna and microorganisms which may help to control pests that attack plant roots

The whole soil profile will contain considerably more. The nutrients become available to plants only as the organic matter is mineralized.

Source of plant nutrients

The raw materials such as cereal straw and mature leaves that are added to soil have a wide C/N ratio, ranging from 50 to 100. They are decomposed by the soil fauna and heterotrophic microorganisms that use the carbon, nitrogen, phosphorus and sulphur contained in the material to synthesize their cells and also use the carbon compounds for cellular processes such as respiration.

During decomposition, populations of active organisms rise and fall, CO_2 is released into the atmosphere, and some of the mineralized nitrogen, phosphorus and probably also sulphur is re-absorbed by the organisms to be re-mineralized again later. Under aerobic conditions the end products are CO_2, NO_3^-, $H_2PO_4^-$ and HPO_4^{2-}, and SO_4^{2-}.

Plants have access only to the nutrients that are surplus to the demands of the soil organisms. An illustration is the well-known effect of incorporation of cereal straw, which leads to the absorption from soil by microorganisms of NH_4^+ and NO_3^- for synthesis of their cells, leaving little or none for plants. The nitrogen becomes available to plants only when the C/N ratio has narrowed sufficiently (to around 20). The nitrogen that is incorporated in microbial and faunal cells becomes available to plants when the cells are decomposed, a process that is stimulated by wetting and drying the soil (Birch, 1960). Other plant nutrients are also released, as has been demonstrated for phosphate (Turner and Haygarth, 2001).

Although the mineralization of soil organic matter provides an important source of nutrients for crop plants, the process is not under man's control and can have disadvantages. The amounts of nutrients that are mineralized might exceed crop requirements; nitrogen can then be lost by leaching as nitrate, and as nitrogen (N_2) and nitrogen oxides to the atmosphere. An example from southern Nigeria is that during 15 months after forest clearance, two crops of maize removed $276\,kg\,N\,ha^{-1}$ compared with $509\,kg\,N\,ha^{-1}$ that was mineralized in the soil (Mueller-Harvey et al., 1985, 1989). Mineralization at a time when crop demand is low will often lead to loss of nitrogen. Measurements at three sites in southern England growing winter wheat showed losses of 25, 57 and $69\,kg\,ha^{-1}$ of NO_3^--N below 90 cm depth between ploughing grassland in September/October and the following April/May (Cameron and Wild, 1984). Some of the environmental problems from nitrate leaching arise from the lack of synchrony between mineralization of soil organic matter and organic manures, and the uptake by crops (Goulding, 2000; Jarvis, 2000).

Maintaining organic matter in soil

The amount of organic matter in soil is determined by the relative rates of additions and decomposition. In freely drained soils, the rate of decomposition to carbon dioxide and mineral products depends on temperature throughout the year, length of period the soil is moist, alternate wetting and drying periods, the composition of the organic material, and soil properties, especially pH and clay content. The effect of temperature, other factors being constant, is to double the rate of decomposition with each rise of 10 K, although this might not apply to forest soils (Giardina and Ryan, 2000). Because of the importance of soil organic matter, models developed from measured rates of addition and decomposition have been used to predict the effects of management practices and of global warming (Jenkinson, 1988, 1990; Jenkinson *et al.*, 1991; Powlson *et al.*, 1996).

Maintaining organic matter in freely drained soils of tropical regions is of particular importance (Greenland *et al.*, 1992; Woomer and Swift, 1994; Syers, 1997). One reason is its contribution to the cation exchange capacity of the soil, highly weathered soils in the tropics having low-activity (low cation exchange capacity) clays. Other effects are that it provides nutrients as described above and it helps to increase the infiltration of rain water. The difficulty is its high rate of decomposition when the soil is cultivated. It is maintained in forested soils which receive large amounts of litter and are kept relatively cool by the tree canopy.

4.6 NUTRIENT CYCLING AND BUDGETS

The cycling of nutrients in agricultural systems is their transfer between components of a field or farm. Nutrients removed in harvested crops and in animals that are sold off the farm might be returned in sewage sludge or animal products (e.g. bone meal) but are then usually classed as losses and gains in a nutrient budget rather than being part of a nutrient cycle.

Nutrients are returned to the soil when crop residues are ploughed in, and in animal excreta. Grazing animals return most of the plant nutrients in their food to the soil surface in faeces and urine, only a small part being retained. There can be a substantial loss of nitrogen by volatilization of ammonia and leaching loss of nitrate from the waste products that animals excrete on patches of soil. Ammonia is also lost from the dung and urine of penned animals under dry conditions and as nitrate when there is leaching.

Nutrients are recycled in various systems of agroforestry (see Section 9.7). Probably the most effective recycling system is one that includes a bush (tree) fallow for several years. Such systems also increase inputs during the fallow by capture from the atmosphere and from deep mineral weathering. The cycle is not closed, however, whatever the form of biomass production, farmed or not. There are always losses and additions. The biggest input is usually of nitrogen by biological fixation, which can be incorporated in soil organic matter.

At sites near oceans, inputs of sodium and chloride are high. Weathering of rock minerals can release substantial amounts of nutrients other than nitrogen, although they might be too deep in the subsoil to be taken up by roots. Loss of nutrients occurs in through-drainage, runoff and eroded soil, and nitrogen is lost as ammonia, nitrous oxide and nitrogen gas.

Agriculture in all its forms exacerbates nutrient losses. There is the removal in harvested crops and animals and their products that are sold off the land, and in increased runoff and eroded soil. Loss of nitrate by leaching occurs especially after the ploughing of grassland or if excessive amounts of nitrogen fertilizers have been used. Large applications of animal waste, for example cattle and pig slurries, can cause leaching of phosphate in organic compounds from light-textured soils. Gaseous loss of nitrous oxide and ammonia can also be increased. Inputs from fertilizer can make up for the losses but this requirement can be kept to a minimum by keeping the cycle as closed as possible (see Stevenson and Cole (1999) for an account of nutrient cycles).

Nutrient budgets

Investigations of nutrient budgets have a long history, dating back to the field experiments of Boussingault in the 1830s (Browne, 1944). Data for the United Kingdom as a whole showed that addition of nutrients (N, P, K) in fertilizers and imported feed stuffs exceeded removals in crops and by domesticated animals (Cooke, 1967). There were similar, positive nutrient balances in the USA and for phosphate in Australia, but for India there was a negative balance at that time for all three nutrients. Cooke also reported data for additions of nutrients and their removal in individual crops and rotations of crops. Typical amounts of nutrients removed per unit weight of the main crops at harvest are given in Table 4.1; the actual amount varies with the crop variety, nutrient supply and growing conditions.

Nutrient budgets and data on the transfer between soil nutrient pools in a wide range of agricultural ecosystems were presented by Frissel (1978) and Lowrance et al. (1983). The budgets showed that many extensive systems and some intensive systems (that received fertilizer) were being depleted of nutrients (Floate, 1978). Recent studies of the nutrient budgets of African soils (Table 4.5) point to nutrient depletion in many countries and also on individual farms (Smaling et al., 1997; see also earlier references therein). As the authors state, they made generalizations in order to obtain nutrient budgets for each country, and they had to use indirect data for some of their inputs and outputs. Their calculations nevertheless indicate that nutrient depletion is common in the soils of sub-Saharan Africa. Another example is the slash–burn

Table 4.5. *Nutrient budgets in Amazonia and sub-Saharan Africa calculated using data from Vlek et al. (1997)*

Region	Fluxes ($kg\,ha^{-1}\,a^{-1}$)		
	N	P	K
(A) Eastern Amazonia[a]			
With fertilizer			
Input	18.8	3.6	6.4
Output	36.7	2.2	14.3
Balance	−17.9	+1.4	−7.9
Without fertilizer			
Input	16.2	0.8	2.4
Output	30.3	1.4	11.7
Balance	−14.1	−0.6	−9.3
(B) Sub-Saharan Africa[b]			
Input	10.7	1.8	4.9
Output	32.6	4.4	21.7
Balance	−21.9	−2.6	−16.8

[a] Fluxes are annual means for a nine-year rotation of a seven-year fallow and two years of cropping with maize, cowpea and cassava; traditional slash and burn of the fallow vegetation; data from a region of highly weathered Ultisols.
[b] Fluxes are based on regional crop yields and fertilizer consumption, and estimated values of other inputs and outputs.

system (seven years fallow, two years arable under maize, cowpea and cassava) of the eastern Amazon region of Brazil (Table 4.5). Here, nutrient depletion was caused largely by nutrient removal in harvested crops.

Nutrient balances for rice reported by Greenland (1997) include inputs in rainfall, flood water, sediments and manures and by biological nitrogen fixation; outputs include the harvested crop, percolation and volatilization. Losses of nitrogen and sulphur also occur when the straw is burned.

Items of a nutrient budget that can be measured without too much difficulty include inputs in fertilizers and manures, and outputs in crops and in animals and their products. Outputs in drainage water from a field can be obtained from the water flux and the solution concentration or, more rarely, from the composition and flow of water from drainage pipes overlying a sealed subsoil. Inputs to and from the atmosphere require relatively sophisticated techniques, which makes a nitrogen balance sheet difficult to establish. Also difficult to establish is the gain from mineral weathering, but losses from water erosion and runoff can be measured. At best, however, nutrient budgets are only approximate.

The purpose of a nutrient budget for a particular farming system is to indicate whether crop nutrient supplies will increase or decrease over time. This information can also be gleaned by monitoring the levels in soil of extractable nutrients, as is the practice for phosphorus and potassium in arable fields in some countries. Nitrogen does not lend itself to this method, although the amount of soil organic matter, which can be monitored over a period of years, provides a rough indication of the supply of mineral nitrogen to crops.

4.7 BIOLOGICAL NITROGEN FIXATION

The total amount of nitrogen in the organic matter of soils of the world is about 220×10^9 tonnes (Stevenson and Cole, 1999). Most of this huge amount has been fixed from the atmosphere by microorganisms. The amount fixed per year has been estimated to be between 10×10^6 and 100×10^6 tonnes (Evans and Barber, 1977). The main genera of microorganisms that contain nitrogen-fixing species fall into two groups: non-symbiotic (free-living) microorganisms that obtain their carbon from organic compounds in the soil (heterotrophs) or from carbon dioxide (autotrophs); and symbiotic microorganisms that obtain their carbon from higher plants. The various species have been described by Harris (1988b) and Sprent and Sprent (1990). Non-symbiotic heterotrophs occur in most arable soils but fix little nitrogen (less than $2 \, \text{kg} \, \text{N} \, \text{ha}^{-1} \, \text{a}^{-1}$), whereas the autotrophs, mainly cyanobacteria (blue-green algae), which occur commonly in waterlogged soils especially in the tropics, can fix much more, perhaps up to around $50 \, \text{kg} \, \text{ha}^{-1} \, \text{a}^{-1}$.

The genus *Anabaena*, a member of the cyanobacteria, has a symbiosis with the water-fern *Azolla* which colonizes paddy fields in China and southeast Asia. The amount of nitrogen that the symbiosis can fix is highest in irrigated paddies that receive phosphate fertilizer and is depressed by the addition of nitrogen fertilizer (Greenland, 1997); annually, fixation can exceed $100 \, \text{kg} \, \text{N} \, \text{ha}^{-1}$. A different form of association is found in the rhizosphere, where several species of microorganisms may fix nitrogen although amounts are small. Most important in rainfed agriculture, however, is the symbiosis between rhizobia and plants of the Leguminosae.

Rhizobia–Leguminosae symbiosis

Many species of plants, including trees, of the Leguminosae have a symbiosis with rhizobia. The three main genera of bacteria that fix nitrogen symbiotically are *Rhizobium*, *Bradyrhizobium* and *Azorhizobium*, each with several species and strains (Singleton *et al.*, 1992). The symbiosis is of considerable agricultural importance, particularly because several leguminous crops can be inoculated with a more effective strain of *Rhizobium* that increases crop yield by fixing greater amounts of nitrogen than the native strain. A possibility for the future is that genetically modified non-legumes might have a symbiosis with rhizobia.

The amounts of nitrogen fixed by the symbiosis are commonly 40–100 kg N ha^{-1} a^{-1} for grain legumes and 100–200 kg N ha^{-1} a^{-1} for herbage legumes. The amounts fixed in tropical environments by grain legumes, legumes grown for green manuring, and shrubs and trees have been reported by Giller *et al.* (1997).

Inoculation with rhizobia has been adopted when new plant species are introduced in a region or country, for example with lucerne (alfalfa) in England, soybeans in the United States and subterranean clover in Australia. The appropriate strain infected the plant and was effective in fixing nitrogen. Inoculation has been less successful in the tropics, although there are a sufficient number of positive responses to justify a continuation of the research to develop suitable strains (Singleton *et al.*, 1992).

4.8 EFFECTS OF CULTIVATIONS

Cultivations have two main effects on the supply of nutrients to crops. Firstly, by loosening the soil they create voids through which roots can grow, increasing the depth of soil from which roots can take up nutrients and giving root laterals and root hairs greater contact with soil. Secondly, by disturbing the soil they increase the mineralization of soil organic matter. Minimum-tillage and no-till systems, although advocated primarily to reduce runoff in the tropics, lead to less rapid mineralization which might be more in synchrony with the requirements of crop plants than that under conventional tillage.

4.9 SUMMARY

When soils are first brought into cultivation the stock of nutrients is, under most conditions, sufficient for crops to be grown for a period without addition of fertilizers. This period might be as short as two or three years after a bush fallow in the humid tropics, or several decades, as was the experience when the prairies of the USA were brought into cultivation. Sooner or later the stocks of nutrients become insufficient for cropping to be economic, as cultivations and the crop harvest lead to losses by leaching, volatilization and removal from the farm. The period of cropping can be lengthened by the recycling of nutrients in straw, stubble and animal excreta. Additions can be made by biological nitrogen fixation and from the water and sediment in paddies and other flooded soils. During a long fallow, trees transfer nutrients from depth in the soil profile to the soil surface and also capture nutrients from the air. These sources are often sufficient for low or moderate crop yields, of the order of 1–$2\,t\,ha^{-1}$ of wheat and 2–$3\,t\,ha^{-1}$ of paddy rice. Increasing populations require greater food production, which in turn commonly requires the use of fertilizer to raise yields (see Chapter 6).

5

Land degradation and its control

Land degradation may be defined as the loss of actual or potential production of biomass and of the capacity to regulate the environment as a result of natural or anthropogenic factors (derived from Lal, 1997).

Loss of productive land adds to the difficulty of feeding an increasing world population and, at the same time, retaining the area of natural or semi-natural ecosystems. The loss may be due to man's activities or to natural causes. An example of loss by natural causes is that during the last 10 000 years a change in climate, particularly to less or no rainfall, has led to the extension of deserts in northern Africa and the Arabian peninsula. Other natural processes include erosion, acidification and salinization of soils, all of which have affected large areas of land. Important as these natural processes are, this chapter deals primarily with degradation caused by man. As will be shown, almost one-sixth of the land area of the world has already been degraded to a greater or lesser extent (although not all by man alone). Techniques for its control and for the recovery of damaged land are economically viable, but are not sufficiently applied.

The effect of degradation may be to lose the whole soil, as occurs in extreme forms of soil erosion, or to result in less capacity to produce biomass in agricultural or natural ecosystems. Environmental consequences follow. Erosion leads to less retention of water in the soil and more sediment deposited in river beds, and together these cause more severe flooding. When crop yields fall farmers may move to land which is a habitat for wild plants and animals, which is then lost to nature, and more land degradation follows. Unless degradation is halted it will become difficult to produce the required amount of food in countries

Table 5.1. *Harmful effects of various agricultural activities on soil properties*

Activity	On-site effects
(1) Destruction of vegetation by burning, felling and ring-barking	• Breaks the natural cycling of nutrients • Increases rate and amount of runoff, leading to erosion
(2) Cultivations and growth of arable crops	• Reduces the level of soil organic matter • Exposes soil surface to erosive actions of wind and rain • Depletes soil nutrients
(3) Use of fertilizers	• Fertilizer containing ammonia, ammonium salts or urea can cause acidification
(4) Irrigation	• Can cause waterlogging and salinization
(5) Overgrazing	• Compacts soil • Removes vegetative cover and together with compaction leads to erosion

where the population is increasing most rapidly; also, whole ecosystems will disappear.

5.2 DEGRADATION OF SOILS: CAUSES AND EFFECTS

Several processes have adverse effects on soils. Most common, and usually the most serious, is erosion: the loss of part of the soil or the whole soil through the action of water or wind. There can also be various chemical changes (nutrient depletion, salinization, pollution, acidification) and physical changes (compaction, sealing and crusting of the soil surface, waterlogging and subsidence of organic soils) that reduce the capacity of soil to support biomass production. All these changes occur naturally, but have been accelerated by the activities of man such as the clear-felling of forests, overgrazing of grasslands and cultivation of land using techniques that are not appropriate for the local conditions (Table 5.1).

An estimate of the areas of land affected by the various processes of degradation is given in Table 5.2. Although the areas are not

Table 5.2. *Global areas (Mha) of the types of soil degradation and the causative factors.*

Notes:

(1) For comparison with the degraded areas, the total land area of the world is about 14 800 Mha.

(2) Four levels of the degree of soil degradation are recognized:

- *light* – the terrain has somewhat reduced agricultural suitability, but is suitable for use in local farming systems. Restoration to full productivity is possible by modification of the management system. Original biotic functions are still largely intact.

- *moderate* – the terrain has greatly reduced agricultural productivity but is still suitable for use in local farming systems. Major improvements are required to restore productivity. Original biotic systems partially destroyed.

- *strong* – the terrain is not reclaimable at the farm level. Major engineering works are required for terrain restoration. Original biotic functions are largely destroyed.

- *extreme* – the terrain is unreclaimable and beyond restoration. Original biotic functions are fully destroyed.

	Causative factor					
Type of soil degradation	Deforestation of natural vegetation	Over-exploitation of natural vegetation	Over-grazing	Agricultural activities	Industrial activities	Total
Water erosion	471	36	320	266	—	1094
Wind erosion	44	85	332	87	—	549
Chemical degradation[a]	62	10	14	133	23	240
Physical degradation[b]	1	+	14	66	—	81
Total	579	133	679	552	23	1964

Source: Oldeman *et al.* (1991) and Oldeman (1994); reproduced with permission from Elsevier Science.

[a] Chemical degradation comprises nutrient depletion (56%), salinization (32%), pollution (9%) and acidification (3%).

[b] Physical degradation comprises compaction, sealing and crusting (82%), waterlogging (13%) and subsidence of organic soils (5%).

definitive, being dependent on the subjective judgement of local experts, they indicate that of the 14 800 Mha of total land area of the world almost 2000 million (13 per cent) is affected to some extent by degradation. About 38 per cent of the degradation is described as 'light',

46 per cent as 'moderate' and 16 per cent as 'strong' and 'extreme'. Of the various forms of degradation, water and wind erosion affect 84 per cent of the degraded area, chemical degradation 12 per cent, and physical degradation 4 per cent. The continental areas that are most affected are Africa and Central America, although all are affected to some extent.

There are two general reasons for man-made degradation of land, which tends to occur particularly during periods when countries are undergoing economic development (Harris, 1995). First, an increase in population leads to cropping of less suitable land, overgrazing and increased demand for wood as fuel and timber for buildings. Fallows are replaced by continuous cultivation, steeply sloping land is brought into cultivation, and plant nutrients are removed and not replaced (nutrient mining).

The second reason is that national policies usually encourage industrialization and create pricing structures for agricultural products that favour urban populations at the expense of farmers; cheap food is imported. The infrastructure in rural areas is neglected, investment in agriculture is insufficient, and farmers receive too little information to improve their techniques. These reasons do not apply to all countries or provinces, but are given here to show that social, economic and political factors have usually to be taken into account if land degradation is to be avoided.

The degradation of soil has both on-site effects on biomass production from the land and off-site effects on surface water and on the atmosphere. These effects are summarized in Table 5.3.

Soil resilience

Some of the on-site effects listed in Table 5.3 are irreversible over a time span of a few hundred years, as with severe erosion. Other types of degradation can be reversed more quickly and easily. Soils that have been acidified can be limed, those depleted of nutrients can receive fertilizers or organic manures, and those that have been only moderately eroded can be allowed to recover under the protection of undisturbed vegetation.

These examples illustrate a concept termed 'soil resilience', which is 'the ability of soil to revert to its original or near original performance or "state" that existed before the impressed forces altered it' (Eswaran, 1994). In an agricultural context 'performance' is measured by crop yield or herbage production. 'State' refers to particular components: thickness of soil horizons, content of organic matter, content of plant

Table 5.3. *Processes of soil degradation that affect soil fertility and the environment*

Process	Effect on soil fertility	Effect on the environment
Erosion	Topsoil removed, nutrients lost, capacity to regulate water supply reduced	Deposition of soil material in rivers and dams, pesticide carried into rivers, flash floods
Loss of organic material	Reduced storage and supply of nutrients, more rapid acidification, less structure	Increased erosion, release of CO_2 into the atmosphere
Nutrient depletion	Reduced biomass production	Increased bare soil leading to more erosion
Salinization	Adverse effect on crops	Increased bare soil, more wind erosion
Acidification	Alumunium and less commonly manganese toxicity to crops	Toxicities of leached aluminium to fish and other inhabitants of surface waters
Chemical contamination	Toxicities to crops, health hazards to animals including humans	Toxicities of chemicals in runoff, eroded soil and drainage water
Compaction and surface sealing	Reduced infiltration of water; reduced germination, emergence of seedlings and root growth	Increased runoff and water erosion

Source: After Carter *et al.* (1997).

nutrients, degree of acidity or salinity, or compaction. Other definitions refer to the ability of soil to return to its equilibrium state before the imposition of the stress that caused degradation (Blum and Santelises, 1994).

The concept of soil resilience is useful in directing attention to those forms of soil degradation that can be reversed comparatively easily or at low cost from those that cannot. One problem with the concept is that the condition of the soil before degradation is often not known; also, this condition may not suit crop production if, for example, the soil was originally acidic. The concept is more fully discussed by several authors in Greenland and Szabolcs (1994).

5.3 SOIL EROSION

Soil erosion is the removal of part or all of the soil by the action of water or wind and deposition of its components elsewhere. The process moulds the landscape, the deposits forming alluvial soils that are usually fertile. It is a natural, geological process. Considerations here are limited to accelerated soil erosion, which is the erosion caused by the activities of man.

Accelerated soil erosion

Erosion often occurs when hillslopes are cultivated and, especially in dry regions, when land is overgrazed. It has been occurring for several millennia (Jacks and Whyte, 1939; Hyams, 1952; Hillel, 1991; Bell and Boardman, 1992) and was recognized by Roman writers as a cause of the impoverishment of their soils. It became an issue of general concern following the dust storms of the 1930s, which led to the formation of soil conservation services in the USA and other countries. Many accounts have been written of the extent of erosion, its causes, effects on agricultural production, off-site effects and conservation techniques (Kirkby and Morgan, 1980; Lal, 1988, 1993; Boardman et al., 1990; Pimental, 1993; Hudson, 1995; Morgan, 1995; Troeh et al., 1999). The discussion that follows considers the effects on agricultural production.

Erosion by water and wind affects about 1643 Mha of the surface area of the world, that is, about 11 per cent of the land area, and is by far the most widespread form of soil degradation (Table 5.2). Rates of soil loss from cultivated land vary greatly from slight to over $100\,t\,ha^{-1}\,a^{-1}$, and may involve loss of the whole soil. To put these losses into perspective, loss of $100\,t\,ha^{-1}\,a^{-1}$ for 10 years is approximately equal to the top 10 cm of soil.

Effect on crop yields and total economic cost

Loss of topsoil by erosion reduces crop yields because of the attendant loss of nutrients, water storage capacity and structural aggregates. The amount by which crop yield is depressed depends on how much of the topsoil is lost, on the relative properties of topsoil and subsoil, and on whether there are compensating inputs of fertilizer and, where possible, water. Erosion causes particularly large reductions in yield from shallow soils and those which have subsoils that are compact, stony or are almost devoid of one or more nutrients. Gullying makes cultivation impossible.

One method that has been used to measure the effect of loss of topsoil is to remove the topsoil by hand. When this was done on a silt loam, claypan soil in central Missouri (Troeh et al., 1999) the yield of maize was reduced to about one-fifth in years with only spasmodic rainfall; however, yields were comparable on the truncated and normal soils when rains were adequate and well spaced. In this experiment adequate fertilizer was applied.

It is apparent from the above discussion that an average of country-wide yield loss calculated from a few point sources may be inaccurate. However, there are, nevertheless, reports from many parts of the world of yield reductions caused by erosion (Lal, 1997), for example reductions of 30–90 per cent on some root-restrictive soils of West Africa and 20–40 per cent in some parts of the American Midwest. Estimates of the total economic cost of loss of soil nutrients by erosion and of the associated water runoff are about $44 billion annually in the USA (Pimental et al., 1995) and about $400 billion globally per year (Lal, 1997). Although these are only estimates it is certain that the costs are substantial. Perhaps more serious is the possibility that reduced yields and loss of cultivated soils will add to the difficulty of raising agricultural production to the level required during this century.

Causes and processes

The agents of erosion are water and wind. Soil particles detached from the soil mass by raindrop impact and runoff are displaced downslope. When soil is dry and soil structure is weak, wind can carry sand grains a few centimetres or metres and small particles (less than 0.1 mm diameter) for distances of several kilometres. Both kinds of erosion occur most readily when the soil surface is bare of vegetation. The processes involved have been discussed by Hudson (1995), Morgan (1995) and Marshall et al. (1996).

Water erosion

The first process is the detachment of mineral grains or small aggregates from larger aggregates, caused by the impact of large, fast-falling raindrops. Some of the soil particles are splashed into the air and on a hillslope fall predominantly downhill. Infiltration of water is reduced as the large pore spaces become blocked by collapse of the larger aggregates and deposition of the splashed particles. When the rainfall intensity is greater than the infiltration rate, water runs off the soil surface.

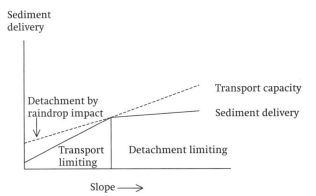

Figure 5.1. Schematic representation of the processes of particle detachment and transport in relation to slope on inter-rill areas. From Foster (1990); reproduced with permission of John Wiley & Sons.

The second process is the transport of some of the detached particles in the runoff water. As it flows downhill with its suspended load the runoff water may detach and transport more particles (Figure 5.1). The flow, initially as a sheet over the soil surface (inter-rill flow), becomes concentrated in small channels called rills that coalesce into larger and deeper rills as the flow becomes turbulent. The suspended load is deposited when the flow rate decreases either because the slope decreases, or because there is vegetative cover or some other form of protection. On a long, unprotected slope or with a prolonged, severe storm the rills tend to join together and the turbulent flow produces gullies. Whereas rills can be eliminated by cultivations, gullies require special treatment.

Wind erosion

Wind erosion is most pronounced in dry or semi-arid areas that have sparse vegetation (Wilson and Cooke, 1980). Wind causes movement of sand in sandy deserts and in the areas around deserts where the soil is composed largely of wind-blown material; erosion is most likely to occur during long dry spells. Topsoil with small granules (0.1–0.5 mm diameter), peaty soils and salt-encrusted soils are also subject to wind erosion during dry spells, especially during the heat of the day. Turbulence at the soil surface drags particles into the air; turbulence in the air is less, and so sand grains, after being carried forward a short distance by the wind, fall back to the surface. They bump into other grains that are then carried into the air. This process (termed saltation) has the effect of creating a moving sea of sand that is arrested only when the wind drops or when the sand is held by some impediment such as vegetation. The famous dust storms of the 1930s in the Great Plains of the USA (similar ones have occurred in several other countries) were composed of fine particles of topsoil that were transported several kilometres from their origin.

Both forms of erosion remove topsoil, the most valuable part of the soil for agricultural production. Wind erosion may leave a surface of stones or gravel when the fine particles have been blown away. Water erosion may leave the less productive subsoil or, where erosion is severe, bare rock.

Measuring soil loss   Method

The usual reason for measuring soil loss is to test the effectiveness of soil conservation techniques. For agricultural purposes soil loss is measured on the field scale, whereas for geomorphological, and environmental purposes the unit is a catchment (drainage basin) – loss is measured in the stream or river that leaves the catchment (Walling, 1988). This loss from the catchment underestimates soil loss at the field scale because there is deposition within the catchment, which is difficult to measure accurately.

Water erosion

Soil loss from agricultural land is commonly measured from field plots that usually include conservation treatments. The types of plots used by conservationists in the United States to develop the Universal Soil Loss Equation (USLE; see below) are probably the most widely used. The standard plot is 22.1 m long on a uniform length-wise slope of 9 per cent, and 1.83 m wide. Runoff and eroded soil are measured at the lower end of the plot (Mutchler *et al.*, 1988; Morgan, 1995). Small plots have also been used to establish the order of magnitude of erosion (Hudson, 1995) and for research. Also used in this context is caesium-137 from the atmospheric fall-out of thermonuclear weapons testing in the 1950s to 1970s. It acts as a tracer to measure the downslope transfer of soil (Loughran *et al.*, 1990; Walling and Quine, 1990; Chappell *et al.*, 1998). Other methods for measuring slope processes are described by Goudie (1995).

The methods described above are suitable for measuring rill and inter-rill erosion. Gully erosion has been measured as the increase in the volume of the gully over time, including the retreat of the headwall. Aerial photography is used to measure the frequency of gullying and the rate of growth of gullies (Mitchell and Bubenzer, 1980; Morgan, 1995).

Wind erosion

Wind erosion is more difficult to quantify. Aerial photography and satellite imaging have been used to measure the advance of sand dunes, and on-site collectors have been used to measure the rate of movement of particles of different size classes (Ploey and Gabriels, 1980; Morgan, 1995). Two difficulties in the latter method are lack of definition of the area of origin of the particles and the interference of the collectors with wind flow. Rates of deposition are easier to measure than rates of erosion. Goudie (1995) reports deposition rates of 5–181 t km^{-2} a^{-1}, the highest being in northern Nigeria and New Mexico. As with water erosion, wind erosion is spasmodic, and so average values should be treated with caution.

Modelling soil erosion

The purpose of most soil erosion models is to predict the amount of soil that will be eroded from a field, hillslope or catchment area. The prediction is usually intended to inform decisions on conservation measures required. A model may also predict where the sediment from the eroded soil will be deposited and how much there will be. There are several models of water erosion (Foster, 1988; Hudson, 1995; Morgan, 1995), but few of wind erosion (Skidmore, 1988).

For water erosion the data required are rainfall and soil characteristics, slope of land surfaces, and cropping practices (or such of these as are relevant). The period of time for which prediction is required may be anything from the duration of a single storm to several years. Prediction of erosion is usually required because of the potential loss of crop yields, or because of off-site damage such as siltation of reservoirs. No one model meets these diverse requirements.

The Universal Soil Loss Equation (USLE; Wischmeier and Smith, 1978) is an early example of a model designed to predict the rate of soil loss from fields and hillslopes. The equation is

$$E = RKLSCP,$$

where E is the mean annual soil loss, R is the rainfall erosivity factor, K is the soil erodibility factor, L is the slope length factor, S is the slope steepness factor, C is the crop management factor, and P is the erosion control factor. Rainfall erosivity is the product of the kinetic energy of a storm and its 30-minute intensity. Soil erodibility is usually measured by rainfall tests under laboratory conditions. The factors are multiplied to give a predicted rate of soil loss. If this rate is unacceptably high, crop management (C) and the length of unprotected slope (L) can be changed to reduce the loss.

An unacceptable rate of erosion is one that exceeds the rate of soil formation. Values of $0.3–2\,t\,ha^{-1}\,a^{-1}$ have been reported for soil formation under temperate and tropical conditions; a rate of around $1\,t\,ha^{-1}\,a^{-1}$ is a useful average (Pimental, 1993). Conservation measures should therefore aim to prevent erosion exceeding $1\,t\,ha^{-1}\,a^{-1}$. The acceptable rate is less for soil on consolidated, hard rock. For deep soils a higher rate might be acceptable in the short term.

The Universal Soil Loss Equation has been found to be most useful east of the Rocky Mountains in the United States, the area in which it was validated by field experiments. Its structure has been criticized (Kirkby, 1980; Foster, 1990). For regions beyond its database the USLE has been modified to produce the Revised Universal Soil Loss Equation (RUSLE; Renard et al., 1997).

Since about 1980 the trend has been to develop models based more on processes. The two fundamental processes in water erosion are detachment of particles and particle transport, which have been described mathematically using parameters measured empirically (see Foster, 1990). The Water Erosion Prediction Project (WEPP) and the European Soil Erosion Model (EUROSEM) are examples of such models (Morgan, 1995). Both can be used for catchments.

Other models of soil erosion include CREAMS (Chemicals, Run-off and Erosion from Agricultural Management System), which are used to compare the effects of different farming practices, including soil conservation, on the loss of nutrients and pesticides, loss of soil and runoff. They are described by Foster (1988) and Smith and Knisel (1985). Models developed to predict the loss of crop yield because of erosion include EPIC (Erosion Product Impact Calculator) and PI (Productivity Index) (Foster, 1988; Hudson, 1995).

Principles of soil conservation

Loss of soil by erosion can be reduced by various conservation measures that control one or both of the two processes of water erosion (detachment and downslope transport). Essentially this means protecting the soil surface from the direct impact of raindrops and minimizing the amount of runoff and its rate of flow. For protection against wind erosion the soil needs a cover of vegetation, and windbreaks may be needed to reduce wind speed. How the protection is implemented depends on the physical, biological and economic conditions at the site in question. It is important that the farmer is involved, so that he can see the benefits (more secure food production or higher yields) of the measures.

There are various ways of controlling water erosion through good husbandry. They include the use of a mulch of crop residues or weeds to protect the soil from raindrop impact and increase infiltration of water. Crops established well before the most erosive rains and at a high plant density reduce the area of bare soil. Mixed cropping with early and late varieties lessens the period of time the soil is bare. Cultivation and ridge and furrow systems should be on or close to the contour to minimize rill formation. Strips of grass, hedges and trees on the contours can also be used, to slow the rate of runoff. Water infiltration can be increased by incorporating crop residues, weeds and other organic materials. No-till planting has the same effects (Lal, 1989a,b).

There is also a wide range of physical practices for protecting the land. To a large extent they vary according to the water regime. Hudson (1995) identifies three possible objectives: (i) to retain the water where it falls or to lead it on to arable land (water harvesting), (ii) to retain as much rainfall as possible, but to cater for infrequent heavy rains, and (iii) to manage unavoidable runoff. To meet these objectives various kinds of terraces and conservation banks can be used (Hudson, 1995), depending on the slope of the land, rainfall characteristics and properties of the soil.

In low-rainfall areas, objective (i) is to retain rain water in the soil. The requirements are a sufficiently high rate of infiltration, a sufficiently deep soil to provide storage of the water, and no severe storms. Banks are laid out on the contour using soil excavated from the uphill side. Between the banks the absorption terraces are used for cropping. The banks retain water and soil.

To meet objectives (ii) and (iii), runoff has to be controlled. A commonly used method is to construct retention banks that are graded at a small angle to the contour, with channels on the uphill side. Runoff water that collects in the channels flows at a low gradient into a natural water course or via a grassed waterway into the water course. Eroded soil that collects in the channels is excavated and spread on the terraces. Where ridge and furrow cultivation is practised, the furrows are drawn off the contour and the same principles are followed, to guide the water into a water course.

Wind erosion of land that is cultivated can be controlled by retaining a covering of crop or stubble for as long as possible. Where soil is tilled, erosion is reduced if the soil is left in a cloddy condition. Planting in the stubble (no-till) provides some control. Overgrazing, a common cause of wind erosion, must be avoided. Where they can be established windbreaks of trees or hedges at 90° to the prevailing wind are used to reduce windspeed (Morgan, 1995).

5.4 DEGRADATION OF SOIL CHEMICAL PROPERTIES

Nutrient depletion

Depletion of nutrients is the most common form of chemical degradation (Table 5.2). Nutrients are lost by removal from the land in drainage water, crops, and animal products, and to the atmosphere. The five natural sources of nutrients to replace those lost are (i) biologically fixed nitrogen, (ii) weathering of soil minerals, (iii) deposition of river silt, (iv) volcanic ash and lava, and (v) dry and wet deposition from the atmosphere. Before the introduction of fertilizers during the nineteenth century, these sources were usually insufficient to prevent depletion, the most notable exception being land flooded annually with silt-bearing water.

The techniques that have been used to counteract nutrient depletion include using dung from penned animals, bush fallows, rotations that include legumes (especially herbage legumes), deposition of dung and urine by animals that had grazed elsewhere, and burning of vegetation collected from elsewhere. As populations increased, fallow/ cropping ratios decreased, and as people moved into cities there were fewer labourers to undertake heavy work such as carrying and spreading dung and carrying vegetation into the field for burning.

As described in Chapter 4, the depletion of nutrients has been most serious in regions where fertilizers have been little used. The two examples given in Table 4.5, of Amazonia and sub-Saharan Africa, show output of nutrients exceeding input, that is, nutrient mining.

Soil acidification

Soil acidification is estimated to affect only 3 per cent of the 240 Mha of land affected by chemical degradation, that is, an area of 7.2 Mha

Table 5.4. *Main sources of soil acidity*

---

(1) Deposition (both wet and dry) of acids and acid-forming substances from the atmosphere

(2) Use of nitrogen fertilizers containing ammonia, ammonium salts or urea

(3) Removal of base cations in harvested biomass and by leaching

(4) Greater uptake by plants of cations than anions (more strictly, where electrical charge on total cations exceeds electrical charge on total anions)

(5) Biological fixation of nitrogen

(6) Leaching of bases associated with organic and inorganic anions

(7) Volatilization of ammonia from ammonium compounds

(8) Increase in soil organic matter content

(9) Oxidation of reduced sulphur compounds

(Table 5.2). Although the area is small relative to other forms of soil degradation, it is of particular concern (i) in regions with industrial air pollution ('acid rain'), (ii) in weakly buffered soils that receive nitrogen fertilizers, and (iii) close to intensive animal production units that release ammonia into the atmosphere. Soils that are naturally acidic occur over wide areas in Amazonas (Smyth and Cassel, 1995) and under forests in temperate and boreal zones. Soil acidity has deleterious effects on plant growth and aquatic organisms because it raises the concentration of aluminium in the soil solution and in drainage water.

Soil acidification can be defined as (i) a decrease in the pH of the soil solution or suspension, or of an aqueous extract of the soil, or (ii) a decrease in the acid neutralizing capacity (ANC) of the soil (van Breemen *et al.*, 1996). pH measures acid intensity and is commonly used when considering the effect of acidity on plants. The ANC is used when quantifying the effects of acids and acid-forming substances on soils and water.

Causes of soil acidification

The main causes of soil acidification are listed in Table 5.4. Uncontaminated rain water has a pH of about 5.5 (with the present concentration of CO_2 in the atmosphere). The pH can be 4 or below in the presence of strong acids such as HCl, HNO_3 and H_2SO_4 generated by industrial activities (Legge and Krupa, 1990). In addition, ammonium ions in rain water cause acidification when they are oxidized in soils. Dry deposition of the gases NH_3 (followed by oxidation in soils) and SO_2 also causes acidification.

The effect on soils and ecosystems depends on the amount of acid, acid-forming and alkali-forming substances deposited from the atmosphere, the acid neutralizing capacity of the soil, and any internal processes that generate acidity or alkalinity (Reuss and Johnson, 1986). Soils containing calcium carbonate and minerals that readily react with acid are resistant to acidification, whereas other soils are not. This is the basis of the concept of critical loads of deposition that soils can accept without long-term harmful effects (Nilsson and Grennfelt, 1988; Hornung and Skeffington, 1993).

Deposition of sulphate has decreased in Europe and North America since the 1960s and 1970s (Jenkins, 1999). Soil acidification will, however, continue. Nitrate and ammonia/ammonium (that oxidize to nitrate), and sulphate which is still being deposited and also desorbed from the soil, lead to loss by leaching of basic cations (Stoddard et al., 1999; Alewell et al., 2000).

In cultivated soils the main cause of acidification is usually the use of nitrogen fertilizers that supply urea, ammonia or an ammonium salt which, on oxidation by soil microorganisms, produce nitric acid (see Section 6.6). Acidification is also caused by the biological fixation of nitrogen and an uptake by plants of cations in excess of anions (see Section 4.4). The effect of all these processes on soil pH is greatest in soils with low buffer capacity, and results in leaching from the soil of anions (NO_3^- and SO_4^{2-}) that carry with them base cations (Ca^{2+}, Mg^{2+}, K^+). The base cations are also removed in the crop harvest.

Generation of acids within the soil is also a cause of acidification. Mineralization of organic matter produces nitrate and sulphate; if leached from the soil they are accompanied by base cations. Oxidation of sulphide minerals, as often occurs when submerged soils are reclaimed, produces sulphuric acid (there are records of the pH falling as low as 1) that also increases loss of base cations.

Effects of soil acidification

A direct effect of soil acidification is to increase the solubility of aluminium, which is toxic to most plants. Manganese can also reach toxic concentrations. Uptake of nutrients, especially phosphate, is reduced and several metabolic processes are affected. The overall effect is to reduce crop yield; with severe acidification, plants die before harvest (see also Rowell, 1988; Marschner, 1995).

The die-back of trees has been attributed to the acidifying effect of deposits from the atmosphere, possibly causing aluminium toxicity or a deficiency of base cations, especially close to heavily industrialized regions. The die-back of trees has also been attributed to poor forest management and to a change in climatic conditions (Schulze and Freer-Smith, 1991).

Another effect is acidification of rivers and lakes by the drainage from acid soils (Mason, 1992; Howells, 1995). When the pH drops below 5 the affected waters have fewer species of fish and often lower numbers as well. Evidence points to aluminium in the water altering respiration across the gills of the fish (Potts and McWilliams, 1989).

Management of acid soils

The solubility of aluminium and manganese, and hence the risk of their reaching toxic levels, is reduced by raising the pH by the addition of lime. The amount to be added in the field can be determined by laboratory experiment, as the amount required to raise the pH to a certain level, or to reduce the exchangeable aluminium to a particular value, and adjusted as necessary for use in the field. More rarely there is a deficiency of calcium or magnesium; this can be corrected by application of lime or limestone containing magnesium or a salt of the metals.

Where there is no local source, as in many parts of the tropics, liming materials are expensive. An alternative is to grow crop species or varieties that are more tolerant of acid conditions. In the tropics the main plantation crops grown on acid soils are oil palm, rubber, tea and pineapple; the main arable crops include cassava, varieties of upland rice, and the grain legumes cowpea and pigeon pea. Grasses grown on acid soils include *Panicum maximum*, *Hyparrhenea rufa*, *Melinis minutiflora*, *Paspalum* spp. and *Brachiaria* spp.; the pasture legumes *Stylosanthes humilis* and *Desmodium intortum* are also acid tolerant. In temperate regions the arable crops potato and rye are grown on acid soils (pH as low as 4.9). Rowell (1994), describes methods for measuring the lime requirement of soils, and Sanchez (1976) lists several crop species and varieties suitable for acidic soils in the tropics.

Salinization

As with acidity, there are soils that are saline through natural causes. Naturally saline soils are present in inland areas of Australia, Hungary and the USA, where rainfall is low and there is little drainage to the oceans. Many coastal areas are affected by salt of marine origin and incursions of the sea. Soils can also become saline under irrigation because of poor planning or poor management, often associated with waterlogging (Umali, 1993). An estimated area of 77 Mha of land is affected by salinity (Table 5.2), and 10–15 per cent (24–35 Mha) of irrigated land is affected (Alexandratos, 1995).

Salinization and waterlogging of irrigated land are commonly caused by inadequate drainage, leakage from canals and excessive application of water (see also Section 7.5). Irrigation water itself contains dissolved salts at concentrations that in dry regions are often high. Also, if the aquifer is saline, when waterlogging occurs the soluble salts are carried towards the soil surface. The ions present in largest concentrations are usually Na^+, Ca^{2+}, Mg^{2+}, Cl^-, SO_4^{2-} and HCO_3^-. All these ions decrease the osmotic potential of soil water; plants are then less able to take up water. This causes a physiological drought; growth rate is reduced and yields suffer. If borate ions are present at a high concentration there may also be a direct toxic effect.

The concentration of salt in irrigation water is determined by measuring its electrical conductivity, and the same method is used for soils, using saturation extracts (Rowell, 1994). The values can be used as a quick guide to the appropriate choice of crops.

A problem related to soil salinity is soil sodicity. This occurs when the level of exchangeable sodium expressed as a percentage of the total exchangeable cations (ESP) exceeds a certain value, often 15 (although in some soils a lower value is used). With a high ESP and low salt concentrations, as can occur when salt is leached out, dispersion of the soil occurs. Soil aggregates swell and clay particles disperse, blocking the soil pores and reducing permeability to water. The recommended treatment is to increase the calcium content of the soil by adding gypsum (calcium sulphate).

Another related problem occurs when irrigation water has a high concentration of bicarbonate. If the sodium concentration is also high, the soil pH can increase to over 9, resulting in less availability of some nutrients and, if the salt concentration is low, soil dispersion. The presence of high concentrations of bicarbonate also causes precipitation of calcium and magnesium carbonates, which can form an impermeable layer in the soil.

Control measures

As with acidification, the three kinds of action that may be needed are prevention, reclamation and adaption. Where salinization is a threat on irrigated land, the aim of good management is to prevent the concentration of salt increasing to a level that is harmful to the crop. This can be done by leaching the salt into piped drains or into a natural drainage system. Commonly, the irrigated land has little or no gradient, the water table is high and drainage requires the water to be pumped into a water course. The salt may be leached out by rain if there is sufficient, but more usually there is too little rain and excess irrigation water has to be applied.

Farming systems for saline and saline/sodic soils can be based on crops that are tolerant of the conditions. The date palm, barley, sugar beet, fodder beet and cotton are tolerant, but varieties differ in their sensitivity and with all crops there is an upper limit to the concentration of salt they can tolerate. In dryland areas used for grazing by sheep, goats or cattle, various halophytic forage species can be planted (Qureshi et al., 1991). A review of experiments (Davidson and Galloway, 1991) describes the establishment of trees (e.g. *Acacia* spp., *Eucalyptus* spp., *Melaleuca* spp.), bushes (e.g. *Atriplex* spp., *Maireana* spp.) and grasses (e.g. *Spartina* spp., *Sporabolus* spp.) in saline and saline/sodic soils in India, Pakistan and northeast Thailand. These species provide grazing and also protect the soil from wind erosion.

Pollution

One of the beneficial properties of soils is their ability to adsorb and decompose chemicals, for example pesticides, that might otherwise contaminate surface waters or the atmosphere and pose a hazard to plants and animals. There is evidence, mainly from *in vitro* studies, that herbicides, fungicides and insecticides can affect the soil biota and its biological processes, some effects being stimulatory and others depressive (Watrud and Seidler, 1998). As yet, however, there is no evidence of any long-term harmful effects on soil fertility from pesticides applied at recommended rates. With the exception of DDT and its decomposition product DDE, pesticides are not persistent in soil because they volatilize and microorganisms decompose them.

Soil pollution is thus mainly a problem caused by hazardous elements and to a lesser extent by organic wastes. Globally, affected soils account for only a small proportion of the total soil degradation (Table 5.2). Accounts of soil pollution have been published by Assink and van den Brink (1986) and de Haan and Visser-Reyneveld (1996), of metal toxicity by McBride (1994), Alloway (1995), Alloway and Ayres (1997) and Hayes and Traina (1998), and of problems with radionuclides by Fellows et al. (1998). Monitoring of pollution has been reviewed by Schulin et al. (1993).

Toxic elements

Soil contaminated with elements at concentrations that give rise to toxicities are commonly close to metal ore mining and smelting operations. Local contamination of alluvial soils and their vegetative cover can occur from water used to wash the ore, which contains suspended mineral particles. Tailings that have dried may be spread over a greater area by wind. Particles carried into the atmosphere in smoke produced during smelting may also be spread over a wide area.

Sewage sludge and industrial wastes are another source of toxic elements. The concentrations of elements vary with the source of the waste, particularly with the materials used in the industrial processes. The elements presenting the greatest hazard are cadmium, chromium, copper, nickel, lead and zinc. Guidelines on the use of sewage sludge have been in operation in many countries for several years to prevent the accumulation of these elements to harmful concentrations on agricultural land. European regulations are now based on the maximum concentrations of potentially harmful elements permitted in soil (HMSO, 1996). Contamination from all sources and naturally high concentrations are taken into account.

Landfill sites contain decomposable organic waste that initially releases carbon dioxide by microbial activity. Later, as the waste becomes anaerobic, it releases methane, which can form a potentially hazardous explosive mixture with air. Drainage from the anaerobic waste may contain noxious organic substances and reduced forms of metals such as Mn^{2+} and Fe^{2+}. Regulations restrict the siting of landfills to areas usually sufficiently far from water courses to avoid contamination from drainage and overflow. When the site has been filled and topsoil added it can be turned to agricultural, forestry or amenity uses. It should not be used as building land because of the danger of subsidence, as well as the hazards from methane and from toxic elements that could contaminate the topsoil.

Organic contaminants

Organic contaminants such as pesticides, mineral oils and other industrial pollutants range widely in nature of compound, source and concentration. At low concentrations volatilization and biodegradation generally prevent accumulation to harmful concentrations. Adsorption isotherms measured in the laboratory show that many contaminants are adsorbed by soil, although they may reach water courses in drainage through wide pores and in eroded soil. Localized heavy contamination of abandoned factory and waste disposal sites creates problems for the environment because the organic materials, for example mineral oil, can pass into the ground water. Loch (1996) has reviewed the problems caused by organic contaminants.

Appropriate remedial treatment for polluted soils depends on the type of pollution. Liming to about pH 6.5 reduces the solubility and hence toxicity of most metals (Alloway and Ayres, 1997). Metals can also be immobilized by the addition of vermiculite and zeolites, and can be extracted by certain plants that accumulate them in their tissues (Adriano *et al.*, 1998). Soil washing is used for soils contaminated with metals, pesticides and polynuclear aromatic hydrocarbons (Skipper and Turco, 1995; Adriano *et al.*, 1998).

5.5   DEGRADATION OF SOIL PHYSICAL PROPERTIES

Neither the areas of land affected by degradation nor the severity of the adverse physical conditions are known with any certainty. Estimates of the effects of human activities on the degradation of soil physical properties are given in Table 5.2.

For the successful growth of arable crops it has always been necessary to manipulate the physical properties of soils. Until the twentieth century, when tractors came into use, soils that could not be cultivated by hand or animal traction were generally left uncultivated.

The cultivations required for arable cropping have inevitably changed the physical properties of soils. Their aim is to make the soil optimal for crop growth, but some effects, for example soil compaction, surface sealing and crusting, and waterlogging, have been adverse (for a fuller discussion see Lal and Greenland, 1979). It is estimated that compaction of soil within the root zone and sealing of the surface account globally for 82 per cent of the physical degradation of soils (Table 5.2).

Soil compaction

Compaction results from the passage of machinery, the treading of animals and the use of the mouldboard plough in conditions that lead to the formation of a plough sole (ploughpan). Bulk density is increased and pore space, particularly of pores that transmit water under gravity (above about 0.05 mm diameter), is decreased (Soane and Ouwerkerk, 1994).

Compaction affects root growth and hence plant growth in two different ways. First, vertical and lateral growth of roots is restricted unless the soil is sufficiently compressible for them to force their way into narrow pores and enlarge them. The result of poor root development is reduction in the growth of plants that depend on water and nutrients from within and below the compacted soil.

The second effect of compaction is to create anaerobic conditions where water accumulates in the soil because of a low rate of through-drainage. Although some plant species can transfer oxygen from their shoots to their roots, for example varieties of rice, most require oxygen from the soil air for aerobic respiration in their roots. Under anaerobic conditions microbial products of reduction such as NO_2^-, Mn^{2+}, Fe^{2+} and S^{2-} can be toxic, as also can organic products such as ethylene (ethene). These effects on roots have been reviewed by Gregory (1988a).

Compaction can be avoided by good practices. For example, soil to be tilled should be friable; it should not stick to implements or cause slippage of tractor wheels. Similarly, heavy machinery should not be used on soil that is wet, because soil is more easily compressed when wet than when dry. Pans created by ploughing to the same depth for a period of years can be broken by subsoiling.

Sealing and crusting

Sealing of the soil surface results from the destruction of aggregates by raindrop impact, the deposition of sediment from erosion, and the slippage of the wheels of machinery. The seal reduces infiltration of water and when it dries may form a hard surface crust. Sealing of the soil surface may create anaerobic conditions, but the more harmful effect is usually the increased runoff and hence erosion. Emergence of seedlings is also reduced, especially when the soil dries to form a crust. The problem is most acute in soils with weak, unstable aggregates and where the soil surface is exposed to intense rainstorms. Sealing and crusting can be minimized by a cover of vegetation or mulch.

Waterlogging

Waterlogging of soil occurs when the rate of through-drainage is less than the rate of input of water, and also when the level of ground water rises to close to the surface. The first of these two causes can result from compaction (see above). It can also result from irrigation of soils having a horizon of naturally low permeability. The second common cause is leakage from unsealed irrigation canals and channels, and excessive use of irrigation water (which may also cause salinization).

Waterlogging can be prevented or remedied by an effective drainage system. Usually a piped system is needed, and often the drainage water has to be pumped into a water course.

5.6 DESERTIFICATION

The succession of low-rainfall years in the African Sahel (between the 200 mm and 700 mm isohyets) that started in the late 1960s resulted in reduced harvests, or complete crop failure, and the death of large numbers of domesticated animals. The drought caused widespread famine in the countries affected. The response of the United Nations General Assembly in 1974 was to call for a UN conference on desertification. With the subsequent attention from the United Nations Educational, Scientific and Cultural Organization (UNESCO) and the United Nations Environment Programme (UNEP), desertification has become a widely discussed and debated topic, which has suffered from the lack of an agreed definition and of reliable measurements of its geographical extent (Thomas and Middleton, 1994).

Desertification is generally understood to refer to land degradation in dryland areas, with the implicit assumption that it is caused by both a run of years of low rainfall and inappropriate forms of land use and management. Some authors emphasize low rainfall as the cause, others the activities of man.

Dryland areas that have been affected are at the margins of land used for crops and grazing. Seasonal rainfall that is below the average of the previous few years, or a period of several days without rain, may result in crop failure. In these areas the rainy season is usually too short for the crop to be replanted. The production of herbage grazed by cattle, sheep, goats or camels is similarly affected. Years of drought occur in many parts of the world, but the effects are most severe in the marginal dryland areas.

In the African Sahel there is evidence that several years of drought have followed periods of above-average rainfall (Nicholson, 1989, 1993; Long et al., 2000). During the years of high rainfall, longer-season crops were grown and more cattle were kept, neither of which could be sustained when the succession of dry years began. The bare soil of overgrazed pastures and of fields that had been cultivated was then eroded by wind. Other contributing factors were (i) the sinking of boreholes to provide water for the greater number of cattle, which caused zones of compacted soil and destruction of vegetation, (ii) cutting down of trees and bushes, and (iii) less nomadic pasturalism because of political boundaries which concentrated cattle in less favourable areas. These issues have been discussed by Thomas and Middleton (1994) and Agnew (1995), who give references to primary sources.

The perennial components of natural ecosystems in dryland areas have in-built survival systems, including deep roots; annuals have seed banks in the soil that enable them to survive several years of drought. Growth resumes when the rainy season starts or the rains arrive after a dry period of several years, that is, there may be a cycle of several years between growth of vegetation and no growth. This cycle can be broken by cultivations or excessive numbers of livestock, which kill the perennials and annuals by overgrazing. Cutting down trees and bushes for fodder, firewood and charcoal causes loss of soil by wind erosion.

There is a doomwatch scenario that attributes the spread of deserts primarily to the activities of man. The primary cause is, however, the fact that several years of low rainfall destroy crops and pastures. For example, measurements made by satellite between 1980 and 1990 at the southern fringe of the Sahara showed that the area of vegetation contracted and expanded with changes in rainfall (Tucker *et al.*, 1991). Fluctuations between wet and dry years also brought about changes in the grassland species (Peyre de Fabrègues, 1992).

Dryland areas will continue to suffer from droughts. Management techniques were considered at an international workshop (Sivakumar and Wills, 1995). Mortimore (1989) has described the human responses to drought.

5.7 SUMMARY

Of the main forms of land degradation, soil erosion is the most extensive and most costly to remedy. Nutrient depletion, soil salinization, acidification, chemical pollution, waterlogging, crusting and compaction are other forms. Their causes and possible control measures and reclamation procedures are discussed.

Present evidence is that 13 per cent of the land area of the world has been degraded to some extent. Natural processes such as erosion, soil acidification and soil salinization are exacerbated by man's activities. These activities include cultivations, irrigation and the use of nitrogen fertilizers, techniques on which agricultural production depends and will continue to depend if production is to be increased and be sustainable in the future.

The effects of land degradation are two-fold: on-site effects that reduce crop yields, and off-site effects such as the deposition of silt in storage dams and river beds, and acidification and eutrophication of surface waters. Reduction, and if possible prevention, of land degradation is therefore essential for economic reasons as well as to preserve natural ecosystems. Land that is degraded should be reclaimed where this is economically viable.

Over the last few decades it has been shown that degradation can be prevented on land that is cultivated. The careful planning of land use, using the knowledge and techniques now available, including land surveys, should allow us to conserve our limited land resources.

6

Raising yields: use of fertilizers

During the early part of the nineteenth century, sodium nitrate (Chilean nitrate) and Peruvian guano were imported into Europe, and more significant developments followed. They included the manufacture of superphosphate in England from 1843, by treating first bones and then rock phosphate with sulphuric acid. Two industrial by-products came into importance in the nineteenth century: ammonium sulphate as a by-product in the manufacture of coal gas, and basic slag which contained phosphate from the impure iron oxide used in the steel industry. From 1861 potassium salts became available for use as fertilizer from deposits in Germany, and later from elsewhere. In the twentieth century three important manufacturing processes were (i) the synthesis of ammonium fertilizers by the Haber–Bosch process, which originated in Germany during the first two decades, (ii) the manufacture of triple superphosphate, which was started by the Tennessee Valley Authority (USA) in the 1930s, and (iii) the manufacture of urea from atmospheric nitrogen and natural gas from oil drilling, which became a cheap and increasingly popular nitrogen fertilizer from the 1950s.

6.2 FERTILIZER USE DURING THE TWENTIETH CENTURY

Fertilizer use is essentially a phenomenon of the twentieth century. Many books and thousands of scientific papers have been published on the need for fertilizers and on their uses. The books include those by Cooke (1967, 1982), Sanchez (1976), Wild (1988), Rengel (1998, 1999) and Laegreid et al. (1999). By 1913, according to Cooke (1988), global use of N, P and K in fertilizers was 1.4, 0.9 and 0.7 Mt, respectively. After 1960 their use grew rapidly, reaching 82.1, 14.2 and 18.0 Mt of N, P and K,

Table 6.1. *Fertilizer use $(N + P_2O_5 + K_2O)$ in arable land $(kg\ ha^{-1})$*

	1980/81	1990/91	1998/99
Near East, North Africa	45	67	71
Latin America, Caribbean	64	63	84
Sub-Saharan Africa	8	10	9
East Asia, southeast Asia, China	121	179	234
South Asia	37	80	107

Source: FAO (1999).

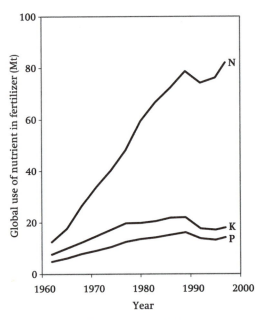

Figure 6.1. Annual global use of fertilizer nutrients as N, P and K from three-year averages. From FAO (1999).

respectively, by 1996–1998 (FAO, 1999). The rate of increase in the use of nitrogen and phosphate fertilizer was almost linear during the period 1965–1990 and of potassium fertilizer until 1979 (Figure 6.1).

The rates of application of fertilizer vary greatly between regions of the world (Table 6.1). Inter-related reasons in regions where the rate of use is small are economic (unfavourable cost/benefit ratio of using fertilizer) and biological and physical (low crop yield potential often because of the limit imposed by water supply).

Table 6.2. *Global fertilizer use and mineral reserves*

Fertilizer nutrient	Global use 1996/98 $(Mt\,a^{-1})$	Reserves (Mt)
N	82.0	No practical limit to gaseous nitrogen; energy supplies might become limiting
P	14.2	>3400
K	18.0	>29 000

Source: FAO (1999) and Vlek *et al.* (1997).

During the period of linear growth the use of nitrogen, phosphate (as P) and potassium (as K) increased annually by 2.6, 0.45 and 0.79 Mt, respectively. According to the FAO data, during the early 1990s the use of all three fertilizer nutrients decreased, in part because of reduced use in eastern Europe and the former Soviet Union. This was followed during the second half of the 1990s by increased use of nitrogen, a small increase in use of phosphate but no increase in potassium use.

Extrapolation to future use

The changes during the 1990s make it difficult to predict global fertilizer use in the future. If the trends in global fertilizer use follow countries such as the UK, which has a long history of using fertilizer, the requirement for phosphate and potassium will stabilize as initial deficiencies are corrected and smaller maintenance applications are needed. Fertilizer nitrogen, by contrast, will be needed in increasing amounts as long as an increase in crop production is required. It differs from fertilizer phosphate and potassium in having little or no residual effect under most conditions, because of losses in gaseous form and by leaching. Requirements for fertilizers will rise, possibly by 50 per cent or more during the next 50 years, but many factors, particularly economic ones, make any forecast uncertain.

The mineral reserves that can be exploited to manufacture fertilizers will be sufficient for the foreseeable future (Table 6.2). A few large deposits of phosphate and potassium minerals are currently exploited to provide the main world supply. Geological surveys have discovered several relatively small deposits of phosphate rock in recent years, and others might remain to be discovered. The atmosphere is the source of nitrogen for the manufacture of nitrogen fertilizers, and the only limitation in the future might be the fuel needed to provide energy for the manufacturing process.

Nutrient deficiencies

Fertilizers are applied to rectify nutrient deficiencies that limit crop growth and yield. They may supply a single nutrient such as nitrogen or phosphorus, or a combination of nutrients. Most are soluble in water. The common sources of nitrogen are urea, ammonia, ammonium nitrate and ammonium phosphate; phosphorus is supplied as soluble calcium phosphate (single or triple superphosphate), ammonium phosphate, and rock phosphate (water insoluble), and potassium as the chloride or sulphate. The general references at the beginning of this section give fuller information.

The nutrients most commonly deficient in soils are nitrogen and phosphorus. Sulphur is often deficient in regions where there is little input from the atmosphere, that is, in regions remote from mining, smelting and manufacturing industries. Potassium deficiency can occur when soils are first brought into cultivation, but often becomes more severe by repeated removal of potassium in cereal straw, herbage from grassland, and fruit crops. Calcium deficiency is relatively rare and limited to acid soils where aluminium toxicity is more usually the factor limiting crop growth. Magnesium deficiency can also occur in acid soils, and can be caused by a high K/Mg ratio in the soil.

Deficiencies of micronutrients are known throughout the world. They are generally caused by lack of availability rather than by absolute deficiency in the soil. Most metals become less available at high soil pH (molybdenum is an exception). Copper availability is low in peaty soils and zinc deficiency may occur at a soil pH of 7–8.5, and also after large additions of phosphate fertilizer. Deficiency of boron occurs in several fruit and root crops in a wide range of soil conditions. Deficiencies of micronutrients differ markedly between crops and their varieties; they are remedied by incorporating the required micronutrient with the fertilizer that is used, by foliar sprays, or by application to the soil of an organic complex that only slowly becomes unavailable to the crop.

6.3 DIAGNOSTIC TECHNIQUES FOR FERTILIZER USE

The purpose of the methods to be described is to identify the nutrients that need to be supplemented by addition of fertilizer and where possible indicate how much fertilizer is needed. The four methods that can be used are field experimentation (trials), analysis of soil samples (usually taken to a depth of 15–20 cm), plant analysis, and recognition of visual symptoms of deficiencies in the crop. Although field experiments are expensive they are the only reliable method of finding the amount of fertilizer required to achieve the expected yield. They are discussed in Section 6.4.

Methods of plant analysis and critical levels of nutrients in parts of plants are described by Walsh and Beaton (1973). The disadvantage of these methods for annual crops is that application of the nutrient that is in short supply is usually too late to prevent reduction in yields. The methods are more commonly used for tree crops.

Soil analysis

Two general points need to be made about the use of soil analysis to test whether fertilizers are likely to be required for arable crops and grassland. Firstly, chemical analysis of the total content of a nutrient in soil is of little value because most is held in organic matter and within the structure of soil minerals where it is not available in the short term for uptake by plant roots. Secondly, the various acids, alkalis, salt solutions and complexing agents that are used to extract samples of soil give an index of nutrient availability rather than the amount that is available to the crop during its growth. The index becomes a useful guide to nutrient sufficiency or deficiency when it is compared with the index of similar soils on which field experiments have tested the effect of increments of fertilizer on the yield of the same crop.

The commonly used extractants and interpretation of the measurements are described by Brown (1987), Carter (1993), Havlin and Jacobsen (1994), Rowell (1994) and Hood and Jones (1997). Briefly, for phosphate in most soils sodium bicarbonate is the usual extractant, various acids being used for acid soils. Potassium, calcium and magnesium are extracted with a solution of an ammonium salt, and sulphate is extracted by a solution of calcium phosphate. Nitrogen as ammonium and nitrate is extracted by a solution of potassium chloride, and most micronutrients are extracted by complexing agents. The sample of soil that is analysed has to represent a relatively uniform area of land. Several samples have therefore to be taken and mixed before taking a subsample for analysis.

A limitation of soil analysis for nitrogen (as NH_4^+ and NO_3^-) is that samples of soil are usually taken either before the crop is sown or at an early stage during crop growth so that a timely application of fertilizer can be made. More nitrogen becomes available by mineralization of soil organic matter, which is favoured by the same conditions that encourage crop growth, but it may be insufficient for the crop or may leave mineral nitrogen in the soil at harvest. Another limitation is that because of the high mobility of nitrate, deep sampling of the soil to 50 cm or more is needed.

Soil analysis is important for efficient use of fertilizers when they are first introduced in order to ensure that the soil nutrients in short supply are supplemented. Later, for all nutrients except nitrogen, maintenance applications of fertilizers can be made and soil analysis is then used every three or four years to check that soil nutrients are not being depleted.

6.4 FIELD EXPERIMENTS WITH FERTILIZERS

Most field experiments have been conducted with fertilizers that supply one or more of the nutrients nitrogen, phosphorus, potassium and sulphur. Many experiments have investigated methods of getting the largest crop response from fertilizers at the least cost; in others, fertilizers have been included in a range of agronomic treatments aimed at optimizing crop yields.

The general purpose is to obtain a ratio of benefit to cost that is as large as possible. Where fixed costs, for example land prices, are high, the only objective that is commercially viable is to aim for large yields; often for this purpose large amounts of fertilizer are required. Where fixed costs are small but fertilizer is expensive, efficiency of use to give a reliable increase in yield is more important.

The response of a crop to the application of fertilizer depends on four general factors: (i) properties of the soil, especially its supply of nutrients, (ii) application of the required nutrients at the right time, right place and in the right amount, (iii) the climatic conditions, especially rainfall, and (iv) the crop variety and its management (Table 6.3). If the purpose of the field experiment is to provide the basis for advising farmers on fertilizer use, it will need to be conducted for more than one growing season and at a sufficient number of sites to cover the soils and climatic conditions in the area for which generalizations are intended. Because the results relate only to the sites and seasons where the experiments are conducted, it is essential to supplement the yield response with information on the soils, climate and crop management.

Table 6.3. *Factors affecting the response of crops to fertilizer applications*

Crop	• crop variety and its yield potential • planting density • control of pests, weeds and disease
Climate	• total rainfall and its distribution during the growing season • temperature • solar radiation • day-length
Soil	• available nutrients in soil and in organic manure • physical conditions, especially for germination of seed, emergence of seedlings, and root growth • soil depth • presence of toxic substances, e.g. aluminium, salinity
Fertilizer	• application of required nutrients • timing of application(s) • placement • amount applied and, for phosphate, the solubility • loss from soil, particularly of nitrogen; also immobilization in soil

Long-term experiments are of obvious relevance to achieving sustainable production. Not always recognized is that they also provide explanations for year-to-year variations in crop yield and long-term trends of increases or decreases in yield, on both of which the economic performance of fertilizer depends. The importance of long-term experiments has been clearly stated by Leigh and Johnston in the preface to their book (Leigh and Johnston, 1994), which refers to several long-term experiments. They are discussed further in Section 9.7.

Three examples of fertilizer experiments

The results of a very large number of field experiments have been reported, and the results of probably thousands more remain unpublished. The three that are to be discussed here include two from Africa, where several early experiments showed that applications of phosphate fertilizer gave larger yields, as did nitrogen fertilizer at sites with adequate rainfall (Greenwood, 1951; Nye, 1953, 1954; Boswinkle, 1961; Goldsworthy and Heathcote, 1963; Goldsworthy, 1967a,b). Later work is reviewed in Buresh *et al.* (1997). The third experiment is from an area in Syria where rainfall is marginally sufficient for crop production.

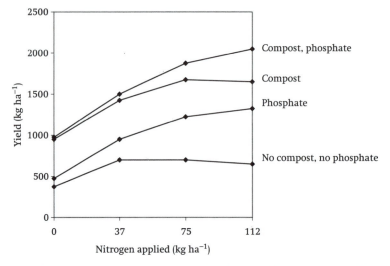

Figure 6.2. Effect of compost and phosphate fertilizer on response of seed cotton to fertilizer nitrogen at Ukirigura, Tanzania. From Le Mare (1972).

Experiment 1

Many of the early experiments with fertilizers in Africa compared them with organic manures such as composts or dung, supplies of which were limited. An experiment begun in 1952 in Tanzania compared the effect of compost ($15\,t\,ha^{-1}$ every three years) with that of triple super-phosphate ($168\,kg\,ha^{-1}$ every three years) on the yield of cotton. Lime ($13.5\,t\,ha^{-1}$ as $CaCO_3$) was applied after the sandy loam soil had acidified from annual applications of ammonium sulphate (three rates, usually 11, 22 and $45\,kg\,ha^{-1}$ of N). Potassium chloride was applied in 1965 and 1967. During the last three years the rates of nitrogen application were increased to 37, 75 and $112\,kg\,ha^{-1}$, and during the last two years nitrogen was applied as calcium ammonium nitrate. The average yields of seed cotton during 1966–1968, after 14 years of continuous cropping, are shown in Figure 6.2.

In all treatments the crop responded to application of nitrogen fertilizer. The response to nitrogen was (compost + phosphate) > compost > phosphate > (no compost, no phosphate). Crop yields increased more with additions of both nitrogen and phosphate fertilizers. The experiment shows the potential for increased yields of cotton with the combined use of nitrogen and phosphate fertilizer and further increase in yield with the incorporation of compost, probably because its content of calcium and magnesium increased the soil pH.

Table 6.4. *Effects of fertilizer and weeding on main-season grain yield of maize in Ibadan, Nigeria. Rate of fertilizer application (kg ha⁻¹) to the main-season maize crop was 120 N, 39 P, 50 K and to the minor-season sweet potato crop was 40 N.*

Treatments				Yield (kg ha⁻¹)	
Before 1976		In 1976			
Fertilizer	Weeding	Fertilizer	Weeding	1975	1976
No	No	Yes	Yes	356	5735
No	Yes	Yes	Yes	2466	5865
Yes	No	Yes	Yes	4369	5895
Yes	Yes	Yes	Yes	5877	6031
LSD (0.05)				1221	NS

Source: Kang and Fox (1981).
LSD, least significant difference; NS, not significant.

Experiment 2

This experiment, at Ibadan, Nigeria in the humid tropics, showed the effect of fertilizer application on yields of maize that had been weeded or not weeded (Table 6.4). The experiment was begun in 1971 to investigate the potential for sustained high crop yields with continuous cropping (Juo and Lal, 1977; Kang et al., 1977). In 1975 yields of maize were in the order (fertilizer, weeding) > (fertilizer, no weeding) > (no fertilizer, weeding) > (no fertilizer, no weeding). When all the maize crops were weeded and fertilized in 1976, there was little difference between yields. The experiment gave a clear demonstration that weed control is essential if crops are to respond fully to application of fertilizer.

Experiment 3

We have seen above from fertilizer experiments in Africa that phosphate applications very commonly increase crop yields and, with adequate rainfall, applications of nitrogen fertilizer also increase yields. These observations apply elsewhere, as shown by the following example from northern Syria.

Seventy-five experimental fields growing barley received four rates of nitrogen fertilizer (ammonium nitrate) and four rates of phosphate

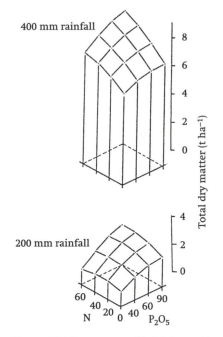

Figure 6.3. The response of total dry matter of barley to nitrogen and phosphate fertilizers at two levels of rainfall, in northern Syria. From Jones and Wahbi (1992).

fertilizer (triple superphosphate) in all combinations (Jones and Wahbi, 1992). The experiments were in an area between the 200 mm and 300 mm isohyets but with variable rainfall between the years of experimentation. Yields were expressed as total dry matter, the straw being almost as valuable as grain as fodder for sheep. The effects of phosphate and nitrogen fertilizers on yield at two different rainfall levels were obtained from regression equations, and are shown in Figure 6.3 for one type of soil.

Of particular interest to cropping in marginally dry areas is the fact that in the absence of applied nitrogen the crop yield responded to applied phosphate at low rainfall (200 mm). The response increased with application of nitrogen but response to nitrogen was very small unless phosphate was also applied. At high rainfall (400 mm) the crop responded to nitrogen and phosphate fertilizer applied separately, and more so in combination; these responses were greater than at low rainfall. These results were conducted on farmers' fields by professional staff, and similar results were obtained from experiments conducted by farmers themselves (Wahbi et al., 1994).

Summary

The three experiments assessed the crop response to applications of nutrients in fertilizers in three different farming systems. They show that the response of crop yield to application of fertilizers depends on rainfall, weed control, the application of all nutrients that would otherwise limit yield, and whether organic manures are also used. These and many other experiments have shown that the response of crop yield to fertilizer applications usually depends on a package of inputs.

6.5 IMPROVING THE EFFICIENCY OF USE OF FERTILIZERS

First to be considered is the efficiency of uptake of nutrients by crops. Later in this section the problem of soil heterogeneity is discussed, under the heading of precision agriculture.

The economic definition of efficiency is profit/cost. The problem with this definition is that this ratio fluctuates with market prices and the provision of subsidies and other forms of financial support (see also p. 190). More commonly used is response of crop yield per unit of fertilizer nutrient, both expressed in $kg\,ha^{-1}$; for example, the yield response of a cereal crop may be 10 kg grain per kg fertilizer nitrogen. However, this provides no explanation for a low or a high value. Another measure of efficiency is the fraction, or per cent, of the applied nutrient that is taken up by the crop, measured as:

$$\text{Per cent apparent recovery} = [(U_w - U_o)/A] \times 100, \qquad (6.1)$$

where U_o is uptake of the nutrient by the crop without applied nutrient, U_w is the uptake with applied nutrient, and A is the amount of applied nutrient. The assumption is made that application of the fertilizer does not affect uptake of the native soil nutrient, hence the recovery is 'apparent'. More useful, although more difficult to achieve, is to account for all the nutrient whether taken up by the crop, lost from the soil or made unavailable within the soil. With this information, which requires an understanding of the reactions of fertilizers with soil, it becomes possible to improve their efficiency of use, as will now be shown.

Phosphate fertilizers

Phosphate ions are adsorbed, especially in acid soils, on to mineral surfaces containing -Al-OH, -Fe-OH and probably -Mn-OH. Adsorption is greatest in soils containing the clay mineral allophane or iron and aluminium oxides with a high surface area (e.g. Oxisols). These soils usually require large additions of phosphate fertilizer to give maximum crop yields. In neutral and calcareous soils, phosphate forms calcium phosphates, for example apatite, of low solubility. These reactions account for the low recovery of phosphate, often 10–30 per cent or less, in the year of application, and at a decreasing rate in successive years. The phosphate that remains in the soil after two or three years may not give a statistically significant crop response as measured by field experiments, but the evidence is that it can still be taken up by crops, although at a low and decreasing rate, for several years (Russell, 1968; Goedert, 1983). For a quick return on the outlay on phosphate fertilizer, placement below or with the seed is usually a better option than broadcasting because it minimizes the adsorption reactions and the phosphate can be more readily taken up by crop roots.

A consequence of the adsorption of phosphate by soil is that leakage to drainage water is usually small. Exceptions are large additions of phosphate fertilizer to soils with low adsorption capacity, for example sands, applications to soils with cracks or channels followed by heavy rainfall, and large additions of organic manures such as slurries from animal (especially pig) excreta.

Nitrogen fertilizers

Nitrogen is lost from soils much more readily than phosphate. Often no more than half of the fertilizer nitrogen is recovered by the crop to which it is applied. In whatever chemical form it is applied, the dominant form in the soil solution of cultivated soils is nitrate (ammonium is also often present in small concentrations), which is not adsorbed by most soils and is therefore readily leached in drainage water. The only exceptions are the lower horizons of acid soils in the humid tropics which have positively charged oxides of iron and aluminium that adsorb nitrate (Kinjo and Pratt, 1971; Wong et al., 1990).

Denitrification

Under anaerobic conditions nitrate undergoes microbial reduction to nitrous oxide (N_2O) and dinitrogen (N_2), the process known as denitrification. Several groups of microorganisms reduce nitrate when oxygen is absent, or present in low concentrations, and when there is decomposable organic matter. They are most active in warm soils at a pH of around 7. Denitrification can occur inside wet soil aggregates in an otherwise aerobic soil, but is most pronounced under waterlogged conditions such as paddies, where nitrate has been produced by nitrification when the soil is aerobic between periods of flooding. Although losses of nitrogen from fertilizers by denitrification vary greatly, they are often around 10 per cent of that applied. A further concern about the process is that N_2O is a gas that contributes to global warming (see Chapter 11).

Immobilization

Immobilization occurs when nitrogen fertilizers are applied to soil containing organic matter with a high C/N ratio, for example ploughed-in cereal stubble. Immobilization is temporary: the mineral nitrogen which is taken up by the soil microorganisms is released when oxidation has lowered the C/N ratio to around 20 (see also Section 4.7). The two processes of immobilization and mineralization run concurrently during the decomposition of carbon-rich organic matter, immobilization dominating first and mineralization dominating later. When the two processes are occurring at the same rate, some of the nitrogen atoms supplied in fertilizer will be absorbed by the soil microorganisms and the same number will be released by mineralization.

Volatilization of ammonia

At pH 7 about 1 per cent of the ammonium plus ammonia is present as NH_3, and the percentage rises as the pH increases. The greater is the concentration of ammonia in solution, the greater is the concentration in the gas phase, other conditions being equal. It follows that in soils of pH 7 and above ammonia is at risk of volatilization, especially under warm and dry conditions. Under these conditions fertilizers containing ammonia or urea are therefore best injected into the soil. Similarly, organic manures such as farmyard manure lose nitrogen as ammonia unless they are incorporated in the soil.

Fertilizer nitrogen should be applied so as to prevent, or at least minimize, losses by leaching, denitrification and volatilization. Urea and ammonium fertilizers should be incorporated in the soil, and nitrate fertilizers should be avoided in anaerobic soils, such as those growing wetland rice. In the humid tropics applications can be split to minimize losses by leaching, and in temperate regions with excess winter rainfall most of the nitrogen for winter crops such as wheat should be applied in early spring. Fertilizers that contain urea, ammonia or ammonium salts have another important effect in that they acidify soils (see Section 6.6).

Precision agriculture

Farmers know from experience that some fields and parts of fields give larger yields than others. These differences commonly arise from differences in supply of crop nutrients or water, or both, in waterlogging or in weediness. Where the differences arise from the supply of nutrients in the soil, application of fertilizer at the same rate over the whole field will be too small in some parts and too large in others, that is, its use is not as efficient as it might be. For efficient management the requirements are (i) to identify the causes of heterogeneity of yield, for example spatial variability of nutrient supply in the soil, (ii) to locate and identify the positions in the field of the large and small crop yields (and related soil nutrient levels), and (iii) to adjust the rate of fertilizer applications according to the spatial requirements of the crop. In practice more information is usually needed, particularly on water content of the soil and temperature, which influence nutrient supplies and crop growth and vary with space and time.

Some machinery now in use has a global positioning system for recording harvest yields and applying fertilizers in a site-specific manner. When using this system the expectations are for higher yields, more efficient use of fertilizer and better protection of the environment. These and other techniques are discussed by several authors (Anonymous, 1997; Pierce and Sadler, 1997; Stafford, 1997, 1999). Their application will probably be limited to large fields in developed countries. Smallholders may know from experience how to vary the rate of fertilizer applications.

6.6   ACIDIFICATION FROM NITROGEN FERTILIZERS

The commonly used nitrogen fertilizers supply nitrogen as ammonium or nitrate salts or as urea. In the soil solution the nitrogen is present in ionic form as NH_4^+, NO_3^- or $CO(NH_2)_2$ (urea), all of which can be absorbed by plant roots. Being positively charged, NH_4^+ is adsorbed in soil by exchange with Ca^{2+}, Mg^{2+} and other cations on the negatively charged clay and organic matter. NO_3^- usually remains in the soil solution. Urea is rapidly hydrolysed by the enzyme urease to release ammonia:

$$CO(NH_2)_2 + H_2O \rightarrow CO_2 + 2NH_3. \tag{6.2}$$

Acidification occurs as NH_4^+ and NH_3 are oxidized by nitrifying bacteria:

$$NH_3 + 4O \rightarrow NO_3^- + H^+ + H_2O; \tag{6.3}$$

$$NH_4^+ + 4O \rightarrow NO_3^- + 2H^+ + H_2O. \tag{6.4}$$

According to these equations, for the application of 14 kg N (1 kg atom of N) the acidity (kg atom H^+) produced by nitrogen fertilizer is 1 for NH_3, 2 for NH_4^+, and 1 for urea. The protons (H^+) undergo cation exchange, displacing adsorbed Ca^{2+} and Mg^{2+} into the soil solution. They can then be leached out of the soil in drainage water accompanied by NO_3^- and SO_4^{2-}.

The acidifying effect of nitrogen fertilizer is, however, usually less than the above equations indicate, for three main reasons. Firstly, crop plants will absorb NH_4^+ before it is oxidized; the acidifying effect then depends on the relative uptake of cations and anions (see Section 4.4). Plant roots taking up NO_3^- may release HCO_3^-, also depending on the relative uptake of cations and anions, which neutralizes H^+. Secondly, the leaching loss of Ca^{2+} and Mg^{2+} occurs only with excess rainfall. Thirdly, acidification from ammonium fertilizer depends on the accompanying anion: phosphate is absorbed by soils much more strongly than sulphate and therefore results in a smaller loss of Ca^{2+} and Mg^{2+}. The overall effect of these reactions is the loss of calcium and magnesium accompanied by nitrate and other anions.

Acidification from the use of nitrogen fertilizers has the most serious effect in weakly buffered soils because of the leaching loss of the small reserve of exchangeable cations, the increase in aluminium concentrations in the soil solution, and reduction of the soil buffer capacity. Soil pH should therefore be monitored, particularly in the tropics where the buffer capacity of the soil is often low.

6.7 SUMMARY

Fertilizers play a key role in providing global food supplies and will continue to do so. They are effective in raising crop yields, particularly as one component of a package of inputs that remove constraints on yield. Deficiencies of nitrogen, phosphate, potassium and sulphate, and of micronutrients that limit crop growth, can be corrected by application of fertilizers containing the required nutrients.

Because fertilizers are relatively expensive, especially in many developing countries, and have to be bought several months before there is a return on the expenditure, it is important for them to be used efficiently. For this to be achieved they should supplement the nutrients that are deficient in the soil, as shown by chemical analysis, and those added in organic manures. This requires an understanding of the status of mineral nutrients in soil, their cycling through plants and animals, and their budgets. Uptake of fertilizer nitrogen by the crop can be increased if drainage and gaseous losses are reduced by its application when required by the crop and at an optimum rate based on experiment or experience.

Fertilizers, especially those containing nitrogen, have effects on the environment, including release of nitrous oxide to the atmosphere and nitrate to surface water (although all sources of soil nitrogen, e.g. incorporation of organic manures and plant residues) can have the same effects. These effects are discussed in Section 9.8. Fertilizer use will nevertheless continue to be essential if the required increase in food production is to be attained.

7

Raising yields: water for rainfed crops and irrigation

The context in which soil water and irrigation have to be considered is (i) irrigated agriculture accounts globally for one-half to three-quarters of total water consumption, including domestic and industrial use (Postel *et al.*, 1996); (ii) about one-third of the global harvest is from one-sixth of the agricultural land area that is irrigated; and (iii) much of the five-sixths of the land area that grows rainfed crops has marginally sufficient rainfall. Because of the limited supplies of fresh water for irrigation (see Chapter 2) and, in marginally dry areas, of the need to conserve rainfall, efficient management of water for agricultural use is essential. In order to understand how this might be achieved, an outline of the main concepts used to describe soil water and its use by crops is first given.

By the end of the nineteenth century significant progress had been made in understanding the physics of soil water (Warington, 1900). It had been shown by then that the amount of water held in a soil against gravity was related to its particle size distribution, and that water moved in soil under the influence of gravity, by capillary action and in the vapour phase. Warington also referred to practical applications of this information to rainfed and irrigated agriculture.

Probably the two most significant advances in the twentieth century were firstly the unifying concept of the free energy of soil water, usually described in terms of potential or suction, and secondly the use of meteorological conditions to calculate the rate of evaporation of water from crops based on the physics of the process. Research was increasingly directed towards problems that occur under field conditions, water balances in catchments and the development of various techniques to measure soil water. General accounts of soil water are given by Hillel (1980a,b) and Marshall *et al.* (1996), evaporative loss from crops by Monteith (1975) and water catchment studies by Pereira (1973).

7.2 SOIL WATER

Over a fixed period of time the change in soil water content (ΔW) can be expressed by the water balance equation:

$$\Delta W = P + I - (R + D + E), \tag{7.1}$$

where the additions are precipitation (P) and irrigation (I) and losses are runoff from the surface (R), deep drainage (D) and total evaporation (E) from soil and plants.

In a soil that drains freely, the water is held in small pores and as films on the surface of the soil particles. After the soil profile has been thoroughly wetted and then allowed to drain, the amount held on a volume basis varies between about 5 per cent in a soil with a high sand content to about 40 per cent in a clay, corresponding to 50 mm and 400 mm per metre of soil depth, respectively. In most soils the amount lies between these two values. When all the pores are filled with water the volumetric content (vol.:vol.) is between 40 per cent and 60 per cent.

Two terms that are commonly used to describe the amount of soil water available to plants are 'field capacity' and 'permanent wilting point'. Neither has an exact physical meaning, but in terms of potential energy correspond approximately to -10 kPa (0.1 m suction) and -1.5×10^3 kPa (150 m suction), respectively. Between the two limits is the 'available water capacity' of the soil. In the two examples referred to above, the amounts of water held at the permanent wilting point on a volume basis are about 2 per cent in the sand (20 mm per metre depth) and 20 per cent in the clay (200 mm per metre depth), respectively. On this basis the available water capacity of the sand is 30 mm per metre depth, and of the clay is 200 mm per metre depth. These are static values; the flow of water in soil also needs to be considered.

Water flow

The direction of flow is always from high total water potential to low potential. The total potential has three components, which are additive: gravity, matric (originally known as capillary) and osmotic. For each potential acting alone the direction of flow is, for gravity, downward towards a free water surface; matric flow in a uniform soil is from wet soil to dry; osmotic flow is from less salty to more salty soil. The rate of flow depends on the gradient of the water potential and the hydraulic conductivity in the soil.

Downward flow under gravity is fast when it occurs through large pores, cracks or channels, and slower when it occurs through narrower pores. It can be as high as 10 m per day in soil with large pores or cracks, and as low as 1 mm per day in a compacted clay. Under field conditions drainage stops, or becomes very slow, when the pores with an equivalent diameter greater than about 0.05 mm have drained (field capacity).

Flow by matric potential occurs through narrow pores and over the surface of soil particles. It provides water to plant root surfaces and to a dry soil surface. Because the soil hydraulic conductivity falls substantially (1000-fold or more) as soil dries from field capacity towards the permanent wilting point, the rate of flow to plant roots becomes less than the rate of transpiration and the plant wilts.

In outlining principles, reference has been made to static or steady-state systems. These rarely exist under field conditions. For example, the gradient of matric potential between a point in the soil matrix and the plant root surface depends on the rate of transpiration, which varies from night to day and between 24-hour periods. Another example is that when land is flooded by irrigation or heavy rainstorms, water will flow quickly through wide channels and cracks as long as these remain open and there is free drainage. The soil matrix is more slowly wetted by downward flow from the surface and lateral flow from the wetted cracks and channels. Before equilibrium is reached there will be evaporation from bare soil and transpiration from plants. Soil profiles therefore often wet unevenly. The complex flow of water in soils is discussed in the general references given above.

Evaporative loss

The climatic factors that determine the rate of evaporation from a wet soil surface are the same as for a free water surface, namely, temperature, wind velocity at the surface, relative humidity of the air and albedo of the surface. The process is driven by the energy that is absorbed from the incoming solar radiation, which depends on latitude, angle of surface to the incoming radiation, the season of the year and cloudiness.

When a wet soil in the field starts to dry, the rate of evaporation is close to that from a free water surface. Evaporation becomes

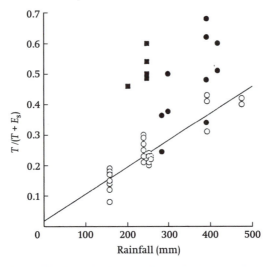

Figure 7.1. Transpiration (T) of water by barley and wheat, expressed as a fraction of total evaporation ($T + E_s$) from crops (T) and soil (E_s), in relation to rainfall. Data points are for Kiboko, Kenya (o), Breda and Tel Hadya, Syria (•), and Merridin and East Beverley, Western Australia (■). From Gregory et al. (1997).

progressively slower after the soil surface has become dry because it depends mainly on the diffusion of liquid water towards the soil surface. Diffusion becomes progressively slower as the length of path increases and the hydraulic conductivity decreases. Some water also evaporates below the soil surface and passes into the atmosphere as vapour.

Loss of water by evaporation from the soil is particularly detrimental in low-rainfall regions, because it leads to increased water shortage for crops and hence lower yields. One of the options to reduce this loss is the application of an organic mulch that reduces the radiant energy reaching the underlying soil and minimizes air turbulence at the soil surface. Cultivations of a bare fallow reduce loss of water by killing weeds that would otherwise take up water from lower parts of the soil profile. Agroforestry systems can also be effective, by providing shade (Wallace and Batchelor, 1997). Under a crop, evaporation from the soil surface can be reduced by early establishment of the crop canopy (Cooper et al., 1987). As shown in Figure 7.1, evaporation from the soil can account for over half the total loss of water by evaporation from soil (E_s) and crop (T), the proportion from soil being greatest in those regions of low rainfall where much of the rain falls in light showers (Gregory et al., 1997).

7.3 WATER REQUIREMENT OF CROPS

Water has three functions in plants: it acts as a leaf coolant when it evaporates, it is essential for maintaining turgor and cellular processes, and the water taken up from soil (the soil solution) contains the mineral nutrients that plants require. The requirement is large: transpiration loss from the canopy of a crop growing in moist soil is usually in the range 3 to 8 mm per day, depending on the climate.

During daytime, evaporation of water from plant leaves (transpiration), which is mainly through the stomata, lowers their water potential. Water then flows from the higher potential of the stems and roots toward the leaves. The effect is to lower the water potential of the roots so that water flows towards the roots from soil that is at a higher water potential. But as the soil becomes drier its water potential decreases. The rate of water transfer to the roots and hence to the leaves then becomes too slow to prevent the plants from wilting. At a soil water potential of about -1.5×10^3 kPa (suction 150 m) the rate of transpiration approaches zero, and the soil is at the permanent wilting point. Before that point is reached rates of transpiration and growth decrease.

In a cool climate the rate of transpiration is low so that a slow rate of water transfer to roots is sufficient to prevent water stress in the crop. A faster rate is required if the transpiration rate is high. Hence in hot dry regions deep rooting is of particular importance because in a moist soil profile crop roots have access to more water than shallow roots and provide a higher rate of supply of water over a longer period. Depth of rooting can be increased by cultivations if the soil has a compact layer such as a plough pan. Most prone to wilting are crops with a naturally shallow rooting system.

In general, grain crops are less sensitive to the soil water potential than crops grown for their vegetative parts although in common with other crops they are sensitive at the flowering stage. These and other aspects of the water requirements of crop plants are discussed much more fully by several authors including Gregory (1988b) and Marshall *et al.* (1996).

Efficiency of water use

Water use efficiency (WUE) of a crop may be defined as the amount of biomass (M) produced by the water taken up by the plants and lost from the soil profile:

$$WUE = M/(T + E_s + R + D), \tag{7.2}$$

where T is transpiration, E_s is evaporation from the soil, R is runoff and D is drainage below the root zone. A useful form of the equation, given by Gregory *et al.* (1997), is:

$$\text{WUE} = (M/T)/[1 + (E_s + R + D)/T]. \tag{7.3}$$

This equation shows that the two requirements for efficient use of water to produce plant biomass are large production of biomass for each unit of water transpired (M/T), and a high ratio of transpiration to loss of water by evaporation from the soil, runoff and deep drainage $(T/(E_s + R + D))$. As mentioned earlier (Section 7.2), evaporation from soil can be reduced by early establishment of the crop canopy and other agronomic practices. Reduction in runoff is one of the main techniques for conserving water in regions of low rainfall (Section 7.4).

Measurement of water use

The amount of water used by irrigated crops needs to be known so that it can be replaced. Two methods are used, one based on the climate conditions that control evaporation, and the other on the depletion of soil water.

A method based on physical principles for calculating the rate of evaporation from a sward of short grass well supplied with water was developed by Penman in the 1950s. Modified forms of this equation using standard data from meteorological stations are available for practical use (Gregory, 1988b). More empirical methods are commonly used. The Blaney–Criddle method uses only the latitude of the site (to give daylight hours) and mean temperature. Where a more reliable estimate of evaporation loss from plants is required, a pan evaporimeter is used to give E_p. To improve accuracy it includes a pan constant, K_p, that depends on the siting of the pan relative to the crop, and a crop factor, K_c, that varies with the stage of growth. The potential evapotranspiration (PET) is then given as

$$\text{PET} = E_p \, K_p \, K_c. \tag{7.4}$$

These and other methods of calculating potential evaporation from a crop are given by Nir and Finkel (1982), James *et al.* (1982), and Murty and Takeuchi (1996). They are of practical value in deciding when to irrigate and how much water to use. The factors K_p and K_c in Equation 7.4 are empirical and are often not included in the equation. Any inaccuracies in the methods, whether using meteorological data or a pan evaporimeter, can be corrected by measuring soil water content.

Commonly used for measuring the water content of soil profiles in the field is the neutron moisture meter. When used over a period of time it gives the rate of loss of water from the soil.

The measurement of soil water potential (strictly matric potential) is useful for indicating when plants need additional water. Tensiometers comprise a porous ceramic cup filled with water and connected to a mercury manometer or vacuum gauge. The suction (negative potential) can be measured up to about 8.5 m (-85 kPa), which is useful for vegetables and ornamental flowers that need to be kept moist. The electrical resistance of absorbent blocks is also used to measure matric potential.

7.4 RAINFED AGRICULTURE

About 83–84 per cent of agricultural land depends wholly on water received as precipitation (rain and snow; subsequently referred to simply as rainfall), the characteristics of which determine to a very large extent the distribution of agricultural systems. These characteristics include the annual total, seasonal distribution, variability between years of both total rainfall and length of rainy system, occurrence of drought and intensity of rainstorms.

Rainfall data have been assembled from a large number of meteorological stations by Landsberg (1985–1995). Global climatology has been discussed by Lamb (1977) and for the tropics by Hastenrath (1991) and McGregor and Nieuwolt (1998). Jackson (1989) has given the scheme shown in Table 7.1 for the geographical distribution of rainfall in the tropics and subtropics, a scheme he describes as a 'great simplification' (he also describes the substantial modifications of this scheme in the individual continents). However, for the present purpose the simple scheme is sufficient.

The influence of climate on cropping pattern is pronounced, although its relationship to crop yield is not simple (Monteith and Ingram, 1998). As defined in Jackson's scheme, regions 1 and 2 are used mainly for perennial crops, including rubber, oil palm, bananas, liberica coffee, coconut and cocoa, and root crops such as yam and cassava, with rice as the main cereal where there is a short dry period, and maize to a lesser extent. In region 3, depending on rainfall and the length of the rainy season, coffee, tea and bananas are grown, the main food crops are rice, maize, sorghum, yam and cassava, and cotton is the main fibre crop. Regions 4 and 6 are cropped mainly by annuals: sorghum, millet, sweet potato, groundnut and sesame, with maize in the wetter areas;

Table 7.1. *Distribution of rainfall regimes in the tropics and subtropics, with approximate annual rainfall*

Region 1	At the equator a double rainfall maximum with no real dry season; annual >2000 mm, all months at least 100 mm
Region 2	A double rainfall maximum in the summer[a] with the two maxima separated by only a slight dip in rainfall and a more pronounced winter dry season; annual <2000 mm, a few months <100 mm
Region 3	A single rainy season and a single dry season; annual 650–1500 mm, rainy season 3–5 months, each with >75 mm
Region 4	A semi-arid region with a short period of summer rainfall; annual 250–650 mm, rainy season 3–4 months, each with >50 mm
Region 5	An arid region; annual less than 250 mm
Region 6	A semi-arid region with a short period of winter rainfall; annual 200–600 mm, rainy season 3–5 months

Source: After Jackson (1989).
[a] Summer and winter are used to describe high sun and low sun periods, respectively.

barley and wheat are grown in region 6 where there are cool winters. Animal grazing is generally important in regions 4 and 6.

Because of the breeding of different varieties, a particular crop can often be grown under a wide range of rainfall patterns, as shown for wheat in Figure 7.2. The mean annual rainfall at the two locations is 461 mm at Tunis, Tunisia and 1644 mm at Passo Fundo, Brazil. The seasonal temperatures and rainfall meet the requirements of the crop, which are to have water for germination, water and cool conditions for vegetative growth, and warm dry conditions by harvest.

Techniques to cope with water shortage

A problem that occurs frequently in rainfed agriculture is a water deficit that restricts crop growth or causes complete crop failure. Even a small deficit shortly after the emergence of seedlings, when roots may extend for only 10–20 cm, may cause their death and require a fresh sowing. A common practice in subsistence farming where shortage of water is prevalent is to grow a short-season crop, for example millet, that can be re-sown if necessary, and on the same piece of land to grow crops such as sorghum, maize, groundnuts and cowpeas that give higher yields in seasons when there is sufficient rain.

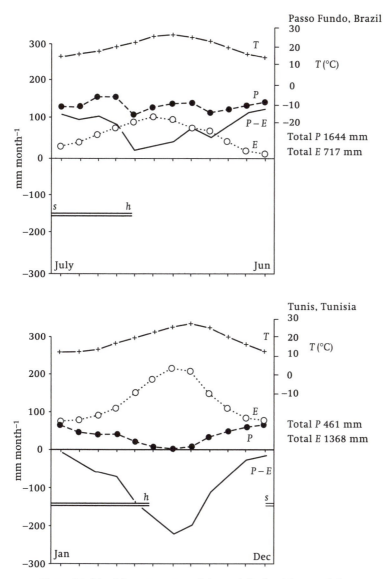

Figure 7.2. Monthly temperatures (+), precipitation (•), potential evaporation (○) and precipitation – evaporation $(P - E)$ for wheat-growing areas near Tunis, Tunisia and Passo Fundo, Brazil. s and h are times of seed sowing and harvest, respectively. From Bunting *et al.* (1982).

Three general methods are used to increase the supply of water to crops: reduction in runoff, reduction in evaporation from soil, and direct increase in water supply other than by irrigation (Table 7.2). The techniques to reduce runoff are also used to control soil erosion, and

Table 7.2. *Methods used to optimize the supply of water to crops in dryland farming*

(1) Reduce runoff	• contour cultivation
	• use absorption terracing
	• use crop residues as mulch
	• timely cultivations to increase infiltration
(2) Reduce evaporation from soil	• establish crops early
	• use mulches
	• supply fertilizer where rainfall is reliable
(3) Increase water supply to the crop	• control weeds
	• collect water during a bare fallow
	• rain harvesting from a catchment
	• grow deeper-rooted crops

Source: Wild (1993).

are discussed in Chapter 5; others have been referred to earlier in this chapter. Bare fallows are used in several farming systems, especially in marginally dry areas for crop production, and are discussed next.

Bare fallows

A bare fallow is effective in accumulating water only when weeds are controlled and where showers of rain are sufficiently heavy to moisten the soil to a depth from which there is little evaporation. The supply of plant nutrients also increases during a fallow by mineralization of organic matter and, having no plants, by a nutrient-sparing effect. In the northern Great Plains of the USA the spring wheat crop had access to an average of 107 mm of stored water after a bare fallow of 15–19 months, compared with 65 mm in annual cropping (Greb *et al.*, 1974). Of the various techniques tested, a combination of weed control and retention of the stubble gave the highest efficiency of water storage. Fallowed soils also contained more nitrate and a higher level of available phosphate. Crop yields were 66 per cent higher than after a previous crop.

In the Mediterranean region, a two-year rotation of cereal/bare fallow is the traditional cropping system. An example of the effect of a bare fallow at Breda in the winter rainfall zone of northern Syria is shown in Table 7.3. The soil is a clay loam overlying silty clay, and average annual rainfall is 278 mm. Total water storage after a fallow period of about 18 months was 29.7 mm greater than after barley, representing

Table 7.3. *Distribution of mineral nitrogen (NH$_4^+$ + NO$_3^-$) and soil water at the start of the 1983–1984 cropping season under bare fallow/barley and barley/barley rotations at Breda, northern Syria*

Mineral nitrogen (mg kg^{-1})			Soil water (mm H$_2$O per depth interval)			
Depth (mm)	Fallow/ barley	Barley/ barley	Depth (mm)	Fallow/ barley	Barley/ barley	F/B–B/B
0–200	13.1	5.2	0–150	14.6	12.3	2.3
200–400	13.7	3.6	150–300	24.9	21.1	3.8
400–600	6.5	3.2	300–450	34.8	27.3	7.5
600–900	6.5	5.7	450–600	39.5	32.1	7.4
			600–750	40.5	35.2	5.3
			750–900	39.4	36.0	3.4
					Total	29.7

Source: ICARDA (1985).

10.7 per cent of the average annual rainfall. The extra water was stored at a depth of 300–750 mm. During a succession of years at the higher rainfall site of Tel Hadya (average annual rainfall 330 mm), during the 18-month fallow period water storage varied between 10 per cent and 40 per cent (Harris, 1995). Increased yields after the bare fallow can be attributed partly to the stored water and partly to the increase in mineral nitrogen.

Another effect in these experiments might have been to reduce the incidence of disease or damage by pests. Reduction of diseases of wheat by soil-borne fungi has been observed at Rothamsted Experimental Station after a one-year fallow (Dyke, 1964). Yields of the first crop after the fallow were higher than the fourth crop at all levels of nutrient addition.

The above observations point to the need to understand the physical, chemical and biological factors that can determine the effectiveness of a bare fallow at a particular location. Economically, the disadvantage of the fallow is that it produces no income. Where economic conditions are favourable it will be advantageous to replace the fallow with use of fertilizer, application of fungicide or use of supplementary irrigation. In addition to having an economic disadvantage, a bare fallow can lead to loss of soil by wind and water erosion.

Where the benefit of a bare fallow is from increased storage of rain water, control of weeds is essential. If herbicide is not used, cultivations should be shallow and as few as possible because each disturbance increases water loss by evaporation. Dead weeds left on the soil surface act as a mulch, reducing evaporative loss of water.

7.5 IRRIGATION

The term 'irrigation' is used here to include the use of naturally flooded land after it has drained and the application of water to land with the objective of promoting crop growth and yield. The practice of irrigation can have several benefits: it raises crop yields in low-rainfall areas, yields are less variable than those dependent on low, erratic rainfall, and the increased yield potential can justify the use of other inputs such as high-yielding crop varieties, fertilizers and pesticides. It can also extend the cropping season, allowing two or three crops to be grown successively each year. Irrigation can, however, lead to waterlogging and soil salinization, as described in Chapter 5.

During the twentieth century there was a large increase in the area of irrigated land (Figure 7.3), from an estimated area of 170 Mha in 1970 to 271 Mha in 1998. As shown in the figure, since 1979 the irrigated area has not kept pace with the rate of increase in population. Whereas the irrigated area increased by 2–4 per cent per year during the 1960s and 1970s, the annual rate since 1979 has averaged only 1 per cent (Postel, 1993). There are several reasons for this decline, including the high initial investment required for the construction of

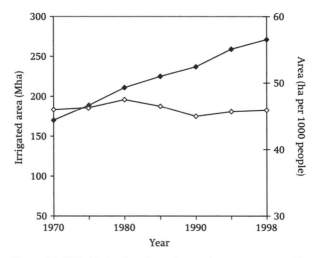

Figure 7.3. Global irrigation. ♦, total area; ◊, area per person. Data from FAO Production Yearbooks.

storage dams, relatively low commodity prices, environmental damage, poor performance of many schemes, and fewer suitable sites for new schemes. Waterlogging and salinization have occurred, severely affecting about 10 per cent (25–30 Mha) of the irrigated land area; a further 60–80 Mha is affected to varying extents (Umali, 1993; Wallace and Batchelor, 1997). Much of the affected area is in developing countries.

The three sources of water for irrigation are off-farm, on-farm wells and on-farm surface supplies. The off-farm sources include rivers, lakes, reservoirs and dams. On-farm water is drawn from wells, usually by pumping, and surface supplies are from small reservoirs (ponds).

Water stored in reservoirs and behind dams is usually also used for domestic and industrial purposes, which means there is competition for its use. Most large dams are used to generate electricity, a complication when costing the water supplied to farmers. Some dams, such as the Three Gorges on the river Yangtse in China, are built primarily to reduce the incidence of flooding downstream and to generate electricity. The most intensive period for the construction of large storage dams was in the 1970s and 1980s, when 277 major dams were built in 53 countries and a further 73 were under construction (Gleick, 1993).

Pumping water from wells carries the risk of exceeding the rate of recharge. When this occurs the wells have to be dug deeper, and greater energy is required to pump the water, thus increasing its cost. Lack of an adequate rate of recharge has become a serious problem in northern China, southern India and in the region extending from southern South Dakota to northwest Texas in the USA (Postel, 1993). It is likely to occur in the future also in Saudi Arabia and Libya.

Crop response

Irrigation is used to grow crops in both arid and humid regions of the world. Perhaps surprisingly, the area under irrigation in humid regions is the greater, because much of the rice crop is grown under controlled flooded conditions in humid regions (Greenland and Murray-Rust, 1986).

Because of the need to optimize the other conditions that limit crop growth and yield, the effect of irrigation is rarely considered in isolation. An example of an early experiment is of the response of cotton to irrigation at three rates of nitrogen fertilizer in the Sudan (Crowther, 1934). The crop showed a positive response to each treatment, and a positive interaction between them (Table 7.4).

Table 7.4. *The effects of three rates of nitrogen fertilizer and three rates of irrigation on the yield of seed cotton (as per cent of control) in the Sudan*

Nitrogen fertilizer applied (kg N ha^{-1})	Rate of irrigation (m^3 ha^{-1})		
	535	890	1250
0	100	112	115
67	141	177	203
134	165	220	281

Source: Crowther (1934).

A major advance in the 1960s was the introduction of dwarfing genes into wheat and rice. The shorter-strawed varieties were less liable to lodge, so that higher applications of nitrogen could be made and the harvest index was increased, both effects increasing yield. The combination of irrigation, more fertilizer use, growth of the new crop varieties and improved land management gave substantial increases in yield of cereal crops. As mentioned in Chapter 4; these changes, together with the breeding of short-season crops, have been called the Green Revolution.

Systems and irrigation efficiency

How efficiently water is used when irrigating crops depends on the system used, but is often low. General references on this topic are James *et al.* (1992), Kay (1986) and Murty and Takeuchi (1996).

Before the water reaches the field losses occur by evaporation from the open surfaces of reservoirs and storage dams, and by seepage from unlined canals. Water from aquifers is not subject to evaporative loss, but if the rate of removal exceeds the rate of replacement this source is not sustainable. Losses can be reduced by using lined instead of unlined canals or by passing the water through wide tubes, as are being used in Libya, but both methods are expensive. Without these more expensive alternatives, up to half of the potential supplies of water can be lost before they reach the farmer.

The efficiency of water use when it reaches the field to be irrigated depends on the system that is used to distribute the water and on how well the crop requirements are met by the rate of application and its timing. The three systems that are in common use are gravity feed to basins or furrows, sprinkler, and drip (also known as trickle), each of

Table 7.5. *Methods of applying irrigation water*

Gravity feed	–	For level or gently sloping land and soil with medium to low infiltration rate; used for basin and furrow irrigation; low capital cost, simple maintenance.
Sprinkler	–	For all conditions of land and soil; affected by wind; high initial cost.
Drip (trickle)	–	For all conditions of land and soil; located on or under soil surface; gives most efficient use of water; prone to clogging; high initial cost and requires regular maintenance.

Source: After Gleick (1993).

which has several varieties. The main characteristics of each system are listed in Table 7.5.

Gravity feed

The traditional system of irrigation is gravity feed, where necessary using lifting devices powered by man or farm animals (as used during early civilizations; see Section 3.4). It is still commonly used because it has low initial cost and requires little maintenance compared with sprinkler and drip irrigation systems. For example, it is used in east and southeast Asia for the cultivation of paddy rice. Water supplied under gravity floods the soil to give a depth of a few centimetres and is retained for much of the period of crop growth by puddling the soil so that drainage occurs only slowly. A uniform supply of water depends on the creation of a flat land surface.

For furrow irrigation the furrows are usually drawn at a slight angle to the contour to give a slow flow of water to the end of the furrow. Before each irrigation the bottom of the furrow is often loosened to allow infiltration. Furrow irrigation is not suitable for soils with a high infiltration rate, for example coarse sands. It is most suited for use on gently sloping land, although it can also be used on steeper slopes where the land is terraced or is in ridge and furrow drawn close to the contour.

Sprinkler and drip systems

Sprinkler and drip systems use water more efficiently. Both are also more versatile than irrigation by gravity in that they can be used on most soils and most land surfaces. The drip system is efficient because it concentrates the water within the root zone, thus minimizing evaporative loss from soil; the efficiency of overhead sprinklers is less, because of uneven distribution, wind drift and loss of water by evaporation from soil.

Both systems require piped water under pressure, which adds to the cost, and the water needs to be free of particulate matter or requires filtration. Both also require daily maintenance. The largest land area under drip irrigation is in the USA, but this system represents the greatest percentage of total irrigated area in Cyprus (71.4 per cent), Israel (48.7 per cent) and Jordan (21.1 per cent) (Postel, 1993). Nutrient solutions are sometimes added to the water, although precipitation of phosphate can block the system.

Efficiency of irrigation

The efficient use of water depends on adding the right amount at the right time, values that can be determined by the methods described in Section 7.3. Computer-based models have been developed to perform the calculations for determining the optimum timing of water application and amounts.

The efficiency of irrigation could be improved substantially by reducing seepage losses from canals, allocating water to farmers based on calculated need, and using an efficient system of application (Stewart and Nielsen, 1990; Postel, 1993). Improvement in this area is needed, particularly considering that the demand for water for domestic, industrial and agricultural use is increasing. The case for irrigation is strengthened when the water is used efficiently.

7.6 SUMMARY

A supply of water is essential for dryland and irrigated agriculture. Successful dryland agriculture depends on optimizing the use of rainfall, mainly by reducing runoff and evaporation from the soil but also, where required, by the storage of water by a bare fallow. When used as part of a package including high-yielding crop varieties, fertilizers, pesticides and suitable soil cultivations, irrigation can produce high crop yields. It is estimated that irrigated crops produce one-third of the global agricultural produce from one-sixth of the agricultural land area. The two systems are often used on the same piece of land, irrigation during a dry season and rainfed cropping during a wet season.

Irrigation is also used to supplement rainfall when there is a period of drought during the growing season.

The use of water for irrigation needs to be as efficient as possible, because demands for water for other purposes are increasing. Improvements can be made through optimizing the timing of irrigations and the amount of water supplied and by the use of an efficient distribution system. Problems can arise from waterlogging and soil salinization (see Chapter 5).

8

Managing change of land use: seven examples

Until 10 000 years ago, hunting, fishing, and gathering seeds, fruits, roots and shellfish provided the food for the small number of people in the world, possibly about five million (Cohen, 1995). By the early part of the nineteenth century the population had risen to about one billion and by the year 2000 to six billion, virtually all of whom depended for their food on the produce from agriculture and fishing. The increase in production from crops has come from an expansion of the arable area and from greater yields per hectare, expansion providing most of the increase until the middle of the twentieth century when technological advances led to substantially increased yields (see Chapter 9).

The evolution of agriculture and its spread into Africa, Asia, Australia, Europe and North and South America was a slow process that occurred over several millennia, starting around 10 000 years ago. Domesticated crop plants and domesticated animals supplied food from land that had previously been the exclusive province of hunter-gatherers; the change to agriculture may be described as the first stage of intensified land use.

Not all was beneficial. Whereas hunter-gatherers relied on the stability of natural and modified ecosystems for their activities, farming inevitably destroyed them. Trees were cut down, pastures were overgrazed, sloping land was cultivated and eroded. Often the end result was impoverishment of much of the land or its entire loss, as described by Chinese, Greek and Roman authors around 2000 years ago (see Chapter 3). Although productive land was lost, more could be brought into cultivation, or food could be imported from more reliable sources such as the Nile valley.

More land was brought into cultivation in northern Europe during the second half of the first millennium AD and during the second millennium, and in North America and Australia between the seventeenth and twentieth centuries. By the middle of the nineteenth century it is estimated that the arable area of the world was about 0.4×10^9 ha and the population about 1.3×10^9 (Evans, 1998). The arable area in the year 2000 was about 1.4×10^9 ha and the population 6×10^9.

As mentioned above, this expansion of the agricultural area was not without its problems. Future expansion is limited to perhaps 0.5×10^9 ha (see Chapter 9), much of which is marginal for agriculture. The present requirement is to increase agricultural production in developing countries in order to raise the dietary levels and relieve hunger, objectives that have already been achieved in many countries by raising yields.

Over a long period of time changes have been made throughout the world to the way land is used to increase production. The two strands for development have been the application of technological advances and the improvement of social and economic conditions, which together have a synergistic effect, as will be illustrated by the examples below. They illustrate the requirements for successful agricultural developments.

8.2 AGRICULTURAL DEVELOPMENT IN A DEVELOPED COUNTRY: ENGLAND

The pattern followed by many countries that are now considered to have developed, are developing, or will develop their agriculture, resembles in many respects the development in England. It is relevant to countries with developing economies because the components of socio-economic change were interwoven with technological innovation in agriculture and in manufacturing industries. The important differences are that the population in England increased only slowly until the nineteenth century (Figure 8.1) – the rate of change in agriculture was correspondingly slow – and that many countries will not develop manufacturing industries on a large scale.

There had been gradual change in England before the Roman period and later, but it was from the sixteenth century (the starting point of this account) that socio-economic and technological developments caused agriculture to evolve more rapidly towards its present condition. The development had some progressive steps and some setbacks,

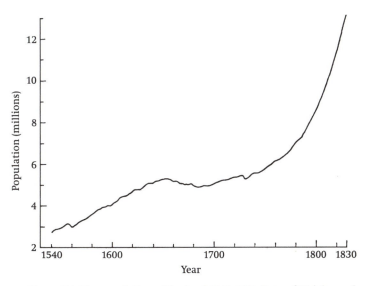

Figure 8.1. The population of England 1541–1831. Data of Wrigley and Schofield (1981), reported by Overton (1996).

caused especially by adverse climatic conditions and by the plagues of the fourteenth and later centuries. This account draws largely on Ernle (1961), Slicher van Bath (1963), Grigg (1974) and Overton (1996).

Socio-economic changes before the middle of the nineteenth century

Three significant changes that occurred between the beginning of the sixteenth century and the middle of the nineteenth century were to the marketing of agricultural produce, land tenure and the country's infrastructure.

Marketing and transport

During the sixteenth century agricultural produce that was surplus to the farmers' needs was marketed under local controls in the local town. In an example given by Overton (1996), the controls at one market in 1564 included a price for grain agreed by the local justices and restriction of the activities of middlemen who might otherwise sell privately at inflated prices. Several changes had occurred by the middle of the nineteenth century. The growth of cities, and especially London, increased the movement of crop and animal produce; roads, canals and railways had created a national market, and middlemen bought most of the grain that was sold by farmers. This greater movement of agricultural produce led to the ending of local price controls and to the creation of free trade for the country's produce.

Government policy on the import and export of corn lasted much longer than legislation on the internal market. Regulation of imports and exports began in the twelfth century. The King's licence was required for the export of corn in the fourteenth century (Ernle, 1961) and a succession of Acts of Parliament regulated trade in the succeeding centuries. Generally, exports were subsidized when prices were low and a duty was paid on imports, which were permitted only when domestic prices were high, a policy that helped to protect both producer and consumer. These Corn Laws that had put a duty on the import of corn (mainly wheat and barley) were repealed in 1846 except for a nominal duty, which was itself abolished in 1869. The effect on agricultural prices in England was felt only when imports increased from North America later in the nineteenth century, made possible by the development of land and sea transport.

The repeal of the Corn Laws was made necessary by the demand of an increasing population, especially of those in the growing cities. The population of England had increased from less than three million in 1500 to 8.7 million by 1800 and to 16.7 million by 1851. The population of London, the biggest city, had risen from 55 000 early in the sixteenth century to 960 000 in 1801, by which time 10 other cities had populations of 13 000 or more. The cities had markets which were supplied with agricultural produce carried on roads that were gradually improved in the sixteenth century and later, by coastal shipping, on canals built in the eighteenth century and later, and on railways in the nineteenth century. Rivers were made more navigable. Livestock was also driven to market. The marketing system, the associated legislation and the required means of transport had changed radically to meet the needs of the people. Of comparable importance was the change in land tenure.

Land tenure

In 1500 the form of tenure and the system of farming, whether mixed arable/animal husbandry or mainly livestock, varied greatly over the country. A common system in mixed farming areas was that tenants paid rent to the lord of the manor for the use of strips of land in 'open-fields' and had the right to graze animals on pastures and stubble and take firewood from woodlands. The farmers of a village needed to co-operate in organizing the work on their strips in the open-fields and in making such decisions as when to leave a field in fallow. The tenant usually had security of tenure for his lifetime as long as he paid his rent (from the sale of arable crops and livestock) and could often pass on the tenancy to his son.

The system slowly changed, and by the middle of the nineteenth century almost all the open-fields and most of the rights to graze on 'common' land had disappeared. The strips were aggregated by the new type of tenant farmer who could thereby keep livestock more profitably and cultivate his fields as he wished as long as he did not offend his landlord. The tenant farmer and landlord paid permanent or seasonal employees for labour. The common route to enclosure was by Act of Parliament. The great benefit was the flexibility it gave to the farmer to change his farming system according to the market price of produce, and to be innovative as new practices became known.

Other socio-economic factors should be mentioned. A spirit of enquiry from the sixteenth century onwards led to a change in the traditional attitudes to both agriculture and manufacturing industries, and particularly to a recognition that agricultural techniques could be improved. The more advanced land management and agriculture of the Low Countries (the Netherlands and Belgium) spread to England in the sixteenth and seventeenth centuries, leading to drainage schemes to reclaim wetlands, the growth of new field crops such as clover and turnips, and better rotations. New crops from the Americas were also introduced; for example, potatoes became widely grown in the eighteenth century. These and other innovations were adopted by the farming community, security of land tenure and access to urban markets having made them profitable.

Technological changes before the middle of the nineteenth century

The average yield of wheat, which may be taken as an index of productivity, increased from an estimated $700 \, kg \, ha^{-1}$ in 1600 to $1400 \, kg \, ha^{-1}$ in 1800, to $2100 \, kg \, ha^{-1}$ in 1900 and to $7000 \, kg \, ha^{-1}$ in 1990 (Cooke, 1967; Overton, 1996). Uncertain though the early estimate is, the slow increase in yield combined with the growth in arable area (Table 8.1) were sufficient to provide for a doubling of the population, from four million in 1600 to over eight million by 1800.

More arable land was created by drainage of wetlands in eastern and southern England and east Yorkshire during the seventeenth century and later. Woodlands, already much reduced in area by 1600, were

Table 8.1. *Estimates of arable area and wheat yields in England, relative to 1700*

	Year				
	1600	1700	1750	1800	1850
Arable area	—	100	—	128	170
Wheat yields	72	100	123	136	180

Source: Overton (1996).

cut down (though there was also some replanting) and heathland was converted to agricultural use. These increases in land use for agriculture were most profitable when food prices were high, such as during the period of wars.

Improvements in yield came in a variety of ways. One of the most effective was the introduction during the seventeenth century of clover to replace bare fallows. In addition, fields were sown with grasses, such as ryegrass, to form temporary grassland (leys) that supported mixed farming (arable/animal husbandry) until more specialized farming became common in the second half of the twentieth century. Also in the seventeenth century turnips became a farm crop although like clover they were widely grown only after the middle of the eighteenth century, when they usually replaced the bare fallow. Other crops included peas, faba beans and sainfoin, a range of non-legumes including Swedish turnips (swedes), mangolds and potatoes, and cash crops such as flax. In the twentieth century they included lucerne (alfalfa), sugar beet, oilseed rape and maize.

The most profound change to English agriculture in the period 1600–1850 can be attributed to the introduction of the Norfolk four-course rotation during the seventeenth century, and its wider adoption in the eighteenth century. The annual sequence was as follows: turnips as fodder for cattle and sheep; wheat or barley; clover used for grazing and hay; wheat or barley. The clover added nitrogen to the soil and the cattle provided farmyard manure from the turnips, straw and hay. Wheat, barley and animal products were sold off the farm. The system replaced the three-course rotation of winter wheat, a spring crop of barley, oats, peas or beans, and a bare fallow in the third year. The Norfolk rotation provided more nitrogen but still entailed some loss of nutrients, as shown by measurements at Rothamsted Experimental Station in the nineteenth century. For N, P and K the losses (in $kg\,ha^{-1}$) over the four-year rotation were 64, 9 and 7, respectively (reported by Cooke, 1967).

Cultivations changed in several respects. During the seventeenth and eighteenth centuries horses replaced oxen for pulling carts and for cultivations, and ploughs were redesigned for light and heavy soils. The seed drill and horse hoe, introduced during the first part of the eighteenth century and widely used by the nineteenth century, reduced the amount of seed required compared with broadcasting, and economized on labour for weeding. For crop harvesting the scythe replaced the sickle early in the nineteenth century. Mechanization developed much more rapidly after the middle of the nineteenth century (see below).

Additives to the soil including lime and marl (calcareous clay) were used for the reclamation of sandy heathland. Many waste materials were thought to be of value as manures in the seventeenth to nineteenth centuries, including rags, wool, and animal and fish wastes, although where they were used and whether on farms or market gardens is not known. Guano from Peru and sodium nitrate from Chile were imported during the early nineteenth century. The second half of the nineteenth century saw the start of the fertilizer industry.

Although there was no breeding of crop varieties before the twentieth century, there is evidence that farmers were aware of different varieties, and some writers advocated the purchase of new varieties (Overton, 1996). An example of the development of a new variety is the barley variety Chevallier, which was raised by the Reverend Dr Chevallier from a single ear selected by a labourer in 1817.

Animal products increased as a result of the greater number of animals that were kept (though the increase was probably small), and through improvements in animal husbandry such as better nutrition and breeding. To judge from paintings of prize pigs, sheep and bulls, the main criterion of the breeder was size, but it is more likely that market prices determined success; with sheep it might have been wool, meat or fat for tallow that at different times brought the best price, and with cattle it might have been beef or milk or both. By the middle of the nineteenth century several named and distinct breeds were known.

Changes since the middle of the nineteenth century

Socio-economic and technological changes during the last 150 years have changed the face of the countryside and raised agricultural output more than in any previous period. It has been a time of intensification, particularly in the second half of the twentieth century, when various technologies improved and were applied together.

The 1850s and 1860s were a prosperous time for agriculture. There was a succession of good harvests, livestock was better fed and housed, and breeds were improved. But in the middle of the 1870s a combination of a succession of poor harvests and the imported grain from America meant that many farmers could not pay their rent. Later, some turned to livestock but subsequently suffered from cheaper imports of refrigerated meat and dairy products from North and South America, Australia and New Zealand. Milk, vegetables and fruit for consumption in the cities were the most profitable products. Two effects were that labourers left the land and that the low price of farmland provided the opportunity for holdings to be increased in size.

Development during the first half of the twentieth century was affected by the two world wars and the Depression of the 1930s. During both wars the government enforced the ploughing of grassland to produce more crops, using local committees to ensure that it was done. During the 1930s prices for agricultural produce were low, and by the time of the Second World War in 1939 crop yields were little larger than in 1900. The experience of food shortage during and after the war, and shortage of foreign currency to buy food, led to generous subsidies to boost agricultural production, and output rose.

Technological changes

During the second half of the nineteenth century the fertilizer industry began, with the manufacture of superphosphate. Ammonium sulphate, a by-product from gasworks, basic slag, a by-product from the manufacture of steel, and potassium salts mined in Europe all came into use as fertilizers. Comparatively little fertilizer was used until the second half of the twentieth century, when the use of nitrogen fertilizers began to exceed that of phosphate and potassium, a trend that continued to the end of the century.

Cultivations in the nineteenth century and into the twentieth century were by implements drawn by horses, until they were replaced by tractors. Instead of using the land to feed horses (about 1 ha of land per horse) it could be used to grow food crops; on the debit side, horse manure was not available to help to maintain soil fertility. Mouldboard ploughs were made stronger and bigger, tine and chisel cultivators came into use on heavy soils, and zero-tillage was used on suitable soils. The scythe was replaced by the reaper-binder and in the twentieth century by the combine harvester. Fewer but more skilled workmen were needed; contractors were used for work such as harvesting. From the middle of the nineteenth century clay pipes were used for drainage of wetlands and in the second half of the twentieth century plastic pipes were introduced.

New crop varieties were also introduced. They were improved by selection of individual plants with the required characteristics and, increasingly in the twentieth century, by breeding. Cereals, root crops, grasses and clovers were all improved. Dwarf wheats were bred which gave high yields and did not lodge when given large applications of nitrogen fertilizer.

Pesticides came into use mainly in the second half of the twentieth century. Previously, control had depended on rotations, bare fallows or burning of severely diseased crops. Potato growers learned the value of buying virus-free seed potatoes from Scotland. A vast array of pesticides came into use, starting with the herbicide 2,4-D in the late 1930s; insecticides including DDT and many others followed.

During the second half of the twentieth century agriculture in England had thus been transformed by the application of technology. Socio-economic conditions, which had also undergone radical change in the nineteenth and twentieth centuries, were also partly responsible for the transformation.

Socio-economic changes

The major changes to agriculture after 1850 were affected by (i) the demand by the increasing population for more agricultural produce, (ii) the import of grain, meat and dairy products, (iii) the two world wars of the twentieth century and the Depression of the 1930s, (iv) the partial replacement of agricultural products with industrial products, and (v) the increase in and spread of knowledge. The first three of these changes were discussed above. The fourth included the industrial manufacture of synthetic fibre that partly replaced wool and linen, and the introduction of new cash crops, such as sugar beet and, later, oilseed rape and sunflowers, for industrial use. The fifth change, which was of crucial importance, included education, research, advisory (extension) services, and farmers' organizations.

The first agricultural college (the Royal Agricultural College) was founded at Cirencester in 1846. In the 1890s government money was provided for agricultural education at eight universities and colleges in England and Wales. In a short period after 1912, farm institutes were set up with government money to teach the skills and practices of farming. Agricultural shows, weekly magazines, books and local lectures added to the spread of knowledge.

Rothamsted Experimental Station, founded in 1843, was privately financed until 1909. It was the only research institute for some time, until others were set up in the twentieth century for research in areas such as grassland, fruit, dairying, vegetables and agricultural economics. The Soil Survey of England and Wales was set up in the 1940s. Research has also been undertaken in universities and colleges, some financed by grants from the Board (later the Ministry) of Agriculture and from the 1930s by the Agricultural Research Council, until more recent changes to funding were made. Industry, charitable institutions and individuals also financed research.

To act as a bridge between research workers and farmers, and also to advise government, advisory officers were attached to the universities and colleges that received finance to teach agricultural courses. They provided advice to farmers and conducted experiments at farm institutes and on farmers' land. In addition, the fertilizer industry ran a scheme aimed at efficient fertilizer use.

In the middle of the nineteenth century there was a 'perpetual contrast between the practices of adjoining agriculturalists. A hundred farmers plodded along the Elizabethan road, while a solitary neighbour marched in the track of the twentieth century' (Ernle, 1961). The situation was changed partly by the government action described above and partly by organizations set up by the farming community. First, in 1838, was the Royal Agricultural Society, which brought together landlords, farmers and scientists from throughout the country. Farmers' Clubs were founded at around the same time. The National Farmers' Union, the body that the government consults over agricultural issues, was founded early in the twentieth century. Labourers' unions were active in the nineteenth century but became less so in the twentieth century.

Throughout the period described here, agriculture did not develop in isolation. Urban populations required food, and markets supplied manufactured goods in return. The growth of manufacturing industries between the eighteenth and twentieth centuries, with their associated urban population, provided a bigger market for agricultural output. Particularly in the twentieth century, there was increased use of agricultural machinery and chemicals, and of the more rapid means of trade and communication that are the characteristics of modern farming. England has been used as an example, but many of these changes have occurred, or will occur, elsewhere in the world.

Table 8.2. *Socio-economic and technological factors that led to the development of agriculture in England after 1600*

Socio-economic factors

- Marketing
  Initially, local controls over sale of home produce to ensure fair prices, later freed from controls; initially taxes on imports and exports, later repealed; increase in urban markets

- Infrastructure
  Roads, canals and railways gave better access to markets; water and electricity supplies improved

- Tenure
  Initially, mainly strip farming with common land, later amalgamation of holdings and enclosure; tenure became more secure

- Knowledge
  Agricultural education, books, lectures, research, advisory services

Technological factors

- Crops
  Introductions from Europe and America; improvement by selection and later by breeding

- Fertilizer
  Waste materials, lime and marl; fertilizers from the middle of the nineteenth century

- Pesticides
  Mainly in the second half of the twentieth century
- Cultivations
  Oxen replaced by horses, these later replaced by tractors; improvement of implements, generally becoming stronger and bigger

- Reclamation
  Drainage of wetlands; woodlands and heathlands converted to agricultural use

Summary

Agricultural output is estimated to have increased about three-fold between 1600 and 1850, through increased area of production and increased yields (Overton, 1996). Yields of wheat between 1850 and the end of the twentieth century increased about four-fold, almost all of which occurred through intensification in the second half of the twentieth century. The two sets of factors (socio-economic and technological) that brought about these increases are listed in Table 8.2. Many of the same socio-economic and technological factors apply to the development of agriculture in other countries, even though they may have different histories and less scope for industrial development and face bigger increases in population.

8.3   THE GEZIRA IRRIGATION SCHEME, SUDAN

The Gezira is a triangular plain lying between the Blue Nile and the White Nile, which reaches its northernmost point close to Khartoum where the rivers meet. Most of the area has soils mapped as Vertisols, with a high (50–70 per cent) content of clay. The mean annual rainfall ranges from 150 mm in the north to 450 mm in the south and east, the short wet season extending from June to September. Rainfall varies greatly between years, especially towards the north, so that before the introduction of irrigation, production of sorghum, the main crop, was uncertain. The account that follows is drawn largely from Tothill (1948) and Gaitskell (1959), and considers the early development of the scheme.

The aim of the scheme was to grow long-staple Egyptian cotton with irrigation for export. Survey of the area to measure land levels and to record land ownership began in 1904–1906. Before the scheme started legislation was put into place to protect the rights of the landowners. Delays due largely to the 1914–1918 war and its aftermath had the fortuitous effect of giving time for agronomic trials to establish the most appropriate cultivations and planting time. The scheme became reality in 1925 with the completion of the Sennar dam on the Blue Nile. When filled, the quantity of stored water was 781 million cubic metres.

The scheme was operated by a triple partnership between the government, commercial companies and tenants. The government allotted land to tenants, supplied water for irrigation and provided the required infrastructure, including roads, hospitals and police. It also set up a research station at Wad Medani. The companies supervised the work of the tenants, kept the records of each cultivator and carried out the ginning, dispatch and sale of the cotton. Tenants were responsible for all the agricultural work on their holdings, including the upkeep of the irrigation channels. Supplies, such as seed, and work done on their behalf, such as ploughing, were debited to them. Advances of cash to meet their costs were made by the companies.

Of the profit from the sale of the cotton tenants were allocated 40 per cent and the government and companies 60 per cent. Each tenant received a proportion of the 40 per cent according to the amount of cotton that had come from his holding, and he retained all the food and fodder crops.

The government purchased land from the original owners, who were offered 40-year tenancies. At the start each cultivator had a standard tenancy of 30 feddans (1 feddan equals 0.42 ha), of which 20 feddans were cropped. For the first six years the required rotation was cotton, dura (sorghum) or lubia (*Dolichos lablab* L.), fallow, cotton, dura or lubia, and fallow. After poor yields of cotton, this was changed to an eight-course rotation; at the same time, the tenancies were increased to 40 feddans. The rotations provided cotton in two years out of six and later two years out of eight, sorghum for local consumption or sale, and lubia mainly for animal feed.

The area under cotton increased from 33 613 ha in 1925–1926 to almost 82 000 ha by 1931. Yields per hectare were low during the first six years, increasing later and fluctuating around 1400 kg ha^{-1} of unginned (seed) cotton. For much of the period between 1930 and 1946, however, cotton prices were very low, and tenant income from cotton was low or nil. In these difficult times the greater reliability of the sorghum crop under irrigation than when fed by rain was the reason most cultivators decided to retain their tenancies.

There were also pest problems with cotton. These seriously reduced yields before they were brought under control by agronomic measures and by the breeding of resistant varieties. Fertilizers were not required, except for nitrogen in the northern part of the scheme, because Nile silt had provided most of the required nutrients in the soil and cropping was not intensive.

Appraisal of the scheme

The following summary is derived from Gaitskell (1959).

(1)	Good water quality and the hot dry season gave good crop yields; research and extension services were provided.

(2)	Farmers had a more secure food supply and a source of income (although low) from the cash crop.

(3)	The weaknesses of the scheme were its dependence on one cash crop, the distance from Port Sudan, the nearest port, and, as emphasized by Gaitskell, insufficient social development until the 1940s. Particularly serious was the low price of cotton on the world market in the 1930s.

This account has focused on the establishment and development of the scheme. After 1956 its area was almost doubled by the development of the Managil Extension. Cotton remains the principal crop, although a wider range of crops, including groundnuts and wheat, is now grown;

fertilizer (mainly urea) and pesticides are used, and rotations have been changed (Craig, 1991).

The groundnut schemes of the late 1940s and early 1950s are now but a vague memory to many, or thought of as unmitigated disasters. After 50 years or so it is easy to forget the conditions of the time: food shortages, especially in those European countries most affected by war, and the near bankruptcy that prevented purchase of food from elsewhere. Similar conditions often prevail today in the developing world.

At the time, much of Africa was under colonial rule, with territories that seemed suitable for large-scale development to produce food crops. The urgent need was for oil crops, to produce the oil required for the manufacture of margarine. As groundnuts were already grown successfully in Africa they were the natural choice. To meet the shortage, large areas of new production were needed, which could be achieved only by mechanical cultivation of land opened up from native bush.

The East African schemes

In the late 1940s plans were made by the British and French governments for vast increases in groundnut production in Tanganyika (now Tanzania), Nigeria and Senegal. The scheme for Tanzania was the biggest and most adventurous; for the account of this that follows I am indebted to Professor A.H. Bunting.

The development was suggested by Frank Samuel, a senior executive of Unilever Ltd, after a flight from South Africa to London, early in 1946, which had carried him over parts of western and central Tanzania in the heart of the wet season. The vast and apparently uninhabited areas of woods and forests below were a rich, dark green. Unilever was at that time the largest participant in the international oilseeds trade, and was consequently largely responsible for the future supply of plant oils for Britain. Samuel proposed that the British government should consider using part of this seemingly potentially productive area for the large-scale mechanized production of groundnuts.

The result was that a three-man mission was dispatched in June 1946 to explore the possibilities in Tanganyika, Northern Rhodesia (now part of Zambia) and Kenya. Of the three members, the leader, John Wakefield, had been director of agriculture in Tanganyika. The others were a Unilever manager of oil-palm plantations in West Africa and

Congo, and a banker. It seems unlikely that either of these had ever raised a groundnut crop.

By June the dry season reigned in all the areas they visited, and the vegetation was grey or brown rather than the lush green that had so impressed Samuel. They spent 'a little over nine weeks covering the ground' (Wood, 1950). Their report (*The Wakefield Report*) recommended that the mechanized production of groundnuts should start little more than a year later, in the wet season of 1947–1948.

The report proposed the establishment of 107 production units, each of 13 500 ha, from which an estimated annual output of 600 000– 800 000 tonnes would be attained by 1950/51 assuming an average yield of 834–1112 kg ha^{-1}, with half the land under groundnuts at any one time. The estimated capital cost was £24 million.

The start was to be in Tanganyika, where three sparsely inhabited areas were designated. The first was to be in what was later found to be the comparatively suitable environment of the Southern Province, even though the lack of ocean ports and land communications would inevitably delay any significant development for at least a further year. Had this choice been accepted, there would have been at least some time to study the soils and climate and the methods of land clearing from tall woodland, and to find out how best to grow the crops by mechanical means – about which nothing appeared to be known in Tanganyika. It would also have given time for similar initial studies of the other two areas. In due course the headquarters were established at Nachingwea (mean rainfall during 1947–1954 of 874 mm, range 697–1080 mm), about 190 km from the sea at Lindi and Mtwara.

The second area was in the Western Province, along the Central railway line from the ocean port at Dar es Salaam to Kigoma on Lake Tanganyika. Its headquarters were at Urambo. This area was almost entirely unsuitable for the production of groundnuts. The wet season was far too long for reliable production of an inherently short-season crop (100–130 days at the wet-season temperatures of Western Tanganyika). The annual rainfall was around 1000 mm. The soils were ancient, mostly light textured, erodible and poorly supplied with organic matter and plant nutrients. Moreover, the rosette virus disease of groundnuts and leaf spot diseases were endemic and severe in the area. In the event the only crop which succeeded was Virginia tobacco – until it too became unprofitable as improvident felling of increasingly remote woodland, without replanting, made the cost of firing the flue barns unsustainable.

The third area that was recommended was in Kongwa district in Central Tanganyika, at the southern end of the seasonally arid Maasai steppe. It was chosen, in London, to be developed first. Consequently very substantial investments in settlements, equipment, workshops and land clearing were undertaken in the environmentally least promising (even forbidding) area.

The mission does not seem to have realized not only that the average rainfall in the area they proposed (438 mm in 1947–1954, range 211–585 mm) was marginal for any form of crop production at tropical temperatures, but also that the rainfall was extremely variable from year to year and that there was a marked dry gap in mid-season in many years. Perhaps the only virtues of the Kongwa area were that some of the soils were 'strong' (although the red earths could not be cultivated after they had become dry) and that there was no rosette disease.

The advance party left for Tanganyika on 27 January 1947, and the first land-clearing tractors were moved into the Kongwa area to start cutting traces through the dense *Commiphora* scrub in February. The United Africa Company, of which Frank Samuel was the chairman, took on the management on a cost basis, with no profit to itself. It was replaced by a government agency, the Overseas Food Corporation, in 1948.

After an initial soil survey in 1947 a more detailed soil survey of part of the Kongwa and Nachingwea areas was undertaken between 1950 and 1954 (Anderson, 1957). At Kongwa three broad groups of soils were described: red earths (probably Oxisols), pallid soils (which seemed to some observers like the relics of an ancient hydromorphic landscape), and calcareous valley soils (seemingly the *mbuga* phase of the red-earth catena). At Nachingwea the soils and vegetation (mostly *Brachystegia–Isoberlinia–Julbernardia* woodland) are more varied. Le Mare (1953) reported the results of fertilizer trials in all three areas of the project.

The scheme was in effect doomed to failure by high-level decisions about the order of development taken weeks before anything had been done on the ground. Had the project been delayed, so that all the necessary information could be accumulated, it might never have been started, largely because mechanization of the crop, though feasible, proved to be both so complex and costly. As it was, for an expenditure of £50 million no commercially significant output of groundnuts was obtained.

The Nigerian scheme

In 1947 a proposal was made by the British government to investigate the possibility of large-scale production of groundnuts in West Africa.

One outcome was the development of an area in central Nigeria north of the river Niger between Bida and Mokwa, an area known to have a low density of population. It became known as the Niger Agricultural Project or the Mokwa scheme (Baldwin, 1957).

The plan envisaged the initial development of 26 300 ha (farming area of 11 700 ha) to be expanded later to an area 13 times as great. Annual rainfall in the area averaged 900–1100 mm between May and October. The soils were believed to be 'red sandy loams', but no land survey was made before the scheme started.

Land preparation began towards the end of 1949. The intention was to use mechanical operations alone, but there were problems from hidden roots, tree stumps and cavities under termite mounds. The area under crops increased from about 890 ha in 1950 to 1460 ha by 1953. Sorghum was more successful than groundnuts, but yields were small and very variable. The scheme was abandoned in 1954.

According to Baldwin, the failure of the scheme was due not to the lack of land, labour or capital but to the inability of the managers to combine these into an economic unit. The original purpose was to grow groundnuts for export and other crops for consumption within the country, but markets were inadequately developed. There was a serious lack of essential information on the soils and climate, suitable crop varieties or the required cultivations. Another underlying factor that was missing was motivation of the farmers.

The scheme developed as a settlement area because land tenure law excluded plantation farming. This meant that the farmers grew crops not as labourers but as share-croppers. Each farmer received one-third of the yield from his 10 cultivated acres; the other two-thirds went to the company that had cleared the land and constructed houses and villages. Although share-cropping is often a success, it failed at Mokwa because there was no shortage of land outside the scheme. A farmer had no incentive to work for one-third of his crop production when he could work on his own farm for nine-tenths (one-tenth to the Emir). It seems that no discussions were held with the local farmers to find out what their views and requirements were. In modern parlance it was a 'top-down' development; it neglected the social requirements of the people and provided them with no economic benefit. The missing ingredient was the lack of incentive for the farmers.

Summary

The groundnut schemes in East and West Africa illustrate the high risk of failure when new land is brought into cultivation without adequate preparations. In both areas, before development began the land had not been surveyed, rainfall data were inadequate, and the soil physical and chemical properties were not known. No pilot experiments had tested the suitability of the land for cropping. In the West African scheme the farmers had no incentive to stay and so returned to their own land. Although these schemes were expensive failures, they do serve to illustrate the need to prepare well in advance for the agricultural use of new land. Broadly based land surveys and pilot experiments are essential pre-requisites; unfortunately for the groundnut schemes, there was no time for them. They need to be in place if the large increases in food production required during the next few decades in developing countries are to be met at least partly by the use of new land.

8.5 THE MAIZE INDUSTRY IN ZIMBABWE

Maize is grown in Zimbabwe as a rainfed crop for local consumption and export. The total production in 1989/91 was 1.84 million tonnes, the fourth largest in the developing countries in sub-Saharan Africa. Between 1965 and 1994, smallholders planted 70 per cent of the national maize area, achieving an average yield of about one-quarter that on large commercial farms. One reason for the large difference is that most of the smallholding land is in the drier parts of the country. The account of the maize industry in Zimbabwe that follows is based on that of Byerlee and Eicher (1997).

Using the terminology of Eicher and Kupfuma (1997), two maize-based Green Revolutions can be distinguished in Zimbabwe. The first was on large-scale commercial farms between 1960 and 1980, and the second was on smallholdings between 1980 and 1986. According to these authors, the foundation for both maize revolutions was laid during the first half of the twentieth century. During this period there was investment in the four 'prime movers' of agricultural development:

- New technology was developed by long-term public and private investment in agricultural research.
- Human capital and managerial skills were improved by investments in schools, training programmes and on-the-job experience.
- Capital investments were made in infrastructure such as dams, irrigation, telecommunications and roads.
- Investments were made in markets, fertilizer and seed distribution systems that were of benefit to the farming industry and its customers.

The first revolution came with the release in 1960 of a long-duration hybrid maize bred in Zimbabwe that was widely adopted by commercial farmers in high-rainfall areas; yields increased by 46 per cent. The necessary requirements in the way of seed production, marketing, etc. were already in place. During the 1960s and 1970s, when the country had assumed independence from the UK, plant breeders released short-duration maize hybrids to replace the tobacco crop (which could not be exported because of sanctions). These new hybrids were adopted by commercial growers and some smallholders in the 1970s.

The second revolution came with independence in 1980. Maize production doubled in the six years following independence, an increase attributed to the cultivation of land abandoned during the civil war, the wider adoption of the new short-duration hybrids, an increase in guaranteed prices for the crop, access to credit for seed and fertilizers, and increased market demand for grain.

Rainfall remained as a controlling factor for production between regions and between years. For example, in 1990–1991 the average maize yield on smallholder farms was $3.6\,t\,ha^{-1}$ in high-rainfall areas but only $1.0\,t\,ha^{-1}$ in low-rainfall ones. In 1985, two-thirds of the record crop was put into the government's maize reserve, whereas in 1992 production was severely reduced by a catastrophic drought. Another problem during the 1980s was that loans for the purchase of seed and fertilizer were often not repaid, because of crop failure caused by drought. In 1990, 80 per cent of the smallholders with loans from the finance corporation were in arrears with repayments. Financial support from government has been pared down in the 1990s because of the high cost.

Summary

Much of the experience of smallholders in developing maize production in Zimbabwe is relevant to other countries in Africa. It was achieved by weaving together improved technology, especially the locally developed hybrids for the high-rainfall and low-rainfall areas, with a system of policies and institutions. The policies and institutions included attractive higher prices for grain, access to credit, extension of markets, education, and an advisory system for smallholders. Zimbabwe had the advantage over several other African countries of having a long history of successful commercial farming associated with research institutes, an extension service, well-trained farmers and a good infrastructure. These helped to kick-start the improved production by smallholders in the 1980s. Although other countries may not have those benefits, so that progress will be slower, according to Eicher and Kupfuma (1997) the five general requirements for development are (i) available markets, (ii) political leadership for a smallholder road to development, (iii) appropriate technology, (iv) efficient public and private farmer support institutions, and (v) a favourable macroeconomic environment for agriculture.

8.6 DEVELOPMENT OF THE BRAZILIAN CERRADO

Cerrados is a collective term for various ecological systems in South America. In Brazil, where they occur at elevations from below 300 m to over 1200 m, the most common system, accounting for over half the total area, is the scattered (open) tree savanna known as cerrado. The rest of the cerrados is seasonally flooded, has no trees or is closed forest, or has mixed ecological systems. The total area of the Brazilian cerrados is a little over 200 Mha, representing one-quarter of the area of Brazil. Goedert (1983) estimated that at least 50 Mha could be used for crop production, compared with 7 Mha actually under cultivation in the early 1980s. According to Wallis (1997), about 137 Mha are 'well suited to large-scale mechanized farming'.

The area had been used for extensive ranching of cattle until the new capital, Brasilia, and new roads and railways were built. Access to markets and the requirements of the population of the capital provided incentives for agricultural development.

Annual rainfall ranges from 1200 to 2000 mm over a period of six or seven months during which there is often a dry period of 1–3 weeks. Crops grown in the region include soybean, maize, rice, coffee and oranges.

The soils were surveyed by Williamson (1963). Using the FAO–UNESCO system, Ferralsols (Oxisols) are the main class of soils, occupying about 45 per cent of the land area, the rest of the area being Podzols and others. Common chemical characteristics of the soils are low pH, low contents of exchangeable cations, low effective cation exchange capacity, low extractable phosphate and high extractable aluminium.

Land that is being opened up for cultivation usually requires the addition of lime and fertilizers before it is cropped, as would be expected from the soil characteristics mentioned above (Goedert, 1983; Wallis, 1997). Additions are typically $4\,t\,ha^{-1}$ of dolomitic lime (adding Ca and Mg and reducing the extractable Al) and phosphate, as rock phosphate or in a soluble form, at rates that might need to exceed $200\,kg\,P\,ha^{-1}$ (Figure 8.2). Gypsum has also been shown to be beneficial.

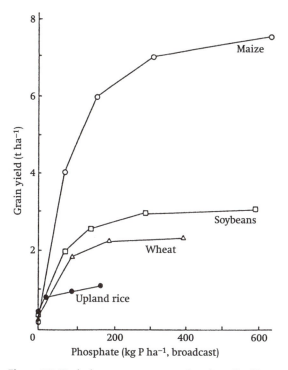

Figure 8.2. Typical crop responses to phosphate fertilizer on virgin cerrado clay soils, Brazil. Data of Lobato (1980), reported by Goedert (1983).

Because gypsum is more soluble than calcium carbonate it overcomes calcium deficiency deeper in the root zone; it also supplies sulphur. Micronutrients, including Zn, B, Cu and Mo, might also be needed. For a crop of maize, after the initial deficiencies have been corrected farmers apply fertilizer at a rate per hectare of 16 kg N, 35 kg P and 66 kg K at planting, and an additional 60 kg ha^{-1} of nitrogen 35 days later. The high rate of fertilizer use is one reason why maize yields have risen to 6 t ha^{-1} in favourable conditions. Other reasons for the success include the growth of improved crop varieties, the use of pesticides, the rotation of two years of soybeans followed by maize, and improved tillage.

An early problem was that cheap credit encouraged purchase of heavy machinery that compacted the soil surface and increased runoff from the heavy storms; erosion followed. Minimum tillage and direct drilling, now commonly used, have reduced the amount of heavy machinery used; they also protect the soil surface from the direct impact of raindrops and reduce runoff. To sustain production, measures to control erosion are needed, as is the maintenance of adequate nutrient supplies and soil organic matter. The importance of organic matter in these soils is three-fold: it provides nutrients, helps to stabilize soil structure, and complexes aluminium.

The traditional ranching of cattle has also changed, with the introduction of better breeds and the introduction of the grass *Brachiaria decumbens*. Legumes would improve the quality of the pastures but it has proved difficult to maintain them.

Summary

The favourable natural conditions that led to the successful development of the Brazilian cerrados include an annual rainfall of 1200–2000 mm over a six-month period, with favourable temperatures that allow the growth of one or two crops per year, and soils that are generally deep, with an initially high infiltration rate. The cost of large inputs of lime and nutrients, especially phosphate, is balanced by the low cost of the land. Roads, railways and port facilities were constructed, and there were internal and external markets, internal and external investment, and cheap credit.

Prior to the 1960s, when development accelerated, the country had good research institutes and universities to supply information, scientists and extension workers. New institutes were built in the cerrado region. Some of the research was done in collaboration with American and European scientists. An important factor was that the Brazilian commercial economy had been established for many years, and entrepreneurs invested in the development.

8.7 PLANTATION CROPS: OIL PALM IN MALAYSIA

Oil palm is an example of a crop that is often grown in a plantation operated by a commercial company, and yields products that bring in overseas currency. In these respects it resembles rubber, cacao, coffee, tea, coconut and others that are also monocropped.

The growth of the oil-palm industry in Malaysia is relatively recent, most of the plantations having been established since 1970. Rubber, grown on estates and in smallholdings, had been the main commercial tree crop from early in the twentieth century, but declined in importance in the 1970s and 1980s because of the low world price for natural rubber and a shortage of tappers. The area of oil palm increased as the demand for palm oil increased. Between 1980 and 1991 the area increased from 1.02 Mha to 2.09 Mha; Malaysia accounted for over half the world production of edible palm oil.

The oil-palm plantations are on land that had been under rain forest or rubber trees. Annual rainfall ranges from about 1800 mm to over 3600 mm, with no prolonged dry periods and a mean annual temperature of about 26–27 °C. The success of oil palm in Malaysia owes much to the earlier infrastructure and experience from rubber plantations: commercial companies had provided financial investment, governments had built roads and railways, and agronomic research and tree selection had been undertaken on private estates and by the Rubber Research Institute. The Palm Oil Research Institute continued the research, appropriate because some of the techniques for establishing oil-palm plantations are the same as for rubber. For example, it is necessary to control soil erosion when the young trees are planted by using a ground cover of legumes or grasses such as *Vetiveria zizanioides*.

One difference from rubber is the large amount of nutrients removed in the harvest of fruit bunches. To maintain nutrient supplies in the soil, common practice is to apply to each tree annually 3 kg ammonium sulphate, 3 kg potassium chloride, 1 kg kieserite and 1 kg rock phosphate. The rates of application are reduced if biomass waste or effluent from the oil mills is applied.

As with other single-tree crops, the plantations of oil palm result in a loss of biodiversity which can have serious consequences for endangered species. In addition, soil erosion has caused siltation of streams and coastal areas that has had adverse effects on fish stocks and coral reefs; further, effluent from oil mills polluted rivers during the early development of the industry. These environmental effects are described by Vincent and Hadi (1993).

Summary

Plantations of oil palm in the humid tropics are sustainable agricultural systems that provide the country with foreign exchange and the workers with income to buy inputs for their farms. Malaysia has been successful in developing the oil-palm industry because of government economic policies, its established research institutes and its early entry to the international market. However, there has been a serious loss of biodiversity, and also loss of soil by erosion during establishment of the trees.

8.8 SEMI-ARID AGRICULTURE: MACHAKOS, KENYA
AND KANO, NIGERIA

Changes to the management of land in the Machakos district of Kenya serve as an example of improvements that can be brought about by the people themselves. The district has low rainfall, soil erosion, soils low in nutrients and a rapidly increasing population (an increase of almost six-fold between the early 1930s and 1990). The conditions are common in East Africa and in other parts of the world. The account that follows is based on that of Tiffen *et al.* (1994).

The seasonal distribution of rainfall is bimodal, with a period of short rains from October to January and a period of long rains from March to June. Management decisions are made difficult by the highly variable rainfall (Figure 8.3) and rain that may fall in heavy, erosive storms. Fourteen droughts that occurred between 1895 and 1987 caused food or fodder crises.

Soil erosion in the Machakos district has a long history, but little terracing of hillslopes was done before the country became independent in 1963. Subsequently more soil conservation measures, particularly terracing, were undertaken. Four important reasons that made this possible were (i) cultivated land had become privately owned, and as it could be bought and sold there was an incentive for its sustainable

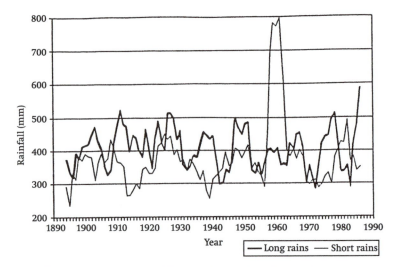

Figure 8.3. Seasonal rainfall at Machakos Town, Kenya, 1894–1988 (five-year running means). Data of T.E. Dowling, reported by Tiffin *et al.* (1994); reproduced with permission of John Wiley & Sons.

use, (ii) the people created informal organizations to undertake terracing, (iii) when extra labour was needed it could be paid for by remittances from family members in the police, army and other non-rural occupations, and (iv) increased water retention on the terraces led to higher yields of food crops and increased the profit from high-value fruit crops and vegetables. On grazing land, crescent-shaped pits were tested to conserve soil and water (Simiyu et al., 1992).

Soil analysis showed that phosphate deficiency was common; also, in field trials there were large responses in yield of maize to applications of fertilizer supplying phosphate and nitrogen. The use of fertilizer has been only slowly adopted, however. Crop nutrients were also supplied in the limited amounts of farmyard (boma) manure and by residual nitrogen from the growth of grain legumes.

An early research success was the breeding of an early maturing maize variety, its seeds being planted with those of the late-maturing local variety to reduce the chance of crop failure due to drought and give large yields in years of adequate rainfall. The effects of crop management and rainfall on the yield of maize have been investigated (Keating et al., 1992; McCown and Keating, 1992).

The package that is now being adopted by farmers to increase their production includes a composite germplasm of maize, soil and water conservation, use of fertilizer and organic manure to supply nitrogen and phosphate when needed, early sowing and higher planting density. More intensive farming has been able to feed more people, and the cultivation of cash crops (coffee, cotton, fruits, vegetables) has produced more income. Local towns and cities have provided markets for the agricultural produce and for products from craft industries based within households or villages, and employment for those with adequate education. The infrastructure has been improved by government and non-government organizations. According to Tiffen et al. (1994), poverty has now been largely overcome.

The conclusion from this study in Kenya that population increase has not led to land degradation is supported by experiences in the vicinity of Kano in northern Nigeria. At Kano itself (population over one million) mean annual rainfall (1906–1985) is 822 mm in a single rainy season of up to five months (May to September). As at Machakos, rainfall is very variable and there are frequent droughts. Mortimore (1993) studied the close-settled agricultural zone extending 65–95 km along the roads from the city. Although the rate of increase in population may have been about 3 per cent per annum (there were no reliable statistics) there was ecological and economic stability between

1964 and 1986, the period of the study. The stability is attributed to the integration of crops and livestock, ensuring a supply of food during droughts and also manure for the crops. Trees provided fuel and supplemented the food supply. As in Machakos district, income was from the sale of vegetables and other crops, from non-farm activities such as weaving and from work in urban centres. The same possibilities exist more generally in Africa (Hyden *et al.*, 1993).

8.9 SUMMARY AND CONCLUSIONS

The examples in this chapter illustrate a few of the many ways by which land use has been changed. Most of the changes increased agricultural production, either of food crops for local consumption or of crop products for export. By no means have all changes been successful. Although the groundnut schemes in East and West Africa are perhaps the best-known examples of failure, other large areas of land went out of production in the twentieth century because of soil erosion, waterlogging and salinization, and other forms of degradation (see Chapter 5). In the examples of successful change reported in this chapter, it often took several years before the change could be considered successful (for example the Gezira irrigation scheme in Sudan or the development of agriculture in the Machakos district of Kenya). Development in England followed a particularly long and tortuous path and, as with the other examples, agricultural systems there are continuing to evolve.

As we consider ways to raise agricultural production in developing countries during the twenty-first century, the examples in this chapter are of value in showing the following: (i) development depends on socio-economic conditions, particularly economic growth, and technological improvements; (ii) the system that is developed depends on the local conditions of land, especially climate, landform and soil, and the available economic resources; and (iii) development requires co-operation between farmers and national government and its intermediaries, the farmers having the crucial role. The chapter has not considered the role of trade in food on the world market; this is mentioned on p. 218).

The several factors that are involved in agricultural development are listed in Table 8.2. The economic incentive for the farmer is to obtain profit from his farm, which requires non-farming people with money to buy his products, markets at which to sell them, and roads, railways, etc. to distribute them. The farmer also requires information that allows him to evaluate inputs, and to be aware of government policy on financial support. For production to be sustained by a high standard of management, security of land tenure is necessary.

The Green Revolution package of modern crop varieties, irrigation, fertilizer and pesticide use and improved cultivations has had the greatest impact in countries where general development was making good progress, as in Asia. The principle of using a package of improvements also applies elsewhere, in modified form. In Zimbabwe, for example, the use of fertilizers with maize varieties that were developed for low- and higher-rainfall regimes was a successful package. In low-rainfall areas, as in the Machakos district of Kenya, conservation of water and soil are part of the package. The possibilities for technological applications are wide-ranging but need research, field experimentation, extension work and on-site trials to show benefits to the farmer.

Some of the examples in this chapter have been of development of new land, while others have been of more intensive use of land. The implications of future changes in land use, which may follow either course, are considered in the next two chapters.

9

Increasing and sustaining agricultural production

9.1 INTRODUCTION

The previous chapter described several routes that agricultural development can take, depending on the biological, physical and economic conditions. In this chapter the requirements for more agricultural land and for higher yields will be considered in relation to the greater population of the twenty-first century, particularly in two groups of developing countries.

Between 1995 and 2050 the world population (on the medium variant; see Figure 1.1) will increase by 3.2 billion (57 per cent), all of which will be in less developed countries, where it represents an increase of 72 per cent (United Nations, 1999). Production of food will need to increase likewise to maintain the present nutritional standards. A greater rate of increase will be needed if the diets of many people in developing countries are to be improved (in terms of both calories and nutritional worth) and allowance is made for the increasing consumption of animal products.

According to FAO data, between 1961 and 1995 production per person rose by 18 per cent as an average for the world population. An increase occurred in all regions except sub-Saharan Africa, where it remained almost unchanged. However, projections for the future by FAO are for the rate of increase in production to become less. A country's food requirements in the future can be met, as in the past, by growing crops on more land, by raising annual yields or by importing food, or by a combination of these methods. The technological requirements for the first two of these possibilities in developing countries are the main themes discussed here. Also discussed are the requirements for sustainable production, and the environmental effects of increasing agricultural production. Importing food, and the trade on which this

Table 9.1. *Populations (10^9) in the world and in developing countries and projections to 2025 and 2050*

	1970	1990	1995	Low variant		Medium variant		High variant	
				2025	2050	2025	2050	2025	2050
World	3.70	5.27	5.67	7.28	7.34	7.82	8.91	8.38	10.67
Developing countries (1)[a]	2.69	4.12	4.50	6.12	6.35	6.61	7.75	7.09	9.31
Developing countries (2)[b]	1.30	2.11	2.35	3.51	3.88	3.80	4.74	4.10	5.73

Source: United Nations (1999).

[a] Africa, South and Central America, Asia (excluding Japan), Melanesia, Micronesia, Polynesia.

[b] As for developing countries (1) but omitting China and India.

largely depends, will not be discussed. First to be considered is the increase in population.

9.2   INCREASE IN POPULATION

In 1950 the world population was 2.5 billion, and by 1999 it had reached six billion. During this century it will continue to increase, but it is uncertain by how much. Uncertainties are the rate of change of fertility (number of children per woman), average life span and the effect of pandemics. In the world as a whole fertility decreased from about five in the 1950s to about three by 1995 (Fischer and Heilig, 1997). The projection is for it to decrease further, to about 1.6, 2.1 or 2.6, giving low, medium and high variants (estimates) of the world population of 7.34 billion, 8.91 billion, and 10.67 billion, respectively, by 2050 (Table 9.1). Almost the whole of the increase will be in developing countries, with the biggest increases in Africa, China and India (which are discussed individually in Chapter 10).

The large differences between the three variants of the projected population give considerable uncertainty in estimating future food requirements. It also has to be recognized that the basis for the projections is the summation of the populations given by the censuses of individual countries, not all of which are accurate. However, revisions are continually being made by the UN Population Division; the latest revision (that used for Table 9.1) was in 1999, and gives lower projections

Table 9.2. *Production, area and yield of all cereals and their average rate of change*

	World	Developing countries (1)[a]	Developing countries (2)[b]
Average 1997–1999			
Production (10^6 t)	2081	1223	542
Area (10^6 ha)	693	465	271
Yield (t ha^{-1})	3.01	2.64	2.05
Average annual change 1970–1999			
Production (10^6 t)	+29 (1.7%)[c]	+22 (2.5%)	+9 (2.3%)
Area (10^6 ha)	+0.1 (0%)	+1.3 (0.3%)	+2.0 (0.8%)
Yield (kg ha^{-1})	+45 (0.6%)	+43 (1.7%)	+24 (1.4%)

Source: FAO Production Yearbooks.
[a] Africa, South and Central America, Asia (excluding Japan).
[b] As for developing countries (1) but omitting China and India.
[c] The numbers in parentheses are the change expressed as a percentage of the period mean.

than earlier versions. Thus projections of future food requirements are likely to be revised as population projections are revised. For the present purposes the latest (1999) projected populations by the medium variant (Table 9.1) will be used.

9.3 FOOD REQUIREMENTS OF THE LARGER POPULATION

The objective of this section is to estimate the food requirements of the population of developing countries in order to provide the basis from which to estimate the future requirements for more cultivated land or larger annual yields. The requirements will be considered for developing countries (1), which include all those in Africa, South and Central America and Asia except for Japan, and developing countries (2), which is the same list but excludes China and India. Developing countries (1) are similar to, but not identical with, those listed by FAO (Alexandratos, 1995). Discussion is restricted to the production of cereals, the main staple of the world; root crops are referred to in Chapter 10. The production of all cereals and the average rates of annual increase since 1970 are listed in Table 9.2. The average rates in this and other tables were calculated by linear regression.

As populations increase during the next few decades more food will need to be produced, particularly in developing countries. Further, the intake of calories is low in several of these countries, and should ideally be increased. In addition there is a trend towards using more cereals as animal feed to produce more animal products for human consumption. The estimates to be reported here are based on the projected increase in population (Table 9.1) and the possible changes of diet in developing countries, with and without China and India. They are intended to show the magnitude of the effects of population increase and change of diet. They take no account of the import of cereals which, on present trends, can be expected to increase.

The future rates of increase in calorie consumption in developing countries and in the consumption of animal products (requiring cereals for animal feed) are both uncertain. The present average intake of calories in developing countries is three-quarters of that in developed countries, but this conceals the very low intake in some countries. For example, in 10 of the 39 countries in sub-Saharan Africa listed by Alexandratos (1995) the intake, was less than 2000 kilocalories per day. Although there is no single value for the required calorie intake, because of its dependence on the physical work being done and on other conditions (Waterlow, 1998), it is estimated by FAO that 800 million people suffer chronic undernourishment that can be attributed to poverty. The assumption will be made here that average calorie consumption in developing countries will increase by 10 per cent by 2025 and by 20 per cent by 2050.

Data from FAO show that the annual use of cereals as animal feed in developing countries increased from 56 Mt in 1969/71 to 160 Mt in 1989/91, representing an increase from 11 per cent to 17 per cent of total cereal consumption. It is predicted to increase by a further 5 per cent, to reach 22 per cent by 2010 (Alexandratos, 1995). A reasonable estimate is that it will increase by 10 per cent between 2000 and 2025 and by 20 per cent by 2050.

A rough estimate will now be made of the cereal production required in developing countries (1) by 2025, assuming self-sufficiency. The population increase will be 35 per cent (from 4.9 billion estimated in 2000), to 6.6 billion on the medium variant. Cereal production in 2000 was estimated to be 1267 Mt. For a 35 per cent rise in population the required increase in production by 2025 will be 439 Mt (Table 9.3), an average increase of 18 Mt per year. If the calorie consumption increases by 10 per cent and feed for animals by a further 10 per cent, the increased population would require an increase in cereal production of 778 Mt, an average increase of 31 Mt per year. Also shown in Table 9.3 are the estimates for 2050, which are less certain.

Table 9.3. *Estimated increase (from 2000)^a in production of cereals in developing countries required by 2025 and 2050*

Year	Developing countries (1)^b Required increase (10^6 t)	(%)	Developing countries (2)^c Required increase (10^6 t)	(%)
2025				
For increase in population^d	439	35^e	246	**45**
For 10% calorie increase + 10% feed increase	339	27	159	29
Total increase	778	**62**	405	**74**
2050				
For increase in population	728	**58**	449	**82**
For 20% calorie increase + 20% feed increase	791	63	399	73
Total increase	1519	**121**	848	**155**

^{a} The estimated production of cereals in 2000 was 1267×10^6 t in developing countries (1) and 560×10^6 t in developing countries (2) (based on FAO Production Yearbooks and the average annual increases listed in Table 9.2).
^{b} Africa, South and Central America, Asia (excluding Japan).
^{c} As for developing countries (1) but omitting China and India.
^{d} Population increase is for the medium variant (see Table 9.1); the estimated populations for developing countries (1) and (2) in 2000 were 4.90×10^9 and 2.62×10^9, respectively.
^{e} Numbers in bold are referred to in Tables 9.5, 9.7 and 9.8.

In developing countries (2) the percentage increase in cereal production that will be needed is greater, required production more than doubling by 2050. This is largely because of the projected rapid rise in the population.

The estimated requirements for cereal production in 2025 and 2050 in Table 9.3 are a rough guide only. They will need to be modified as trends of population growth and the dietary changes referred to above become better known. What is certain is that for self-sufficiency in developing countries a substantial increase in food production will be required year by year for at least the next 50 years, by cultivating more land, raising yields, or both.

Table 9.4. *Area of cereal cultivation required in developing countries by 2025 and 2050 to meet the required production (Table 9.3) with no increase in yield*[a]

		Developing countries (1)[b]			Developing countries (2)[c]	
Year		Required area (10^6 ha)	New area (10^6 ha)		Required area (10^6 ha)	New area (10^6 ha)
2025	+35%	630	163	+45%	399	124
	+62%	757	290	+74%	479	204
2050	+58%	738	271	82%	501	226
	+121%	1032	565	155%	701	426

[a] The required areas are the areas in 2000 (estimated) plus the required percentage increases (Table 9.3). The areas in 2000 were 467×10^6 ha in developing countries (1) and 275×10^6 ha in developing countries (2) (from FAO Production Yearbooks and the average annual increases in Table 9.2).

[b] Africa, South and Central America, Asia (excluding Japan).

[c] As for developing countries (1) but omitting China and India.

9.4   RAISING ARABLE PRODUCTION: USE OF MORE LAND

The two issues to be considered are (i) the area of land that would be needed if the required increase in cereal production (Table 9.3) were to be achieved solely by an expansion of the area of cultivated land (an extreme condition), and (ii) the area that is suitable for cultivation. The total area required is much greater (about double) when all crops and grazing are included.

The total area of land required for cereals in developing countries (1) by 2025 for population increase alone (35 per cent) is 630 Mha, an increase of 163 Mha from the area of 467 Mha in 2000 (Table 9.4). By 2050 the additional land required is 271 Mha, for a population growth of 58 per cent. The increases are larger when allowance is made for the expected changes of diet shown in Table 9.3. In developing countries (2) the requirement is for a smaller increase in land area of 124 Mha by 2025 and 226 Mha by 2050 (from 275 Mha in 2000) and again for a larger increase when the expected changes of diet are taken into account.

Land suitable for agricultural expansion

Estimates of land area that could be used for agricultural expansion have been made by FAO (Alexandratos, 1995), Buringh and Dudal (1987) and Fischer and Heilig (1997). The FAO estimate is based on the concept

Table 9.5. *Estimate of land area in developing countries (excluding China) with potential for crop production*

	Land with potential for crop production (Mha)					
	Land use in 1990				Land use in 2010	
			Land not in use[a]			% increase
	Total	Land in use	A	B		1999–2010
Sub-Saharan Africa	1009	212	797	505	255	20
Near East/ North Africa	92	77	15	(14)	80	5
East Asia (excluding China)	184	88	96	44	103	17
South Asia	228	190	38	9	195	2
Latin America/ Caribbean	1059	189	870	220	217	14
Developing countries	2573	757	1816	791	850	12

Source: Alexandratos (1995).

[a] Column A is total land area; column B excludes land under habitation, forest and protected areas. Data for Near East and North Africa are incomplete.

of agroecological zones, the land area being divided into a large number of distinct agroecological cells with relatively uniform soil, landform and climate. The required data are obtained from the *Soil Map of the World* (FAO–UNESCO, 1971–1981) and measurements of temperature, rainfall, relative humidity, wind speed and solar radiation. They are used to calculate the thermal regime and the number of days of sufficient moisture for plant growth (length of growing season). Each cell is classified as suitable for rainfed crop production if at least one of 21 possible crops would give a yield of 20 per cent or more of that on land with the same climate characteristics but with no slope or soil constraints. (For further details see FAO–UNESCO, 1978–1981 and Alexandratos, 1995.)

An estimate of the land area with potential for agricultural production and not in use in 1990 is given in Table 9.5. The total for developing countries (excluding China) is 791 Mha. The estimate of Fischer and Heilig (1997) is that 550 Mha could be used if wetland and forest ecosystems are conserved.

As indicated above, in developing countries (1) the extra land required for cereals by 2025 is 163 Mha for the increased population alone and 290 Mha when allowance is made for dietary change (Table 9.4). As cereals occupy about 50 per cent of the total arable area ('arable' as defined by FAO), the additional arable areas that would be required are twice those listed in Table 9.4. When allowance is made for dietary change they exceed the estimate by Fischer and Heilig of available land area by 2025 and that of FAO by 2050.

Also to be taken into account is the distribution of the available land area. The geographical distribution of the additional available land is uneven. As shown in Table 9.5, more than 90 per cent is in sub-Saharan Africa and in Latin America (that includes the Caribbean in the FAO data). The estimate of Fischer and Heilig (1997) is that, excluding forest and wetlands, the additional land required by 2050 exceeds that which could be used in six regions of the world (Central America and the Caribbean, eastern Africa, western Africa, western Asia, southeastern Asia and south-central America). The implications for agricultural development in Africa, India and China are discussed in Chapter 10.

The estimates of areas suitable for cultivation have weaknesses, as recognized by FAO. The agroecological cells are often based on sparse data which may be unreliable. The soils are insufficiently characterized at present, and need to be surveyed in detail. Also, field trials are needed before crop yields are known, and it is likely that with the constraints known to exist they will probably be small. The time required to improve the database makes the warning by Fischer and Heilig (1997) apposite: 'the rapid population growth during the next three decades will leave little time to develop land and water resources along a sustainable path'.

Land surveys

Usually, but unfortunately not always, expansion of land use is preceded by a planning stage during which a survey is made of the natural resources of the land. Information may be gathered by satellite and aerial photography, with in addition 'walking the ground' as an essential part. Patterns of landforms and types of vegetation cover can be identified, from which generalizations can be made.

The information that is needed depends on the intended use of the land. For rainfed arable farming it will include temperature, rainfall characteristics and seasonal water balance to indicate the length of the growing season, angle of slope and its length as an indication of the need for erosion control measures, and such soil properties as depth, pH, nutrient supplies, organic matter content and buffer properties. For irrigation, information is needed on water supplies, land levels, water infiltration and drainage rates, and soil salinity and sodicity. The data that are collected in the field and in the laboratory will usually be more comprehensive than mentioned here.

Surveys for intended development should also include socio-economic information, for example on rural populations, future requirements of food for rural and non-rural populations, markets, roads, schools and hospitals. Crops and their management should also be included. The information that surveys might provide and possible recommendations from them have been set out in several FAO publications (Alexandratos, 1995) and by Landon (1991), Webster (1997) and Young (1998).

Summary

Unused land can be brought into cultivation, but for developing countries as a whole there is not enough to provide the increased agricultural production that will be required by 2050. Most of the land which might be used is in less densely populated and wetter regions of sub-Saharan Africa and South and Central America, and a little elsewhere. Where expansion on the new land is likely to occur, land surveys, land planning and pilot experiments should precede the development. Little is known yet about the yield potential of unused land or whether production can be sustained. Effects on natural ecosystems are discussed in Section 11.3.

9.5   RAISING ARABLE PRODUCTION: INCREASING YIELDS

In this section we consider increased yields per harvest and increased harvests per year as the two means of raising production while using the same area of land.

Between 1960 and 1990 global annual yields of the two major cereals rice and wheat approximately doubled (Evans, 1997). During this period new crop varieties were introduced, cheap nitrogen fertilizers became available, the irrigated area increased and pesticides were more widely used. The new varieties of rice and wheat were short-stemmed; they did not lodge (become flattened) as readily as longer-stemmed varieties at higher rates of application of fertilizer nitrogen, they had a

Table 9.6. *Average yield of cereals required in developing countries by 2025 and 2050 to meet the required production (Table 9.3) with no increase in area*[a]

| Year | | Developing countries (1)[b] | | Developing countries (2)[c] |
		Required yield ($t\,ha^{-1}\,a^{-1}$)		Required yield ($t\,ha^{-1}\,a^{-1}$)
2025	+35%	3.6	+45%	2.9
	+62%	4.4	+74%	3.5
2050	+58%	4.3	+82%	3.6
	+121%	6.0	+155%	5.1

[a] The required yields are the yields in 2000 (estimated) plus the required percentage increases. The yields in 2000 were $2.64\,t\,ha^{-1}$ in developing countries (1) and $2.05\,t\,ha^{-1}$ in developing countries (2) (from Table 9.2).
[b] Africa, South and Central America, Asia (excluding Japan).
[c] As for developing countries (1) but omitting China and India.

higher harvest index (more grain as a proportion of total biomass) and responded more to application of fertilizer nitrogen. Early maturing varieties made possible multiple cropping (two or three harvests per year) and also successful cropping in regions with a short rainy season.

On the assumptions that there is no increase in area of cereals (an extreme condition) and that the required increase in production is as shown in Table 9.3, the required yields are as given in Table 9.6. In practice it is expected that production will be raised by increases in both yield and cultivated area (see Section 9.6).

New crop varieties

The new dwarf varieties of rice and wheat give large yields when water is not limiting and the crop receives appropriate applications of nitrogen fertilizer. Yields of maize in the USA have increased largely because of closer planting, in-built resistance to pests and diseases, and use of larger applications of nitrogen fertilizers. Varieties of crops have been bred for different climates and, as with maize, for resistance to pests and disease (see Greenland, 1997, for success with rice in this area).

Potential crop yields in the future cannot be predicted with any certainty. According to Evans (1997), 'Further increase in the harvest index will be limited and, so far, the maximum rates of photosynthesis and crop growth have not been improved genetically.' He adds that yield potential may be increased by routes as yet unforeseen. Accounts of crop improvement have been published by Callaway and Francis (1993) and Hayward *et al.* (1993).

Transgenic crops

Foreign genes have been transferred to crop plants since the 1980s, when antibiotic resistance from bacteria was transferred to tobacco plants. There have since been many other developments, some of which, for example herbicide resistance in soya in the USA, have met with commercial success. The new transgenic crops, known more commonly as genetically modified or GM crops, became widely grown in the late 1990s, especially in the USA. In 1998 transgenic crops were grown on nearly 29 Mha worldwide (excluding China), and in the USA 40 per cent of all cotton, 35 per cent of soybeans and 25 per cent of maize grown were GM varieties (Conway and Toenniessen, 1999).

GM foods have been criticized in several developed countries as being unsafe, although there is no evidence that any of the millions of people who have consumed GM foods have suffered any form of ill health as a result of them. There is also the possibility of transfer of the introduced genes to other species, producing weeds or insects resistant to chemical pesticides. These same arguments are also being used in developing countries. (For discussion of ecological risks see Rissler and Mellon, 1996.)

Whatever the outcome of the debate, there is no doubt that genetically engineered crops have the potential to raise the yield and quality of food crops in the developing world. One example of quality improvement is the introduction of genes to produce β-carotene in rice grain (golden rice) and hence prevent blindness caused by shortage of vitamin A in the diet. This transgenic rice is now being adapted to local growing conditions by conventional breeding, and will then be distributed licence-free to subsistence farmers (news item in *Nature*, 2001, **409**, 551). Possibilities for the future that are currently being tested include tolerance of drought, soil acidity and salinity in cereals, biological nitrogen fixation by rice, and resistance to insect and other pests in the crops grown in developing countries. These and other possibilities referred to by Conway and Toenniessen (1999) demonstrate the huge potential of GM crops to relieve hunger in the world, if they can be shown to be safe. The potential of transgenic crops and their place in agriculture during the twenty-first century has been widely discussed (Conway, 1999; Macilwain, 1999; Trewavas, 1999).

Cropping intensity

If all the arable land in a region is used to grow an average of two successive crops per year, the cropping intensity is 200 and for one crop per year it is 100. The cropping intensity is less than 100 where part of the land is under bare fallow, and over 100 if some of the land grows two or more crops per year and the rest grows one crop. The term is not applied to the system common in parts of semi-arid Africa in which early-maturing and late-maturing crops are interplanted during the growing season to gain an early harvest and also extend the season.

Double-cropping has become more common with the introduction of early maturing crop varieties. This is particularly so with irrigated, transplanted rice, which has a cropping intensity approaching 200 in much of China and in areas such as the Punjab (Evans, 1998). Regional values of cropping intensities calculated by FAO are appreciably larger for irrigated than for rainfed crops (Alexandratos, 1995), which implies that further increases in cropping intensity may be limited by the supply of water for irrigation. Early maturing crops will increase the cropping intensity in humid regions with a double rainfall peak when the 'small' rains are only marginally sufficient for a crop. The projection by FAO is that increase in cropping intensity will account for only 7 per cent of the increase in production in East Asia between 1988/90 and 2010 but 20 per cent in Northeast/North Africa.

Fertilizer use

As discussed in Chapter 6, fertilizers have been an essential component of the package of techniques that have raised crop yields during the twentieth century, and particularly since the 1960s. Further, their use in most farming systems is essential to prevent nutrient depletion during a period of cropping. The amounts that are required can be minimized by using fertilizers efficiently, by recycling nutrients in farming systems such as those that include animal production, and by including legumes in a rotation. Nevertheless, fertilizers remain as essential sources of nutrients for the increased yields required in the twenty-first century.

The amount of fertilizer that will be required is difficult to estimate, firstly because the trend of increase in use has not been constant. World consumption of fertilizers (N + P + K) increased almost linearly from 1970 to 1988/89. The use of all three nutrients increased during this period, then decreased between 1990/91 and 1994/95 before increasing again (Figure 6.1). These trends were partly a reflection of economic policies in developed countries, but they were also followed in developing countries, where world prices of cereals often made it cheaper to import cereals than to produce them at home.

A second difficulty is that in developing countries, where the need for fertilizers is greatest, the amounts of fertilizer required to rectify initial deficiencies (especially of phosphate), as distinct from the later, and smaller, maintenance applications, are not known. A similar uncertainty applies to potassium and sulphur. The experience of countries with a long history of fertilizer use, for example the UK, is that the annual use of phosphate and potassium levels off after time, the use of increasing amounts of nitrogen fertilizer continuing longer. A similar trend may apply to developing countries.

A third uncertainty is that, where fertilizers have to be imported, (for example in developing countries), their cost varies with the exchange rate of the local currency. The variable cost may work its way through to the farmer, who has to judge whether the use of fertilizer is economic.

In many developing countries, and particularly in sub-Saharan Africa, the rate of application of fertilizers is very low (Table 6.1). This is partly because of the limitation of yield by low (and uncertain) rainfall, although experiments in East and West Africa and in Syria have shown positive responses to fertilizer phosphate with a seasonal rainfall as low as 200 mm (Figure 6.3). Other reasons for low fertilizer use are farmers' lack of information on their benefits, unreliable supplies when needed, and, perhaps most important of all, the high cost relative to the expected profit from the harvested grain.

The alternatives of adding nitrogen by biological fixation and of recycling nutrients in animal dung, biomass transfer, composts or plant ash will reduce fertilizer requirements, but will not alone be sufficient in most farming systems. The importance of fertilizers in agricultural production is recognized by most national governments, through direct or indirect subsidies; some instead provide a guaranteed minimum price for particular agricultural products.

Irrigation

The area of irrigated crops increased by about 1 per cent per year during the 1980s and 1990s, a smaller rate of increase than in the previous two decades (see Chapter 7). The projection by FAO is for this current rate of increase to continue to 2010.

This projected increase in irrigated area is based on expansion plans by individual countries; the actual rate of expansion is, however, uncertain, because of cost and the competing claims for water between countries, and within countries for domestic and industrial uses. Large storage dams are expensive and involve the displacement of rural communities. Pumping of ground water has been limited at several locations by insufficient replenishment. These and other issues that affect the expansion of the irrigated area are discussed in Chapter 7.

A major contribution to cereal production would be made by increasing the efficiency of irrigation (see Chapter 7). Seepage losses from canals should be reduced and water should be provided more equitably to farmers' plots, in the right amounts and at the optimal time. Use of trickle irrigation, the most efficient method of irrigation, should be expanded, where appropriate. More use could be made of runoff and waste water and, under good management, of saline water. Irrigated soils that have become waterlogged, saline or sodic should be reclaimed. To achieve these improvements co-operation is required between farmers, hydrologists, soil scientists, agronomists and engineers, a co-operation that is often lacking.

Storage of water in excavated ponds, by individual farmers or small communities, is common in Asia where a surplus in the rainy season is followed by a long, dry season. The use of such ponds in India and possibilities for development are discussed in Chapter 10. Similar small-scale irrigation schemes could be further developed in sub-Saharan Africa using earth dams to store water for domestic use and irrigation during the dry season. There is sufficient rainfall in the Guinea belt of West Africa (around 1000 mm annually) for this purpose.

Water conservation

The various techniques used to conserve water in dryland areas are described in Chapter 7. Where rainfall is marginal or unreliable or where there are dry periods within the wet season, successful cropping depends on the experience of farmers and advice derived from long-term weather records. Water conservation is important, as is the selection of crops, crop varieties and cropping system. Intercropping is often used to provide an early harvest from a short-season crop such as millet, which may be interplanted with groundnuts, cowpea or maize to provide later harvests if the rainfall is sufficient. Another strategy of farmers in seasonally arid areas is to store grain from bumper harvests to eke out grain supplies when yields are small.

Improvements have resulted from the introduction of short-season varieties of crops, such as maize that can be harvested about 100 days after planting, and further developments on these lines might be possible.

9.6 THE BALANCE BETWEEN USE OF MORE LAND AND INCREASED YIELDS

The previous two sections have dealt with the use of more land and increased yields as alternatives for increased food production, with reference particularly to developing countries. The purpose was to highlight the implications of each. Considered here is the relative contribution that each might be expected to make towards feeding the increased population during the next 50 years. The calculation assumes a continuation of the annual rates of increase in yield and area of cereals for the period 1970–1999 listed in Table 9.2. The required increase in production (Table 9.3) is then calculated by iteration, keeping constant the ratio of increase in yield to increase in area.

The requirements for yield and area are listed in Table 9.7. It should be noted that these are not intended for use in land planning, firstly because they do not apply to individual countries, and secondly because radical technological changes might occur (genetic engineering of crops is one example) which would invalidate them. The purpose is to show what land and yield will be needed if past trends continue into this century.

Comparison between Tables 9.4 and 9.7 shows the substantial reduction in additional land area required for cereal production when yields are raised. For example, developing countries (1) require 630 Mha of land by 2025 to meet their cereal requirements if yields are not increased (Table 9.4) whereas they require only 502 Mha if yields continue to increase at the present rate. The reduction is even greater by 2050. More land will continue to be taken into cultivation, but larger yields will reduce this need for additional arable land and so help to conserve natural ecosystems.

FAO predictions

According to Alexandratos (1995), the FAO predictions of increased arable area and increased yield in developing countries are based

Table 9.7. *Contribution of increased yield and increased area to the production of cereals estimated to be required by 2025 and 2050 (Table 9.3) in developing countries; the estimates are by extrapolation using the average rates of change (1970–1999) given in Table 9.2*

Year	Requirements in developing countries (1)[a]			Requirements in developing countries (2)[b]		
	Production $(10^6$ t)	Area $(10^6$ ha)	Yield $(\text{t ha}^{-1}\,\text{a}^{-1})$	Production $(10^6$ t)	Area $(10^6$ ha)	Yield $(\text{t ha}^{-1}\,\text{a}^{-1})$
2000	1267	467	2.7	560	275	2.1
2025	1706 (+35%)[c]	502	3.4	806 (+45%)	320	2.5
	2045 (+62%)	500	4.1	965 (+74%)	345	2.8
2050	1995 (+58%)	498	4.0	1009 (+82%)	350	2.9
	2786 (+121%)	542	5.1	1408 (+155%)	415	3.4

[a] Africa, South and Central America, Asia (excluding Japan).
[b] As for developing countries (1) but omitting China and India.
[c] The percentages in parentheses refer to the increases in the production above those in 2000 (see Table 9.3).

not on historical trends but on available land, the requirement for more production, and expected developments in individual countries. Predictions of the relative importance of yield per harvest, cropping intensity and arable area during the period 1988/90 to 2010 are given in Table 9.8. The greatest dependence on area is in sub-Saharan Africa, East Asia (which excludes China in Table 9.8) and Latin America including the Caribbean, that is, in regions where there is most unused land (Table 9.5). Increase in yield per harvest is greatest in South Asia and Near East/North Africa. For all regions increased yield per year makes a bigger contribution than increase in area. Yield is predicted to account for 66 per cent of the increased production (all arable crops).

These estimates of FAO and those by extrapolation, described above (Table 9.7), do not identify the requirements of individual countries, and differences between countries are large. Rwanda, for example, has an estimated 3.1 per cent annual increase in population between 2000 and 2010, less than 0.1 ha of cultivated land per person, and no unused land that is suitable for cultivation. By contrast, the neighbouring Democratic Republic of Congo has the largest area of unused land in sub-Saharan Africa that could be put into agricultural production.

Table 9.8. *Estimated contribution of yield, area of arable land and multiple cropping to increased crop production in developing countries (excluding China)*

	Contribution to increased crop production 1988/90 to 2010 (%)		
	Yield/harvest	Arable land area	Cropping intensity[a]
Developing countries	66	21	13
Sub-Saharan Africa	53	30	17
Near East/North Africa	71	9	20
East Asia (excluding China)	61	32	7
South Asia	82	4	14
Latin America/Caribbean	53	28	19

Source: After Alexandratos (1995); reproduced with permission of John Wiley & Sons.

[a] Cropping intensity is the ratio of harvested land area to total arable area.

9.7 SUSTAINING AGRICULTURAL PRODUCTION

The need to sustain as well as to raise agricultural production follows from the prediction that the world population will, on the medium variant (see Figure 1.1), continue to increase until at least 2050. Agriculture exploits the natural resources of land by removing nutrients in crop harvests and, to a lesser extent, in animal products. In addition, mismanagement of the land can result in serious degradation, such as erosion, acidification and salinization (see Chapter 5). The depletion of soil nutrients is inevitable under most systems of cultivation, although the rate can be reduced by nutrient recycling. Greenland (1997) has identified four systems that help to sustain yields:

(1) animal-based mixed farming, in which animals graze grasslands and concentrate nutrients in manure that can be used on cropped land;

(2) tree-based systems, in which trees gather nutrients from subsoils and the atmosphere and concentrate them at the soil surface where they can be used by crops;

(3) water-based production, where nutrients are supplied by river sediments, by the water itself and by biological nitrogen fixation;

(4)   fertilizer-based systems, which replace the nutrients removed in crops and increase the supply of nutrients, needed for higher yields.

A common form of the first of these is known as ley farming. This is used in temperate regions, and provides nutrients for crops when the grassland is ploughed. For economic reasons it is now in less common use. The water-based system for rice is discussed in Section 7.5 and fertilizer use is discussed in Chapter 6. A tree-based system of the humid and subhumid tropics is slash–burn, described by Nye and Greenland (1960) and Sanchez et al. (1997). It is sustainable only if the ratio of years of bush fallow to years of cultivation is greater than about 10:1.

Agroforestry

In recent years interest has been directed at the partnership between trees, crops and pastures known as agroforestry. Agroforestry has several forms. It has been described by Lundgren (1982) as a collective name for land-use systems in which woody perennials (trees, shrubs, etc.) are grown in association with herbaceous plants (crops, pastures) or livestock in a spatial arrangement, or rotation, or both, usually with both ecological and economic interactions between the trees and other components of the system.

Two of the most beneficial effects of agroforestry are that it can protect the soil from erosion and control floods by reducing the rate of flow of rain water to streams and rivers. These two related effects are a function of both the tree canopy and the tree litter.

Trees capture nutrients from the atmosphere (Johnson and Lindberg, 1992) and the subsoil, and several genera can also add nitrogen to the ecosystem by biological fixation. The nutrients that are captured are used for growth and are either retained in the tissues of the trees or deposited on the soil surface in litter, especially leaf fall, and in throughfall (rain-wash from leaves).

Although trees have long been partners of crops and pastures, the association was little investigated until the 1970s. Accounts of the more recent work in this area have been given by Nair (1993), Cooper et al. (1996), Sanchez et al. (1997) and Young (1997). One application of agroforestry is to supply biomass for increasing the yield from field crops. For example, in a field experiment on an acid soil in Kenya (Sanchez et al., 1997), a comparison was made between the effect of addition of urea and of Tithonia diversifolia biomass on the yield of maize. Each was added at the same rate of N (60 kg ha^{-1}) and with additional phosphate. Yields of maize were significantly higher from incorporation of *Tithonia* than from addition of urea.

Planting of hedgerows with *Leucaena* and *Gliricidia* at the International Institute of Tropical Agriculture, southern Nigeria, improved the physical condition of an Alfisol, as shown by the higher infiltration rate of water compared with a no-till treatment (Lal, 1989a,b), and can therefore be advocated as a means of controlling water erosion. In addition, the prunings of *Leucaena* provide nutrients for the crop grown between the hedgerows. This system is known as alley cropping. The hedgerows also shade the cultivated area, reducing water loss; on grasslands they provide shade for grazing animals.

Trees are planted for a variety of economic purposes: to provide fuel wood, fodder, fruits and nuts, and to provide wood for the manufacture of furniture. On-going research is investigating how best they will fit into farming systems, especially in the tropics. Whereas much is understood about the supply of nutrients from soil to major crops, much less is known about the supply to native species, including trees.

Long-term experiments

There is no minimum period for a field experiment to deserve the description 'long term', but it will usually be 10 years or more, depending on its purpose (Laryea *et al.*, 1995). During this period the experimental treatments may be changed or supplemented, with the aim of finding a management system that can be sustained.

Sustainable systems have been developed in Europe and elsewhere by trial and error over a long period. In developing countries, where the demand for agricultural production is rising rapidly and farming systems are changing, long-term experiments are required if higher production is to be sustained. Reviews of existing experiments, including those in developing countries, may be found in Leigh and Johnston (1994), Lal and Stewart (1995), Pieri (1995), Paul *et al.* (1996) and Buresh *et al.* (1997).

The treatments to be tested in long-term experiments differ according to soil properties, climate and economic conditions. They may have been identified from surveys, from short-term experiments or from concern about some form of innovation. For example, in francophone West Africa acidification and decline in content of soil organic matter were found to limit the sustainability of the prevailing farming systems (Pieri, 1992). In southern Nigeria, sustainable farming of Alfisols

and Ultisols has been found to depend more on the physical properties and processes of the soils than on the chemical ones, because of
the relationship between water infiltration rate and erosion (Lal, 1995).
Experiments that include rotation of crops or a bush fallow are necessarily long term.

Although the design of the experiment may aim to establish a
sustainable farming system, it may also shed light on some other problems. An early example, from Rothamsted during the nineteeth century,
was the large loss of nitrate by leaching from application of nitrogen
fertilizers in the autumn. Much later it was demonstrated that uranium
accumulates in soils receiving phosphate fertilizers, and organic pollutants accumulate by atmospheric deposition. The experiments have also
been given wider significance by the use of data obtained from them
to develop models of the dynamics of soil carbon and nitrogen (for
these examples see Leigh and Johnston, 1994). The Rothamsted long-
term experiments are of particular value because of the high standard
of management and the retention of soil and crop samples in sealed
containers from the early days of the experiments. These archived samples have been used to demonstrate the changes that have occurred in
the soils as a result of the various treatments and through atmospheric
deposition. These examples show that long-term experiments can be of
greater value than might be expected from their original objectives.

Monitoring change

Regular monitoring of soil properties provides early warning of un-
wanted change. The soils of some farmers' fields in Europe and North
America are sampled every few years to test whether soil organic matter,
nutrient levels and an acceptable pH are being maintained (Skinner
and Todd, 1988, give an example from England and Wales). Other
analyses can be made where there is a recognized hazard, such as
salinization. Routine monitoring of changes to soil properties are, un-
derstandably, rare in developing countries, yet thousands of rainfall,
temperature and other meteorological measurements are made every
year.

Monitoring of the climate and soil properties in both long-term
and short-term field experiments is of particular value in helping to
identify the causes of changes in crop yields. The appropriate frequency
of monitoring has been discussed by Lal and Stewart (1995). In monitoring changes in soil properties over time, depth of sampling must
allow for change in bulk density, which may increase or decrease by

20 per cent or more when soil is disturbed by cultivation and may change even more when a surface organic layer is compacted.

Information required

There is already much information on the causes of land degradation that leads to agricultural production becoming unsustainable. As discussed in Chapter 5, knowledge of these causes can lead to control measures, if suitable techniques are applied. An important aspect is knowledge of the characteristics of individual sites. The essential information can be provided by land surveys that characterize the soils, vegetation and climate. Supplementary information can be provided by soil analyses, short-term experiments and demonstration plots.

Where sufficient information is not available for a particular site, other similar sites may give an indication of whether land degradation is likely to occur. The importance of specific information on individual sites, especially where new land is to be taken into cultivation, cannot be over-emphasized.

In the humid tropics, yields usually fall to low levels within two or three years after a bush fallow unless manure or fertilizer, and often lime, are applied. These and other problems that lead to lack of sustainable yields can be avoided if the requisite information on the properties of the land being cultivated is available and appropriate preventative techniques are applied. Trained staff carrying out land surveys, research and extension work can provide the information needed by planning officers and farmers. Soil management for sustainable agricultural production has been reviewed by Lal and Pierce (1991), National Research Council (1993a), Raglan and Lal (1993), Lal (1994, 1995, 1997) and Syers and Rimmer (1994).

9.8 PROTECTING THE ENVIRONMENT

Discussion will be restricted here to the possible effects on the environment (land, water and the atmosphere) of increasing agricultural production by increasing the area of agricultural land or by raising yields. It is in the developing countries of Africa, Asia and South and Central America where production will be increased most, and where the consequences will need to be closely monitored. Accounts of wider environmental issues are given by Cleary (1989), Binns (1995), Kirkby et al. (1995), Tinker (1997) and GEO-2000 (1999). Land degradation and its control are discussed in Chapter 5.

Effects of using more land

Grasslands and forested land have been converted to managed pastures and arable land for several millennia. During the period 1980 to 1995 the annual loss of tropical forests was estimated as 13–15 Mha (Alexandratos, 1995; GEO-2000, 1999). Most of these losses have occurred in parts of South and Central America, Africa and southeast Asia, often as the frontier has been opened by commercial logging and the construction of roads. The new land is usually acquired at low cost or may even be free. According to an early estimate by the World Bank, quoted by Williams (1981), three-quarters of the settlement is spontaneous and only one-quarter is organized. In regions where arable farming has long been practised, new land brought into cultivation is likely to have been left as less suitable for arable farming. Natural and semi-natural ecosystems will be lost and the land may not sustain agricultural production. It is also probable that the land to be taken over is already in use for extensive grazing or contains trees or other plants that may provide food and other resources for a sparse population.

According to Barbier (1997), the farmers who take over the land are usually too poor to be able to invest in fertilizers or any form of soil protection, crop yields decrease and the farmers move on to new land – if there is any to move to. The expansion is sometimes planned by governments, who give support to the farmers as in Indonesia, and large-scale animal farming may be developed, for example beef production in the Amazon basin (Williams, 1981). Inevitably there is loss of natural ecosystems and biodiversity; probably most serious is the loss of biodiversity in tropical humid forests (Tinker, 1997; Pimm and Raven, 2000).

Effects on the soil

When new land is taken over for farming, small trees, branches of trees, leaves and litter from forests and the grass of savannas are usually burned. Gases, principally carbon dioxide, and partially oxidized particulate carbon compounds are released into the atmosphere. Cultivations, and the higher temperatures of the exposed soil, result in the release of more carbon dioxide. Another effect of the higher temperatures is that organic nitrogen compounds in the soil are oxidized to nitrate more rapidly, and possibly in greater amounts than they are absorbed by crop plants. In freely draining soil the excess passes into drainage water. In humid regions the surface of the exposed soils becomes compacted by rainstorms, leading to erosion on hilly land. In drier regions there may be wind erosion.

Off-site effects

Accelerated soil erosion, which often follows the removal of a vegetative cover, leads to the deposition of sediments in river beds, reservoirs and dams. It also leads to flash floods, which will increase in the future as global warming leads to more intensive rainstorms. Some of the most catastrophic flooding has been caused by the conversion of forested land to farmed land in hilly areas; such flooding has led to serious loss of life and economic loss in several countries, particularly Bangladesh and China.

It is inevitable that land will be taken into cultivation, because there are people who need it to grow crops to feed themselves. Unfortunately most of the conversion lacks any assessment of the farming systems required for sustainable production or of environmental effects. Broadly based land surveys, followed by rational land planning, should be a prerequisite for an extension of farmland. Without these the new farmland will be productive for only a short period, and in the 'at risk' areas environmental damage and catastrophic floods can be expected.

Effects of intensification

As described in Section 9.5, the larger crop yields since the middle of the twentieth century have provided most of the increased production required to feed the extra 3.2 billion people in the world. The process that made this possible can be described as intensification. Our dependence on it will continue during the next half century or so, over which a similar increase in population is expected.

Fertilizers and pesticides are the two components of intensification that have received most public attention. The public concerns are about the effect of fertilizers and pesticides on the quality of food and water, and particularly about any possible dangers to health. There are also the wider issues of their off-site effects on animals and plants, and on the atmosphere. If intensification is to increase, as seems inevitable in developing countries, possible harmful effects need to be recognized and minimized.

Effects of fertilizers

Of the nutrients supplied in fertilizers, nitrogen is the most difficult to control; this applies even more to nitrogen added in organic manures or crop residues and organically held nitrogen in the soil itself. In freely draining soils microorganisms oxidize the nitrogen to nitrate. Because nitrate is not adsorbed by most soils, it remains in solution. If it is not taken up by plant roots it is either washed into the drainage water by excess rain or biologically reduced (denitrified) to dinitrogen gas or nitrous oxide (N_2O).

Nitrate that is washed out of the soil represents an economic loss to the farmer and a possible health hazard if it reaches drinking water. It may also cause algal growth in surface waters. Farmers, water engineers and environmentalists therefore have a shared interest in minimizing the leaching loss of nitrogen.

Leaching of nitrate and its modelling and control have been intensively studied in developed countries e.g. the UK (Goulding, 2000). Measurements at Rothamsted Experimental Station indicated an annual leaching loss of 4–53 kg N ha^{-1} on plots growing wheat and receiving 144 kg ha^{-1} of fertilizer N (optimum application). Losses were greatest in years of high rainfall and increased with the larger applications of nitrogen. Measurements reported by Goulding *et al.* (2000) show the importance of not exceeding the crop requirement for fertilizer nitrogen. One problem in this regard is that even if the requirement is known for an 'average' season a period of drought can reduce yields, and nitrate left in the soil will be leached by winter rainfall. In countries where there is sufficient information on the within-season variation of rainfall, and application of fertilizer nitrogen does not exceed the crop requirement, leaching of nitrate can be minimized. It can never be totally avoided, however, because the system is 'leaky'(Laegreid *et al.*, 1999).

The likely health hazard posed by nitrate in drinking water depends on its concentration. The acceptable upper limit set by the World Health Organization and the European Commission is 11.3 mg $NO_3{}^-$-N l^{-1} (50 mg $NO_3{}^-$ l^{-1}). Apart from in young infants, the health risk from nitrate in drinking water is very small, unless the water is contaminated by faecal microorganisms (as can occur in farm wells).

Fertilizers and manures are also a source of oxides of nitrogen, including nitrous oxide (N_2O). Nitrogen oxides are greenhouse gases, making a contribution to global warming; they also destroy ozone in the stratosphere. They are produced in soils by biological denitrification under anaerobic conditions and by the decomposition of intermediaries during the biological oxidation (nitrification) of ammonium ions to nitrate. Soils and fertilizers are the dominant sources of the nitrous oxide in the atmosphere; fertilizers contribute 14–34 per cent of the total input (Cole *et al.*, 1996; Smith *et al.*, 1997). Organic manures and incorporated crop residues also release nitrous oxide to the atmosphere (Chang *et al.*, 1998; Baggs *et al.*, 2000).

The effect of fertilizers and manures on nitrous oxide release can be minimized through appropriate management practices, particularly by cultivations that prevent soils becoming anaerobic (wetland rice is an obvious exception). It can also be reduced by keeping to a minimum the period that ammonium and nitrate are present in soil, by applying the fertilizer at the time and in the amount required by the crop. These and other measures are described by Cole *et al.* (1996) and Smith *et al.* (1997).

Ammonia, another gas, is released from fertilizers containing ammonium salts or urea, and from manures, when they are applied to soils of pH 7 or higher. It adds to the load of nitrogen in the environment, and when it is absorbed by vegetation or other soils it leads to acidification (Section 6.6). The release of ammonia can be prevented in most soils by incorporating the fertilizer or manure rather than spreading it on the soil surface.

Ammonia from fertilizers and manures can also cause eutrophication (abnormal enrichment) of terrestrial ecosystems. Surface waters can develop algal blooms from nitrate in drainage water and from phosphate in eroded soils and drainage water (see below). Small concentrations of phosphate (about 10^{-6} M) are commonly present in the drainage water from fertilized soils, with higher concentrations from sandy soils. In organic soils and in soils that have received large applications of animal, especially pig, manure, much of the phosphorus is held in organic forms, which is more readily leached than inorganic phosphate. Surface runoff can carry fertilizer phosphate into surface water, and in soils with cracks and wide pores it can be washed into drainage water.

The eutrophication of surface water from nitrate and phosphate, both of which also enter the water from urban and industrial sources, often gives rise to algal blooms. These may kill fish and cause taints in drinking water. The agricultural sources of phosphate can be minimized by controlling erosion and runoff, avoiding excessive use of phosphate fertilizer, and not overloading soils with applications of organic manures (for nitrate see above).

Effects of pesticides

The control of weeds, fungal diseases, and insect and other pests by the application of pesticides is often required to prevent reduction in crop yield and quality. Pest control is an essential component of intensification. It usually involves application of appropriate chemicals, several of which are toxic to animals (including man). They have a wide range of properties, varying in, for example, volatility, degree of adsorption by soil and persistence in soil. The classic example of environmental damage caused by a pesticide was that caused by the widespread use of the insecticide DDT, which is persistent in soil. DDT becomes more concentrated as it passes through the food chain from birds that eat the soil fauna to the predators that feed on the birds. Its use is now prohibited in most developed countries, as is that of the soil partial sterilant methyl bromide, which is volatile and is an agent in the destruction of ozone in the stratosphere.

The environmental and health risks of pesticides have become less than in the early days, largely because of more rigorous testing before new pesticides are released on to the market, lower rates of use and improved methods of application. In addition, pesticide concentrations in drinking water and foods are now routinely monitored to ensure they do not exceed acceptable limits.

Summary

During the twenty-first century agricultural systems will continue to become more intensive. The greater amounts of fertilizer and pesticides that will be used in developing countries will require controls if they are not to create a hazard to human health. The mistakes and improvements already made in more developed countries can serve as guidelines. Biological control of pests may be developed further, and genetic modification may lessen the requirement for pesticides. Given adequate investment in research and extension, intensified agricultural production and the use of more land will provide the food required during this century while causing little damage to the biological and physical environment.

9.9   SUMMARY

During this century, less developed countries will have to increase their food production to support their growing populations. The projected increases (on the medium variant; see Figure 1.1) are from 4.9 billion in 2000 (estimated) to 6.6 billion in 2025 and to 7.8 billion in 2050, increases of 35 per cent and 58 per cent, respectively (United Nations, 1999). In this chapter the cereal supplies of two groups of countries are estimated: developing countries (1) includes all Africa, South and Central America and Asia excluding Japan, and developing countries (2) is as for developing countries (1) but with the exclusion of India and China (which are dealt with separately in Chapter 10). The required cereal supplies are estimated from the expected populations in 2025 and 2050; in addition they are estimated assuming these populations and a change in diet (increased calorie intake and the consumption of more animal products). Tables 9.4, 9.6 and 9.7 show, respectively, how the average area of cereals alone, the average yield of cereals alone, and area and yields together (using average rates of increase between 1970 and 1999) need to increase to give the required production.

For all arable crops the required area alone (no increase in yield) would need conversion to agricultural production of all the land area that is currently not in use (excluding land under habitation, forest and protected areas), and exceed it in several countries. Crop yields and their sustainability on land not at present in use are, however, uncertain. Further, some of the land that may be taken over has not been surveyed; it is probably less productive than land already in use and its rate of degradation is unknown. The need for more land is reduced if yields are raised (compare Tables 9.4 and 9.7), which will usually require more inputs of fertilizer, possibly more use of pesticides, and also improved crop varieties.

There can be harmful effects on the environment whether new land is used or yields are raised by intensification, although they need not necessarily occur. Soil erosion, probably the greatest hazard, can be controlled (see Chapter 5), and the harmful effects of fertilizers, particularly nitrogen fertilizers, and pesticides can be minimized by using them more efficiently.

Land in Africa and South and Central America will be brought into cultivation, because it is cheap. Conversion of such land entails a loss of natural ecosystems and a risk of soil degradation. Raising yields will reduce the amount of land required, thereby reducing these effects. This will require investment in training staff for research and extension and incentives which make higher yields profitable to the farmer. These are economic requirements that depend on political decisions; the technology is there.

10

Increasing agricultural production: the examples of Africa, India and China

Chapter 9 considered how agricultural production could be increased in two groups of developing countries by extending the area of cultivation and by increasing crop yields. Inevitably, generalizations were made that would be grossly misleading if applied to individual countries, regions within countries, village communities or individual farmers.

This chapter extends the discussion to two countries – China and India – and to the continent of Africa except for Egypt and South Africa. All three have large, increasing populations, large rural sectors and expanding urban populations. These conditions create opportunities for a farmer to sell surplus produce and so pay for services (health care, education, etc.), agricultural inputs and manufactured goods. If marketing his produce is profitable he will have the incentive to raise his production. Whether farmers in the two countries and in Africa can do this by extending the cultivated area or by raising crop yields is the main theme of this chapter. The conclusions reached indicate a ladder of development, with larger yields becoming progressively more important.

10.2 AFRICA: THE RECENT PAST AND FUTURE PROSPECTS

In this chapter Africa* refers to all African countries except Egypt and the Republic of South Africa. Egypt is omitted because of its large crop yields, almost the whole of its arable crop production depending on irrigation. South Africa is omitted because of its advanced state of industrial development. The remaining countries are by no means a homogeneous group; they differ in size, natural resources (especially climate and soils), and social and economic development. The conditions they

Table 10.1. *Populations of Africa***,
China and India in 1995 and projections
(medium variant) for 2025 and 2050*

	Population (millions)		
Year	Africa*	China	India
1995	598	1221	934
2025	1156	1480	1330
2050	1598	1478	1529

Source: United Nations (1999).
[a] Africa* is the continent of Africa except
for Egypt and South Africa (see text).

have in common are relatively low crop yields and rapidly increasing
populations.

As shown in Table 10.1, between 1995 and 2050 the projected increase in population in Africa*, at one billion, exceeds that in China
and India combined. The population is set to double by 2025 and increase 2.7-fold by 2050, the greatest rates of increase of any region. In
sub-Saharan Africa the probability of the population reaching a peak
by 2100 is a little under 75 per cent (Lutz *et al.*, 2001). The requirements
for social, economic and agricultural development are therefore considerable. The discussion that follows is limited to the development of
food production.

Historical trends of crop yields

During the period 1970 to 1995 the population of Africa* doubled, from
300 to 600 million. Cereal production increased at a slightly lower
rate, and roots and tubers at about the same rate as the population
(Figure 10.1 and Table 10.2). The trends of production per person of
both cereals and roots and tubers show a fall during the first half of
the period and a small increase in the 1990s. This change agrees with
a small fall in calorie intake per person in sub-Saharan Africa between
1961/63 and 1988/90, followed by a small increase in the 1990s (FAO
Production Yearbooks).

The main cereals grown in Africa* include maize, sorghum, millet, wetland and upland rice and tef, according to the climate, particularly rainfall. We now consider the historical trends of areas and yields
of the individual crops, and possibilities for the future.

Table 10.2. *Average change in production per person per year of all cereals (1970/99) and roots and tubers (1972/99), by linear regression*

			Change in production (kg person^{-1} a^{-1})
Africa*	–	cereals	−0.3
	–	roots and tubers	0
India	–	cereals	+1.5
China	–	cereals	+4.4

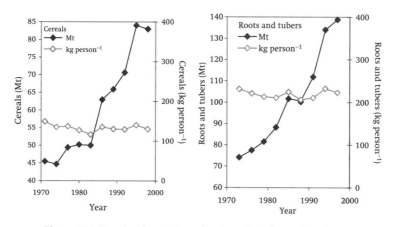

Figure 10.1. Trends of annual production of total cereals and roots and tubers in Africa (omitting Egypt and South Africa). Each point in this and later figures in this chapter represents a three-year average. Data from FAO Production Yearbooks.

Individual crops

The arable crops occupying the largest area in Africa* are maize, millet, sorghum and roots and tubers (Table 10.3). The trends of yields and cultivated areas of these crops are shown in Figure 10.2. Also included is paddy rice, which has the largest yield of all the cereals but occupies a comparatively small area. During the period from the early 1970s to 1999 the areas and yields of each crop increased at the rates shown in Table 10.3. Also listed here are average rates of increase in area, yield and production given by linear regressions.

Yields of cereals and roots and tubers increased more slowly than their areas. Yields of roots and tubers, which are grown predominantly

Table 10.3. *The major food crops of Africa (omitting Egypt and South Africa); harvested area, yield and production for 1997/99 and average annual increases 1970/99 (roots and tubers 1972/99)*

	Data for 1997/99			Average annual increases 1970/99[a]		
Crop	Area (Mha)	Yield (t ha^{-1})	Production (Mt)	Area (Mha)	Yield (kg ha^{-1})	Production (Mt)
All cereals	85	1.0	84	1.02 (1.5%)	9.7 (1.1%)	1.6 (2.6%)
Maize	21	1.2	26	0.35 (2.2%)	8.5 (0.8%)	0.50 (3.0%)
Millet	20	0.7	13	0.14 (0.8%)	1.3 (0.2%)	0.11 (1.1%)
Rice	7	1.6	12	0.13 (2.6%)	11.2 (0.8%)	0.24 (3.3%)
Sorghum	23	0.8	19	0.41 (2.4%)	6.2 (0.8%)	0.42 (3.3%)
Roots and tubers	19	7.9	146	0.23 (1.7%)	89 (1.2%)	2.82 (2.8%)

Source: FAO Production Yearbooks.
[a] Average annual increases calculated by linear regression. The percentage increase is calculated as $x/y \times 100$, where x is the average annual increase and y is the average value for the whole period.

in humid and subhumid zones, increased faster than the yields of other crops. At the other extreme is millet, a crop of regions with little and very variable rainfall. Figure 10.2 shows the large variability in yield, particularly of maize; low yields of this crop can be attributed to low rainfall or drought.

Maize

Maize is a major source of calories in sub-Saharan Africa (Byerlee and Eicher, 1997). It is grown as a sole crop, especially on large commercial farms, and also in association with such crops as millet, groundnut, cowpea and others on small farm plots. According to Byerlee and Eicher (1997), in eastern and southern Africa 'the most important category in terms of production is the medium-scale farmer cultivating 3–10 ha of land using animal power. The second-most important type of farmer, the small-scale farmer, cultivates 1–3 ha manually with a hand hoe. Finally about 5% of the maize area is planted by commercial producers, who usually cultivate 50 ha or more'.

   With the exception of the forest zone that covers most of the Democratic Republic of Congo, maize is one of the main crops between Zimbabwe in the south and the Gambia to the northwest, the region

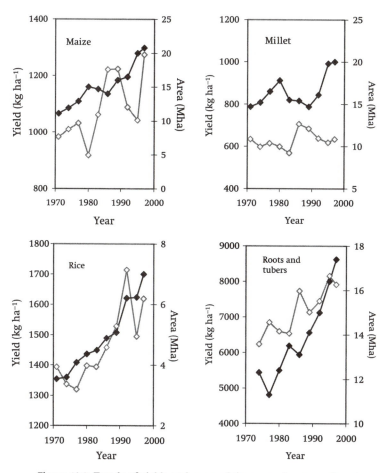

Figure 10.2. Trends of yields and areas of three cereal crops and roots and tubers in Africa (omitting Egypt and South Africa) ◇, yield; ◆, area. Data from FAO Production Yearbooks.

stretching east–west across the continent, omitting the drier parts of East Africa. Varieties have been bred or selected for much of this area to suit the local temperature, length of growing season and required quality of grain, but yields have increased only slowly (Table 10.3). An example of greater success has been development of the maize industry in Zimbabwe (see Chapter 8), success which can be attributed to various factors: the early development by local breeders of hybrids which suited the local soil and climate conditions; an efficient system for distributing the seeds; availability of credit to purchase land, seed and fertilizers; guaranteed prices; and a developed infrastructure and effective research and extension services.

The slow rise in yields might be attributed to lack of one or more of the required inputs; there is also the possibility that, as with all crops, yields on the additional land brought into cultivation are smaller than the average. The extreme fluctuation of yields between three-year periods (Figure 10.2), however, points to climate, and especially rainfall, as having the greatest effect on yield.

Rice

The 12 Mt of rice produced in Africa* in 1997/99 was largely from Madagascar, Nigeria, Tanzania, Ivory Coast and Guinea. Although the amount is small as a fraction of the total cereal production, the yield of rice is larger than that of other cereals and its production is increasing faster than all except for sorghum (Table 10.3). The area of rice cultivation doubled between 1970/71 and 1996/98, from 3.5 Mha to 7.0 Mha (Figure 10.2).

The countries in Asia that have agricultural economies based on rice grow most of the crop under irrigation and obtain yields of up to 6–8 t ha^{-1}. Egypt, using the same system, obtains similar yields. Although yields are at present much lower in Africa* there is potential for them to be raised, and there is scope for extending the area of rice cultivation. There are suitable small valleys with alluvial soils where storage dams under the control of the local community could be used to supply water for irrigation. There are also areas of wetlands where rainfed or irrigated rice could be grown. Greenland (1997) estimates a potential area of rice cultivation of 71 Mha, about ten times the current area. There is also potential for an increased area of rainfed upland rice.

Alexandratos (1995) and Greenland (1997) report the example of increased production of rice in a region of northern Nigeria from 9000 t in 1985 to 98 536 t in 1987, most of which came from planting a greater area. A new short-season variety was grown that was more acceptable in the diet than local varieties and was resistant to blast disease. Rice production was stimulated at the time by a restriction imposed by the Nigerian government on rice imports. Given favourable economic conditions and suitable varieties, it is therefore probable that rice production in sub-Saharan Africa will rise substantially.

Sorghum and millet

Sorghum and millet are indigenous African crops that occupy the drier regions of the continent. The main millets are *Eleusine coracana* (finger millet) and *Pennisetum* spp. There are many local varieties of sorghum that are tall and have a low harvest index. Selections from these varieties have been introduced, as have hybrids. The hybrids are dwarf, have a larger harvest index than the traditional varieties, and where the crop receives sufficient rainfall or irrigation give higher yields with applications of fertilizer. In Egypt, for example, where sorghum is grown with fertilizer and irrigation, hybrids yield about $5\,t\,ha^{-1}$, compared with average yields from traditional varieties of $0.9\,t\,ha^{-1}$ in countries south of the Sahara (FAO Production Yearbooks). The potential of the sorghum hybrids in rainfed agriculture has not yet been realized.

Yields of sorghum have increased more slowly than the area of cultivation during the last three decades, and the same applies to millet (Table 10.3). The grain of both crops is often the staple food for people living in areas with marginally sufficient rainfall. Varieties with a shorter growing season or with greater tolerance to drought would help to relieve food shortages.

Roots and tubers

Roots and tubers, particularly cassava, yams, cocoyams and sweet potato, are important crops in the humid regions of the tropics; cassava is also grown in subhumid and seasonally arid regions. In Africa* these are predominantly subsistence crops; together with plantains they account for about 40 per cent of the calorie intake for about half the population of sub-Saharan Africa (Alexandratos, 1995). Progress has been made at the International Institute of Tropical Agriculture in breeding varieties with large yields that are also resistant to diseases and drought. They provide the potential for greater production where subsistence farmers have access to markets.

Fertilizer use

The use of fertilizer (N + P + K) more than doubled in Africa* between 1970/71 and 1990/93 and then decreased (Figure 10.3). Over the period 1970 to 1988 the average increase by linear regression was 2.8 per cent per year. Although this growth rate was high, the use per hectare of arable land in the countries south of the Sahara averaged only 8–10 kg $(N + P_2O_5 + K_2O)$, a rate that remained almost constant between 1980/81 and 1997/98 (see Table 6.1).

The rate of use is less than one-fifth of the average of all developing countries. The three main reasons for the low rate of use are (i) it is cheaper to increase production from increased area of cultivation than from higher yields, (ii) in a large part of the continent

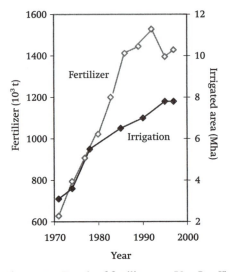

Figure 10.3. Trends of fertilizer use (N + P + K) and irrigated area in Africa (omitting Egypt and South Africa). Data from FAO Production Yearbooks.

yields are restricted by the supply of water, and (iii) fertilizer is relatively expensive and supply to the farmer is often unreliable. For many farmers the response of crops to application of fertilizers is low or difficult to judge, making investment in fertilizers too great a risk. Much will depend on general economic development that provides cash for the purchase of agricultural produce by urban populations, and on national policies to encourage fertilizer use, for example by subsidies or cheap loans, or that guarantee a minimum price for the crop product. In some countries reform of land tenure may be needed (Platteau, 1992).

Critical for the farmer is for him to make profit from the use of fertilizer. As discussed by Heisey and Mwangi (1997), a farmer selling his produce will invest in fertilizer only if the benefit/cost ratio is at least 2 because of uncertainties over both the crop response and market prices, and often of having to pay large interest charges on a loan for the purchase of the fertilizer. Using this figure of 2 and a response of 20 kg grain per kg fertilizer, it is profitable to use fertilizer if the price ratio of kg fertilizer/kg grain is less than 10. For a response of 4 kg grain per kg fertilizer, a more realistic response for a smallholder, the threshold price ratio of fertilizer/grain is 2. If the price ratio is higher than 2 the crop response should be more than 4 kg grain per kg for fertilizer use to be economic. In the early 1990s the price ratio of fertilizer nitrogen/maize grain was above 2 in seven out of nine countries in sub-Saharan Africa (Heisey and Mwangi, 1997), that is, its use would be considered unprofitable unless the response was greater than 4 kg grain per kg fertilizer nitrogen. As always, the economic assessment of fertilizer use cannot be separated from its management.

Larger increases in crop production can follow from applications of fertilizers (where there is adequate rainfall) if the fertilizers are used more efficiently (Quiñones *et al.*, 1997). This can be achieved by addition of the required nutrients in the right amount, at the right time and in the right place, as indicated by field experiments and soil analysis (see Chapter 6). Soil preparation, choice of crop variety and control of pests are part of the required package. Research and extension work will help the farmer and he will respond if there is an economic incentive, as has occurred in the rest of the world.

The future requirements for fertilizer will be large. As mentioned in Section 4.6, there is evidence for nutrient mining in sub-Saharan Africa. In addition, nutrient deficiencies, especially of phosphate, are common (see Section 6.4). With a tripling of the population the requirement for fertilizer by 2050 will be at least three times the present amount. Most will need to be imported; the only large deposits of phosphate rock are in North Africa, and at present only Nigeria and South Africa manufacture nitrogen fertilizers. More attention should be given to nutrient cycling and biological nitrogen fixation, to help keep costs down. With greater input of nutrients there will be more pollution of surface waters, unless the fertilizers are used more efficiently.

Water conservation and irrigation

Irrigated land in Africa* occupies 4.9 per cent of the total arable area (FAO Production Yearbooks). Although the irrigated area is still small (7.7 Mha) it more than doubled between the early 1970s and 1997 (Figure 10.3). An analysis of the water resources and irrigation potential for the whole of Africa (FAO, 1995) shows Egypt, Sudan and South Africa to have the largest areas of irrigated land. There were big differences in irrigation potential and efficiency of water management between countries. In several countries the water supplies are sufficient to extend the area of irrigation, but storage systems to provide the water when it is needed have often not been developed. Small earth dams on streams are cheap to build and can be controlled locally, whereas large concrete dams on rivers are prohibitively expensive in Africa and involve more bureaucracy (see Chapter 7).

Most of the food production in Africa is from rainfed crops. In 1992 and 1994 production of maize in southern and eastern Africa was severely reduced by drought. For example, the production of cereals in South Africa dropped in 1992 to 4.6 Mt, from 11.0 Mt in 1991. A long dry period starting in the late 1960s across the Sahel from West Africa to Sudan resulted in food shortage in several countries. These recent dry spells are a continuation of the fluctuations in rainfall that have occurred in the past and can be expected in the future. Nicholson (1993) has suggested that such fluctuations in rainfall in the Sahel will continue but may be overlain with a gradual, long-term reduction in rainfall. As discussed in Chapter 7, water conservation and short-season crops are essential where rainfall is marginally sufficient for crop production. However, severe droughts will continue to cause food shortages. The response by farmers to drought has been described by Mortimore (1989).

Conclusion

There is reason for optimism about the future production of food crops in Africa* (considered here as all of Africa except Egypt and South Africa), although the effects of climate change are uncertain. Across the continent temperatures are forecast to rise. Rainfall may increase in East Africa and decrease in southeast Africa (IPCC, 2001b).

Reasons for the optimism are the increasing use that is being made of modern crop varieties, fertilizers and irrigation, although the change is slow; also, the potential for rice growing is becoming known. Two serious (and related) problems that may limit production in the future are poverty (due to very slow development of economies) and drought. More farm-based research could help to alleviate rural poverty by more efficient use of inputs, thereby raising profits. Community-based water conservation schemes could be more widely used to reduce the effects of drought. Several of these issues are discussed in Binns (1995); an example of their application can be seen in the Machakos district of Kenya (see Section 8.8).

The historical evidence indicates that increase in area has had a greater effect on production than increased yields (Table 10.3). In the future, success in increasing food production and conserving natural ecosystems will predominantly depend on raising yields, especially in parts of the region that receive adequate rains. Although the trend of using more land will continue where land is available and cheap, its sustainable use will not be achieved if the farming systems continue to exploit the natural soil resources (Sivakumar and Wills, 1995). Land surveys are an essential prerequisite before new land is taken into cultivation. Ultimately yields must be increased more than is occurring at present, by the application of the various technologies described here. Whether this will be achieved will depend on improvement in the economic conditions and particularly on the demand for food by people able to pay for it.

10.3 INDIA: THE RECENT PAST AND FUTURE PROSPECTS

The projected increase in the population of India, from 934 million in 1995 to 1.5 billion in 2050 (Table 10.1), is bigger than that of any other single country. To maintain the present level of nutrition (average of 2400 kcal day^{-1}) the production of cereals, mainly rice, wheat, sorghum, maize and millet, will together need to increase by 63 per cent. To achieve this increase the two components are, as usual, socio-economic (Baker, 1984; Chambers, 1984; Dhawan, 1988; Chambers et al., 1989) and technological (Singh, 1997: Shah et al., 1998).

The total area of cereals in India (101 Mha) remained almost constant between 1970 and 1997/99, while the population increased from 555 million to 970 million (74 per cent increase). During the same period, the production of cereals for food and animal feed increased by 89 per cent, from 117 Mt (1970/71) to 227 Mt (1997/99) (Figure 10.4; FAO Production Yearbooks). According to Shah et al. (1998), districts with mainly drylands contributed 38 per cent of total production in

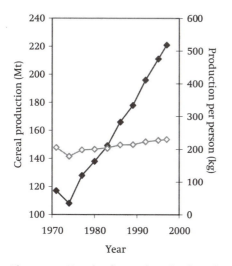

Figure 10.4. Trends of annual production of total cereals in India. ♦, production; ◊, production per person. Data from FAO Production Yearbooks.

Table 10.4. *Production of the three main cereal crops in India (1997/99) and average annual increases (1970/99)*

Crop	Data for 1997/99			Average annual increases 1970/99[a]		
	Area (Mha)	Yield (t ha^{-1})	Production (Mt)	Area (Mha)	Yield (kg ha^{-1})	Production (Mt)
All cereals	101	2.2	227	<0.01	43 (2.7%)	4.3 (2.7%)
Maize	6	1.6	10	<0.01	24 (1.9%)	0.15 (2.1%)
Rice	44	2.9	128	0.20 (0.5%)	52 (2.4%)	2.5 (2.8%)
Wheat	27	2.6	69	0.27 (1.2%)	54 (2.9%)	1.7 (4.1%)

Source: FAO Production Yearbooks.

[a] Average annual increases calculated by linear regression. The percentage increase is calculated as $x/y \times 100$, where x is the average annual increase and y is the average value for the whole period.

1988/90, districts with mainly irrigation contributing the rest. In economic terms, between 1962/65 and 1988/90 the value of productivity (rupees per hectare) increased by 36 per cent on the drylands, and almost doubled on land where there was mainly irrigation. Although there are no data to allow an exact comparison between the total cereal production from irrigated and from rainfed land, the evidence points to irrigation plus the other components of the Green Revolution package as mainly responsible for the increased yields leading to the increased production shown in Figure 10.4. With rainfed crop cultivation, high-yielding varieties and fertilizer use also contributed to the increase.

Production of each of the three main cereal crops (rice, wheat and maize), which account for 74 per cent of the total area of cereals, was raised more by increases in yield than by increases in area (Table 10.4). The yields of these crops in India (Figure 10.5) fluctuated much less than yields in Africa (Figure 10.2 – rice and maize only). In addition, yields of rice and maize were larger in India. These differences can largely be attributed to the increased use of irrigation and fertilizers and the planting of locally adapted high-yielding crop varieties. Much of the food required during the twenty-first century will come from increases in these inputs.

Irrigation

With much of the subcontinent having long dry periods and large rivers flowing into it, it is not surprising that controlled irrigation has long

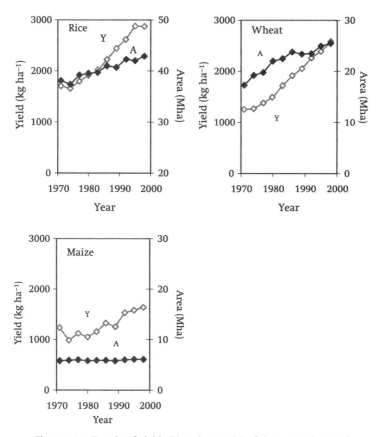

Figure 10.5. Trends of yields (Y) and areas (A) of three cereal crops in India. Data from FAO Production Yearbooks.

been practised. Historical records dating back to the fourth century BC describe the construction of reservoirs and later of diversionary canals (Singh, 1997). Canal irrigation was extended in the nineteenth and twentieth centuries during and following the colonial period. Tube-wells came into use in the 1920s.

In the past few decades there has been a rapid development of irrigation, from 30 Mha of irrigated land in 1969/71 to an estimated 57 Mha in 1997 (FAO Production Yearbook) (Figure 10.6). This represents about 35 per cent of the total arable area of 163 Mha. Shah *et al.* (1998) predict a gross irrigated area of 88 Mha by 2006.

In 1983/84, when the irrigated area was 42 Mha, the sources of water were wells including tubewells (46.5 per cent), canals (38.7 per cent), tanks or small reservoirs (9.0 per cent) and 'other' (5.7 per cent), where the percentages represent the areas under irrigation (Singh, 1997).

Figure 10.6. Trends of fertilizer use (N + P + K) and irrigated area in India. Data from FAO Production Yearbooks.

Tubewells have been used increasingly since the 1970s because of their low cost compared with large storage dams. In India, as in other countries, they have been over-exploited in many areas, that is, the rate of water extraction has exceeded the rate of recharge. 'The crisis of groundwater' in the Indian states has been discussed by Shah *et al.* (1998), who advocate watershed planning to control runoff, and the construction of more farm ponds for supplementary irrigation and in which fish could be raised to supplement the human diet.

In 1979, some 1075 large dams were in use and 479 were under construction, making a total of 1554. Many supply electricity, which has reduced the dependence on firewood for cooking in both rural and urban areas (Singh, 1997). The stored water from these dams irrigates about one-third of the total irrigated area. Large dams have been criticized, however, not only for harming the environment and displacing people from their homes, but also for creating a bureaucracy that is partly responsible for poor management of water for irrigation, leakage from canals (causing waterlogging and soil salinization), and inequitable distribution to farmers' fields. Rural populations facing displacement by proposed storage reservoirs have risen in protest, and social reformers have claimed, as they have against the Green Revolution in general, that only the rich benefit from large-scale irrigation.

Irrigation will continue to be important in the future, if the country is to produce the predicted requirement of 63 per cent more food by 2050. The projection by Shah *et al.* (1998) that the irrigated area could reach 88 Mha by 2006 would imply a greater rate of expansion than during the period 1960–1990. Shah *et al.* estimate that between

1991 and 2006 an additional 17 Mha of rice and wheat will be irrigated, yielding 34 Mt of grain. Improved management of the existing irrigated area will, by extrapolation from recent decades, produce an increase in yield of $0.6 \, t \, ha^{-1}$, giving an extra annual production of cereals of 24 Mt. These authors quote government estimates of the potential area of irrigation by surface water and ground water of 75 Mha and 64 Mha, respectively, a total of 139 Mha. This would double the irrigated area.

Technological problems described by Singh (1997) include water-logging and salinization. Other problems common to irrigation schemes are loss of land by submersion behind high dams, siltation of storage dams and the lowering of ground-water level by tubewells, which in coastal areas is followed by the influx of saline water. There is also the problem of uneven distribution of water from feeder canals. Chambers (1984) gives an example of this from the 180 000 ha Mahanadi Reservoir Project: the yield of paddy rice was $1541 \, kg \, ha^{-1}$ at the top and $218 \, kg \, ha^{-1}$ at the bottom of the feeder system.

Fertilizer use

The huge rise in fertilizer consumption in India is shown in Figure 10.6. Between 1960/61 and 1997 the average rate of application increased from $1.9 \, kg \, ha^{-1}$ of arable land to $88 \, kg \, ha^{-1}$ (amounts expressed as $N + P_2O_5 + K_2O$). This was mostly from increased use of nitrogen fertilizer, which was 10.3 Mt in 1997. The ratio of N:P:K of 7.9:1:0.7 was high, partly because of the use of N fertilizer on sugar-cane.

High-yielding crop varieties

The area under high-yielding crop varieties, especially of wheat and rice, increased rapidly from 2 Mha in 1966/67 to 70 Mha in 1991/92 (Singh, 1997). Together with increased use of fertilizer and irrigation the high-yielding varieties have made India self-sufficient in food production, although this remains vulnerable to the strength of the monsoon.

Dryland agriculture

The importance of dryland agriculture, which is mainly rainfed but may include supplementary irrigation, is shown by the estimate that this sector will be required to produce 51 per cent of the predicted increase in demand for food by 2006 (Shah et al., 1998). Shah et al. argue that, to deal with the diverse conditions of the rainfed area, the planning

Table 10.5. *Requirements for management of watersheds (mainly drylands) in India*

===

(1) *Soil and water conservation*: mechanical and biological control of erosion; water collection in farm ponds; dams on small streams; diversionary dykes to recharge ground water

(2) *Soil improvement*: better cultivations; composting; green manuring; use of animal manures; more biological fixation of nitrogen

(3) *Management of arable crops*: improved varieties for drought and pest control; more efficient use of fertilizers and water; double-cropping and intercropping

(4) *Management of land cover*: agroforestry; improved grassland management, including ley farming

(5) *Management of cattle*: crop varieties with higher value as fodder; improved management of common land and forests

===

Source: After Shah *et al.* (1998).

strategy should be based on individual watersheds (defined as subunits of water catchments) and take into account the socio-economic and ecological conditions. These authors recommend a raft of improvements to raise production and help to relieve poverty, including an improved system of bank loans to farmers, growth of cash crops, reduced costs of fertilizer through better management of crop residues, development of biogas plants (to use animal slurries) to reduce the dependence on wood and charcoal for cooking, and planting of trees to lessen soil erosion and runoff.

Table 10.5 summarizes the possible technologies that might be used in each watershed (for further details see Shah *et al.*, 1998). The proximity to urban centres, length of growing period, terrain and soil conditions, and availability of support from government and non-government organizations will determine what is possible and desirable at particular locations.

Conclusion

India's additional 400 million people by 2025, and 600 million by 2050, will depend for their food mainly on increases in crop yields. Irrigated crops currently occupy about one-third of the cultivated land area. The national government is extending the irrigated area and reclaiming that which has become waterlogged or saline. On existing irrigated areas more efficient use of water would increase yields substantially. In

the two-thirds of the country classed as dryland many improvements
that will increase yields are possible. Some of these improvements can
be made by the individual farmer or village community; others require
government planning and support, and an improved system of bank
loans. There is concern that yields of rice and wheat may be adversely
affected by the future rise in temperature and shortage of water predicted by climatologists (IPCC, 2001b).

10.4 CHINA: THE RECENT PAST AND FUTURE PROSPECTS

The population of China reached one billion in 1981, a little over one-
fifth of the total world population. On the medium variant of the projected increase in population (see Figure 1.1) it will reach 1.48 billion
by 2025 and will not increase further by 2050 (Table 10.1). The magnitude of the increase in population between 1995 and 2025 is second
only to that of India but the growth rate as a fraction of the existing
population is much less.

Data from FAO Production Yearbooks and from Garnaut *et al.*
(1996) show that between 1952 and 1990, when the population doubled
from 575 million to 1155 million, the total grain production increased
2.7-fold. Grain production per person increased from 300 to 360 kg a^{-1},
with a dip in the late 1950s and 1960s. Data for cereal production for
the period from 1970 to 1999 are shown in Figure 10.7. The increase was
achieved with an area of arable land per person of 0.08 ha. Because of

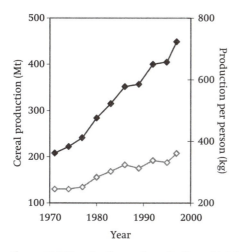

Figure 10.7. Trends of annual production of total cereals in China.
◆, production; ◇, production per person. Data from FAO Production
Yearbooks.

Table 10.6. *Production of the three main cereal crops in China (1997/99)*
and average annual increases (1972/99)

Crop	Data for 1997/99			Average annual increases 1972/99[a]		
	Area (Mha)	Yield (t ha^{-1})	Production (Mt)	Area (Mha)	Yield (kg ha^{-1})	Production (Mt)
All cereals	93	4.9	454	−1.2 (1.2%)	124 (3.7%)	9.1 (2.8%)
Maize	25	4.9	121	0.5 (2.7%)	98 (2.6%)	3.7 (4.8%)
Rice	32	6.4	201	−0.2 (0.54%)	123 (2.5%)	3.4 (2.6%)
Wheat	30	3.9	116	0 (0.0%)	109 (4.2%)	3.3 (4.5%)

Source: FAO Production Yearbooks.
[a] Average annual increases calculated by linear regression. The percentage increase is calculated as $x/y \times 100$, where x is the average annual increase and y is the average value for 1972/99.

the large population and the size of the projected increase, the policy of the Chinese government towards the country's agriculture will affect world food supplies.

Recent technological changes

The farming systems in China have been described by Wenhua (2000). The main cereal crops – maize, rice and wheat – accounted for 97 per cent of total cereal production (454 Mt) in 1997–99; rice accounted for 44 per cent of the total (Table 10.6). Between 1972 and 1998 the yields of all three crops increased substantially, though the area of rice decreased and that of wheat remained the same; only the area of maize increased (Figure 10.8). The decrease in area of rice is attributed to urbanization of the coastal area (Pingali *et al.*, 1997). Intensity of cropping (two-season rice) also decreased, for example from 66 per cent of the land area in 1980 to 58 per cent in 1990 (Huang and Rozelle, 1994), an important factor being loss of labour because of access to alternative employment in new industries.

The increases in crop yield can be attributed to the use of more fertilizer, an increase in irrigated area, the cultivation of modern varieties and pest control, the components of the package that created the Green Revolution. The increases were also made possible by changes in government policy (see below).

Fertilizer use has increased rapidly since the early 1970s, reaching 30.2 Mt (N + P + K) in 1997/98 (Figure 10.9). On the total arable area

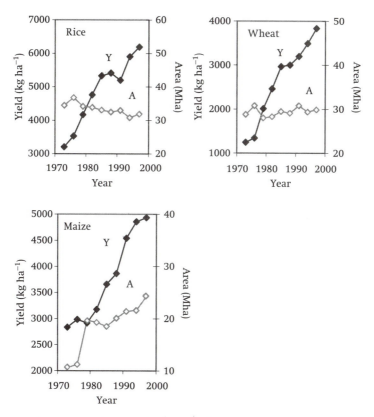

Figure 10.8. Trends of yields (Y) and areas (A) of three cereal crops in China. Data from FAO Production Yearbooks.

of 94 Mha, the average annual use was 248, 44 and 30 kg ha^{-1} of N, P and K, respectively, which are high rates, especially when combined with the application of organic manures.

The irrigated area increased after the construction of large dams between 1950 and the 1970s (Figure 10.9). Although the increase slowed during the 1980s, China is continuing to construct large dams, for example the Three Gorges dam on the river Yangtze and the Xiaolangdi dam on the Yellow river (Huang Ho), partly to extend the area of irrigated land and also to control floods and generate more hydroelectric power.

Modern crop varieties have been widely adopted in China. According to data quoted by Alexandratos (1995), all the rice and 90 per cent of the maize planted in 1991 were of modern varieties. The new varieties of rice and wheat have a large harvest index and incorporate resistance to pests and diseases.

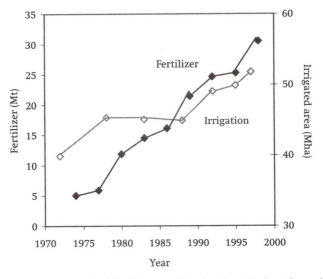

Figure 10.9. Trends of fertilizer use (N + P + K) and irrigated area in China. Data from FAO Production Yearbooks.

Effects of government policies

Major changes in agriculture in China began in the 1950s, with the introduction of collectivization to replace the independent family farm that had been the norm for thousands of years. Agricultural output fell in the late 1950s and 1960s when the 'peoples communes' were forced on farmers; famines followed. Increase in food supplies came with an increase in irrigated area, cultivation of new varieties of rice and wheat, and increase in fertilizer use. Each commune had an obligation to fulfil its quota of production, the price for which was set by the state. The 'household responsibility' system, introduced in 1978 and later modified to make it more productive, transferred the quota obligation from the commune to the individual household (Lin, 1996). Farmers were able to sell part of their production at the prevailing price at local markets, and their income rose. A further step towards a market economy was taken when a relatively free national market was established in the 1990s for almost all agricultural produce (Garnaut and Guonan, 1996). The trade in rice is described by Latham (1998).

Meeting future food requirements

In the future China will have a choice between increasing its production of food crops by intensification and importing food against the export of manufactured goods. These alternatives have been discussed by Garnaut *et al.* (1996) and Kalirajan and Wu (1999).

Production will be increased if the price for the product provides a sufficient incentive. According to Pingali *et al.* (1997), the cost of rice production in China in the early 1990s was lower than that in Thailand, the main exporter of rice, because of higher yields. Although average yields have exceeded 5 t ha^{-1} per harvest for more than 15 years, they could reach 6 t ha^{-1} for a single crop and 10 t ha^{-1} for a double crop (Greenland, 1997). Production of cereals will also be increased, by continuing to extend the area of land under irrigation and possibly by constructing canals to carry water from the southern mountains to the drier north of the country. Global warming might reduce yields of rice, however (IPCC, 2001b).

China has imported relatively small quantities of rice in most years since the 1960s (Lin, 1996; FAO Production Yearbooks). Government policies will determine whether the imports will increase, against the export of manufactured goods, or the rural sector will be supported. As about half the population is still active in agriculture it seems probable that the policies will support both agriculture and manufacturing. If agriculture is made more intensive it will be important that it is sustainable (erosion controls are needed) and for inputs to be used more efficiently.

Conclusion

By 2025 China will be able to feed its additional 260 million people by raising yields or by importing food: the decrease in area of arable land (Seto *et al.*, 2000) seems certain to continue. Yields could increase by more informed use of fertilizers, water and pesticides, and the development of new crop varieties for saline soils and regions with short growing seasons. This will require more research and an effective extension service. The Chinese government might provide the necessary finance and offer an adequate price for agricultural products, or opt for free trade, exporting manufactured goods to pay for food. The latter option would mean large purchases that would affect international prices of some products, especially rice.

10.5 SUMMARY AND CONCLUSIONS

Since the early 1970s (the period considered here) production of arable crops in India and China has increased faster than the population. In

Africa (omitting Egypt and South Africa) production lagged behind the population during the 1970s and 1980s but increased a little during the 1990s. Only time will tell whether these trends will continue.

The three regions have in common large population increases projected for the first quarter of the twenty-first century; the increases in India and Africa are expected to continue beyond the middle of the century.

The regions differ in their level of development and in their possibilities for increasing food supplies. In Africa more land has been brought into cultivation and yields increased, if the required inputs are provided; historical trends are for the cultivated area to increase faster than yields (see Table 10.3). India and China, by contrast, have increased their production mainly by increasing yields.

These contrasting trends reflect those in Europe, North America, Australia, New Zealand and elsewhere. In these areas, in earlier centuries new cheap land was brought into cultivation to raise production. Often the natural fertility of the land fell, and only then were yields raised by inputs such as fertilizer and higher-yielding crop varieties. This 'ladder of development' has met the requirements of the increasing populations in India and China, and there seems no reason why it should not be effective in Africa.

The area of cultivated land in China is decreasing, yields are already high, and, although further increases in production are possible, it might be more economic for the country to import more of its food in the future. India is lower down the ladder and has more potential for increasing yields. Africa is still lower. Although the area of cultivation in Africa will increase, yield increases should be treated as a matter of urgency, for two main reasons. Firstly, new land has usually not been fully surveyed, its cropping potential is not known, and many soils are at risk from erosion and probably have low supplies of mineral nutrients. Secondly, uncontrolled expansion into new areas will destroy natural ecosystems, some of them containing valuable animal and plant species which may be at risk of extinction.

African countries face more difficult problems than India and China. Commonly they import food while having limited amounts of foreign currency to pay for it; high population densities, for example as in eastern Nigeria, have led to near-continuous cultivation of land and decreasing yields; elsewhere droughts are endemic and soil nutrient supplies are often low. In spite of this, more countries could be at least self-sufficient in food if more productive farming systems were developed. Modern varieties of crops to suit the local environmental conditions, increased use of fertilizers and, where appropriate, irrigation are all needed. This will require funding for more on-farm research, extension work and an economic incentive for the farmers, funding which will have to compete with other demands for limited financial resources.

In this chapter generalizations have had to be made, and it should be appreciated that these can be misleading. All three regions are diverse: they have areas of low rainfall where crops may fail because of drought and other areas that are well watered. The vegetative cover and soils also vary greatly, as do population densities and social and economic conditions. There are also political problems and much poverty.

It is for each country to decide by how much and by what route to develop its agricultural sector. The purpose of this chapter has been to show that ultimately the success of arable agriculture depends on raising and maintaining crop yields, a process that can take several years of research as well as an enabling social and economic environment. In those regions where more land can be brought into cultivation, land surveys and planning are essential if land degradation is to be avoided.

11

Prospects and uncertainties

On 2 January 2000 the *Sunday Times* of London carried an article that included the following sentence: 'Some of the most intense debates of the coming century will be about ensuring, amid an exciting and empowering technological revolution, that we do not destroy our environment or forget the legions of the poor'. Within these 'intense debates' there is the issue of food production for a world population which is thought likely to increase by about 50 per cent to about nine billion by the middle of the century.

As shown in Chapter 9, food production in many developing countries will need to double, or more, to meet the demands of a larger population and improve dietary levels. Using more land and raising average yields of arable crops can both be used towards achieving the required production. Crucial questions are whether the increase will be sufficient and can be sustained, and whether there will be irreparable damage to the environment. First to be considered are the reasons for optimism that food production will be sufficient.

At a time when the population of England was increasing, Malthus (1798) postulated that population would outstrip food supplies and people would starve. History has shown otherwise; in the two centuries since, the world population has risen from around one billion to six billion and, although some severe local food shortages have occurred, still occur and seem likely to continue because of poverty, war, drought and floods, most of the extra five billion people are not short of food, for two reasons: more land has been cultivated and technological applications have raised yields (Grigg, 1993; Alexandratos, 1995; Evans, 1998). Much of the discussion in earlier chapters has been on the effect of these two factors, and especially of the technological changes associated with intensification.

Population and technology

Probably the most important reasons for the failure of the Malthusian theory are that it did not foresee the large increase in cultivated area in North America and elsewhere, the effect of population increase on technological change or the developments in the biological and physical sciences. In recent decades the development of modern birth control techniques and greater affluence in developed countries have reduced the size of families, a change that has in some countries been prompted by individual choice, and in others by national policy to control population growth. In agriculture the techniques put together in the Green Revolution (and before) provided food for the burgeoning population of the twentieth century. A larger population creates a bigger infrastructure (roads, schools, etc.), and employs more skilled workers and research and advisory staff. These and several other changes discussed by Boserup (1981, 1985) have lowered birth rates and helped to increase food production to satisfy the increased economic demand.

Application of technologies depends on the local conditions and adoption by the farmer. For example, to attain large yields a high-yielding crop variety needs to be adapted to the conditions of day-length and temperature where it is to be grown, and usually requires good cultivations, the application of fertilizers, and often also of pesticides, and water by irrigation. The principles for attaining large yields are known, as are the techniques that can be applied at specific locations, whether these be water conservation, drainage of irrigated land, addition of nutrients and their management, liming, erosion control, or more general techniques of land management. In all this the crucial person is the farmer.

Adoption of a new technology by a farmer depends on his assessing that it will lead to a reliable profit, for which he requires access to markets where the value of his extra production is greater than the costs of his extra inputs. How he can obtain a profit, and sometimes whether one can be obtained at all, depends on the local physical, biological and socio-economic conditions (Table 11.1). It is the wide range in these conditions that gives the great variety of farming systems of the world.

A farmer makes his decisions according to the local conditions, but some generalizations can be valid. For example, to raise production

Table 11.1. *Four economic and social conditions ('the four I's') for agricultural development*

(1) *Incentive for the farmer*: profit on investment from the sale of products, requiring markets and access to them, and a reliable supply of inputs and their efficient use
(2) *Information*: passed from research and extension workers to farmers by way of demonstration plots, radio, leaflets, etc.; also, costs of inputs, expected market prices for products and opportunities for co-operatives
(3) *Investment*: national or other sources of investment in the infrastructure, including schools, institutes for training farmers, universities, hospitals, roads/railways and food storage facilities; price support for inputs and products
(4) *Innovation*: techniques from research institutes and universities and from other countries to improve efficiency of use of inputs; new crops and crop varieties; alternative farming systems

the Chinese farmer uses the same inputs on his small paddy as are used for large-scale rice production in California, although he uses more labour and has less scope for mechanization – so 'Chinese agriculture will always show Chinese characteristics' (Xu Guohua, 1991). His inputs may include fertilizers, irrigation water, pesticides and modern crop varieties. With other farming systems not all these inputs may be needed, or indeed be available or economic to use, but the principle of raising yields by managing one or more of these inputs, or their alternatives, is a general one (see discussion in earlier chapters).

Population and economics

Generalizations can also be made about the economic conditions for agricultural development. Although they have not been discussed in detail they were referred to in relation to agricultural development in England (Chapter 8), where the conditions are well documented. They are summarized in Table 11.1. An outline of the much debated macroeconomic policies for agricultural development is given in Section 11.4.

The conditions that are usually required for development are now being met to a varying degree in many developing countries, although not all follow the same pattern. Two examples discussed in Chapter 8 – Machakos in Kenya and maize development in Zimbabwe – were driven by groups of farmers. Two different schemes were irrigation in the

Sudan Gezira (Chapter 8), which was the product of the colonial policy of the British government, and secondly, the growth of rice production in China since the middle of the twentieth century (Chapter 10), which was largely determined by the actions of the national government. Viewed retrospectively, in the examples referred to, and others, agricultural production has met the increasing demand when farmers were able to make their own management decisions and the four economic/social conditions (Table 11.1) were in place. It seems safe to assume that the same requirements will apply in the future if there are customers able to pay for the produce.

11.2   IMPLICATIONS OF THE CHOICE: MORE LAND OR LARGER YIELDS?

Until around the middle of the twentieth century agricultural production in the world was increased to a large extent by cultivating more land. Urban spread, degradation of land, particularly by erosion, and protected ecosystems and leisure areas have, on balance, stopped the expansion worldwide (Chapter 9): in 1998 the harvested area of all cereals in the world (700 Mha) was the same as in 1970. More land is being brought into cultivation in the more sparsely populated parts of Africa and South and Central America, where there is potential for expansion. Less is being used in China, where there is urban spread and little potential for expansion, and also in some European countries, where it is cheaper to import food than to grow it.

Raising yields

Annual crop yields can be increased by raising yields per harvest and by increasing the number of harvests per year (cropping intensity) averaged over a rotation (see Section 9.5). With irrigation two or three crops can be harvested each year from the same land, but where there is a bare or bush fallow in the rotation the cropping intensity is very much lower.

Yield per harvest depends on three factors, discussed in earlier chapters: (i) the potential of the crop, (ii) the potential of the site, and (iii) the level of management. Modern, short-strawed varieties of cereals have raised the crop potential by increasing the harvest index (grain biomass/crop biomass) and their resistance to lodging when receiving applications of nitrogen fertilizer. The site potential includes the depth and physical, chemical and biological properties of the soil, and climate (the amount and seasonal distribution of rainfall, temperature, solar radiation and day-length), and water for irrigation. Management includes cultivations to prepare the seedbed (or wet land for rice plants), timely planting of seed, application of fertilizer, water conservation or application of water for irrigated crops, and control of weeds, insect pests and disease, requirements discussed in Chapters 4, 6, 7 and 9. The farmer's aim is to achieve the most profitable yield at the least risk, which depends on the economic conditions at the time and his experience of risks.

Although more land will probably be brought into agricultural use (mainly in sub-Saharan Africa and South and Central America) the general trend, as in the past, is towards increased yields (see Chapters 9 and 10). This trend will become more pronounced as less land becomes available and natural (and semi-natural) ecosystems receive more protection. The intensification that is needed to raise yields in developing countries requires the same environmental monitoring of food and water that is used in developed countries to ensure their safety and to avoid damage to the environment (see Section 9.8).

11.3   PROTECTING THE ENVIRONMENT

As a component of the environment, land, and particularly soils, have important functions that affect the environment. The most obvious function of soils is that they support plant growth. They are also the medium in which leaf litter and other plant residues are decomposed so that they sustain the recycling process for nitrogen and other mineral nutrients and carbon.

Soils both hold water against gravity and reduce its rate of flow into streams and rivers, thereby reducing the risk of floods, particularly flash floods. They buffer changes in temperature and changes in pH, creating better conditions for soil-inhabiting organisms and plants. They are effective ion exchangers, at least for cations, which allows them to hold and provide ammonium, potassium, magnesium, calcium and other cations to plant roots; they absorb many organic substances, including pesticides. Over the Earth's surface soils differ considerably, however, in their properties and hence in their effectiveness as environmental filters and buffers. Further, they leak nitrate, aluminium when acidic, and phosphate when overloaded with phosphate from organic and inorganic manures. These environmental functions of soils have been discussed by Wild (1993). Their influence on the composition of the atmosphere is discussed below (Section 11.4).

Soil quality and soil health

These two terms came into use during the 1980s in recognition of the need to show that soil functions both as a component of the environment and as the medium in which crop plants are grown. There have been several definitions of the terms. The broad definition of Karlen *et al.* (1997) of soil quality is: 'the fitness of a specific kind of soil to function within its capacity and within natural or managed ecosystem boundaries, to sustain plant and animal productivity, maintain or enhance water and air quality, and support human health and habitation'. Definitions of soil health give more emphasis to the biological properties of soils, although the two terms are often used interchangeably. For example, 'Soil health is the continued capacity of soil to function as a living system, with ecosystem and land-use boundaries, to sustain biological productivity, promote the quality of air and water environments and maintain plant, animal and human health' (Doran and Safley, 1997).

Essential when using these terms is to state the intended use of the soil and its physical and economic environment. For example, a soil rich in nutrients may have a high rating to grow grass cut for silage, but a low rating as a natural ecosystem because it would contain few plant species. Several publications discuss the concepts and applications of soil quality and soil health, and how soils might be rated (e.g. National Research Council, 1993b; Doran *et al.*, 1994, 1996; Carter *et al.*, 1997; Gregorich and Carter, 1997; Pankhurst *et al.*, 1997; Huang, 1998; Pierzynski *et al.*, 2000).

Protecting land and soil

The history of land use emphasizes all too clearly that we should not be complacent about future development. About 1200 Mha of land in the world is described as moderately to excessively degraded, mainly by erosion (see Chapter 5). The area is greater than that of the USA. The proportion from agricultural activities, as distinct from natural soil erosion, is uncertain because the two are interlinked, but it is probably well over half. The land can generally be protected from erosion, and good management prevents physical and chemical degradation (Chapter 5). Before new land is brought into cultivation the risk of erosion and salinization needs to be assessed (from land surveys) and appropriate action taken.

Protecting natural and semi-natural ecosystems

There are two separate issues. Firstly, there is concern that ecosystems should be conserved for utilitarian and ethical reasons; utilitarian because they may contain organisms, or are themselves, useful to man, and ethical because we should be guardians of our heritage and avoid the extinction of species.

The utilitarian argument is usually more persuasive. Two early examples of benefits to man are quinine from the bark of the cinchona tree, a native of South America, that was used to treat malaria, and the antibiotic streptomycin derived from the soil bacterium *Streptomyces coccus*. More recent examples are given by Beattie and Ehrlich (2001). Many ecosystems, however, have not been investigated, large numbers of species have not been identified and, for example, the ecology of organisms involved in the decomposition of leaf litter and in soils is poorly understood. It would be foolish to destroy what might prove to be of value. Further, whole ecosystems are of economic value in reducing the rate of runoff of rain water, as discussed above, and many attract tourists who bring foreign currency and create opportunities for employment.

The second issue is the function of natural ecosystems, particularly of forested land, in the carbon cycle between land and the atmosphere. FAO estimates that gross deforestation in the tropics was about 15 Mha per year between 1980 and 1990 (Alexandratos, 1995). Globally, 56 Mha of forest were lost between 1990 and 1995, the greatest loss occurring in Latin America, at a rate of 5.8 Mha per year between 1990 and 1995 (GEO-2000, 1999). The significance of the carbon cycle to climate change is discussed below (Section 11.4).

In regions where the number of people is increasing and land is available and cheap it will be used to produce food. Ecosystems and their range of species (biodiversity) are therefore at risk of destruction. 'Settlement for agriculture is the main cause of extinctions, because fragmentation, habitat loss, introductions, and hunting all follow from this' (Tinker, 1997). These effects of the use of more land for agriculture can be made less if annual yields are increased.

11.4 UNCERTAINTIES IN MEETING FUTURE FOOD REQUIREMENTS

Since its beginnings about 10 000 years ago agriculture has changed by adaptation to the prevailing conditions of the land (climate, terrain and soil) and to social and economic demands. When it has failed to adapt, especially to climate change, civilizations have collapsed. The early civilizations of the Indus valley, the city states of Sumer in southern Mesopotamia and probably the Mayan civilization of Central America are examples (see Chapter 3).

More commonly agriculture evolved to provide food, fibre and animal products such as wool and leather for local use and trade. Production increased as the human population increased, in earlier periods largely by increasing the area of land devoted to agriculture and later, particularly in the latter half of the twentieth century when the world population increased from 2.5 billion to six billion, largely by raising yields. Uncertainties in the future are how agriculture will adapt to changed conditions in this century, and centre around four issues: (i) the size of the increase in population in regions and individual countries; (ii) the effect of climate change; (iii) the resources (water, soils, crop varieties and inputs including energy, fertilizer and pest control) required for greater production; and (iv) the macroeconomic conditions.

Increase in and distribution of population

The population of a country is measured by a census. The numbers may themselves be unreliable, but a greater uncertainty in the future is the rate at which the fertility (birth) rate will change. The general trend is downward: the world average of children per woman was around 5.0 in 1955–1960 and 2.9 in 1990–1995. If the rate falls by 2050 to 2.6 (high variant), 2.1 (medium variant) or 1.6 (low variant) the population increase from 1995 will be 5.0 billion, 3.2 billion and 1.7 billion, respectively. The corresponding increases by 2025 are 2.7 billion, 2.2 billion and 1.6 billion (Fischer and Heilig, 1997; United Nations, 1999). These numbers will become more accurate as the trends of fertility and increased life expectancy become better established and the effect of pandemics such as AIDS is better known.

Almost certain is that the biggest increase in population by 2050 will be in India, followed by China, Nigeria, Pakistan and Ethiopia which, with several others, have been classified by FAO as developing countries. It is in developing countries where increases in food production will need to be substantial (see Chapters 9 and 10). However, developing countries differ considerably in population, density of population, and natural resources. In China, for example, the birth rate has fallen rapidly so that the population is predicted to be almost stable by

2025, whereas in Nigeria it will increase rapidly to over 300 million by 2050 and probably continue to increase.

Developing countries also differ in size, urbanization, development of infrastructure, gross national production per capita, and natural resources (including actual and potential agricultural land per capita). Agricultural development to meet the needs of increasing populations must therefore take account of the conditions in individual countries, a requirement that is outside the scope of this book. Two generalizations can be made, however: (i) that more land can be used for agriculture, particularly in sub-Saharan Africa and South and Central America, and (ii) that in these regions and throughout the developing world there is a need to increase annual yields of crops.

Climate change

Much has been written about climate change, its causes and its effects (e.g. Bolin *et al.*, 1986; Bouwman, 1990; Scharpenseel *et al.*, 1990; Rounsevell and Loveland, 1994; American Society of Agronomy, 1995; Houghton, 1997; Lal *et al.*, 1999; IPCC, 2001a,b; O'Neill *et al.*, 2001). The account that follows, which relates only to the changes that might affect agricultural production in the future, is based mainly on Houghton (1997), IPCC (2001a,b) and Fischer *et al.* (2001). Four changes are predicted to affect agricultural production: increased temperature, increased concentration of carbon dioxide in the atmosphere, changes to the geographical distribution and intensity of rainfall, and a rise in sea level.

The projected rise of globally averaged surface temperature during this century is in the range 1.4–5.8 °C (IPCC, 2001a). This temperature rise will be uneven over the Earth's surface, being greatest at northern latitudes and less pronounced at lower latitudes. The temperature increase may shift the northern limit of arable agriculture 500–1000 km northwards. Problems from pests and diseases of crops are expected to increase as the temperature rises.

A rise in temperature will increase evaporation of water from the sea, soils and plants. The hydrological cycle will become more intense, causing more rainfall and more erosive rainstorms. The change in rainfall will vary, however: mid-latitude regions, which generally have low rainfall at present, are predicted to receive less in the future, and high latitudes to receive more in winter. The models on which these predictions are based are not sufficiently refined to predict the size of the change, the rate of change or the changes over small regions. The effects of the change in rainfall on agricultural production in individual countries are therefore uncertain, but some regions are likely to be at risk of lower production because of more frequent droughts while elsewhere crops may be damaged by more floods.

Increased concentrations of carbon dioxide increase photosynthesis. The growth response of C3 plants (wheat, rice, barley, soybean) is greater than that of C4 plants (maize, sorghum, millets, sugar-cane). The response varies with temperature and other environmental conditions, and also differs between species, but growth response and crop yield can be expected to increase.

The fourth effect of climate change is a rise in sea level, which is predicted to be 5 mm per year with a range of uncertainty of 2–9 mm per year. The rise relative to the land surface depends on the local rise or fall of the land itself; for example, in the two areas likely to be most affected – Bangladesh and the Nile delta – land subsidence is predicted to be 0.7 m and 1 m, respectively, by 2050 (Houghton, 1997), compared with an average rise in sea level of 0.25 m over the same period. Other low-lying areas in Europe and elsewhere will lose land, and some of the low-lying islands and coral atolls of the Indian and Pacific oceans may be lost entirely. Inland intrusion of salt water will also affect more land.

Based on one model of climate change, Fischer *et al.* (2001) have assessed its quantitative impact on the production of cereals. Of the major producers, production will increase in Canada and Russia and decrease in France, the Ukraine and the USA, resulting in little change in the world as a whole. In Africa, Kenya and South Africa will benefit but several other countries, including Angola, Cote d'Ivoire, Sudan and Tanzania, will lose production. Elsewhere, China will benefit in its northern region whereas India will lose some of its rainfed production. It should be noted that there are several models of climate change, each of which may give different quantitative changes of cereal production. However, the global distribution of changes in temperature and rainfall referred to above are generally accepted.

Summary

Of the four effects of climate change, increase in temperature will probably shift the northern limit of arable agriculture in the northern hemisphere and increase the risk of flooding in low-lying areas at high latitudes. In mid-latitudes droughts are expected to become more common. Increase in atmospheric carbon dioxide, considered to be the main cause of climate change, will probably increase crop yields, although it is not yet known to what extent. In the world as a whole agricultural output might not be affected, with some countries producing more and others less; the losers are expected to be countries that currently have a low rainfall.

Available resources

The requirements for resources have been discussed earlier: land in Chapter 9 and Section 11.2, fertilizers in Chapter 6, and water in Chapters 2 and 7. Mineral reserves in the world are likely to be adequate for the manufacture of phosphate and potassium fertilizers to meet the expected demand during this century, and for urea the only eventual limit to its manufacture might be a source of cheap energy. Availability of water and productive land is another matter. Shortage of water for arable and tree crops and pastures is probably the biggest biological and physical limitation to agricultural development in developing countries. Rainfall can be conserved by reducing runoff (see Chapters 5 and 7) and irrigation can usually be made more efficient (see Chapter 7), but several countries depend on supplies from rivers that cross country boundaries, creating the difficulty of having to reach international agreements on water use. As mentioned above, supplies of water may become less or greater as a result of climate change.

Finally, areas of land that might be developed for agriculture are known at least approximately (see Chapter 9). Much more needs to be known, however, from soil surveys and pilot experiments of land's potential for agricultural production in both the short and long term. Assessment is also needed of the risk of degradation of the land, particularly by erosion, and of the inputs that will be required.

Macroeconomic conditions

To be successful, agricultural development requires both the application of technology and favourable economic conditions. Neither is successful without the other. Most of this book has concerned itself with technological developments, with some reference to local social and economic conditions (see Chapter 8 and Table 11.1). A few comments are also needed on national and international economic policies that affect agricultural development and particularly international trade.

Governments of most countries provide support for agriculture directly, as subsidies on inputs, guaranteed prices of products or cheap loans, or indirectly, by providing infrastructure including roads, railways, electricity, grain storage, etc. and financing research and extension work. They may also finance the building of water storage dams, the development of irrigation and other settlement schemes and the reclamation of degraded land. This support, which is provided to a different extent in individual countries, is justified by the benefits from the production of food and fibre for internal use or export.

The support provided in Europe, North America and elsewhere in developed countries has often changed as economic conditions have changed. The requirements for government support in developing countries are the same, but with rapidly rising populations they need to be flexible. The difficulties of many of the countries are made more severe by the limitations of their natural and financial resources.

Since the second half of the twentieth century the means of stimulating agricultural growth in developing countries has been debated by economists concerned with the possibility of industrialisation, the effects of international loans, taxation policies, responsibilities of governments and other issues (Alexandratos, 1995). There is no single requirement, but rather a package is needed comparable to that of technological inputs in the Green Revolution, which will differ between countries. The economic requirements include 'price stability, a competitive exchange rate, and an interest rate that reflects the balance between credit and savings' (Alexandratos, 1995).

One uncertainty in the future for each developing country is its exchange rate on the international money market, which sets a limit to imports and exports if a long-term balance is to be achieved. Countries importing cereals depend largely on exports from North America and to a lesser extent on those from Australia and Europe. Apart from the exchange rate, the cost of imported food depends on the surplus available from the producer countries, which is affected by drought, the level of price support, and the amount held in storage. The conclusion must be that developing countries with limited scope for exports, or for generation of foreign currency by such means as tourism, should, where possible, aim for self-sufficiency in food production, thereby reducing their dependence on the uncertain cost of imports.

11.5 SUMMARY

(1) Among the few certainties of the future is the substantial increase in the world population. Most of the increase will be in countries classified by FAO as developing, with the largest absolute increases

projected for India and China and the largest growth rates for Africa. The challenge that lies ahead is to provide sufficient food for this burgeoning population by increasing agricultural production in the developing countries themselves. Some may be able to import it from the few countries that can produce a surplus over their own requirements. The greater agricultural output will need to be sustained throughout the twenty-first century and probably beyond.

(2) The countries classified as developing vary greatly in size, land, climate and human resources, and in extent of economic development. The requirements for agricultural development must therefore be based on the specific conditions in each country.

(3) Production of cereals, the main component of the human diet and considered here as an index of agricultural production, can be increased by raising annual yields or by increasing the area of land under cultivation each year. Since 1970 production in developing countries as a whole has been increased by both means (see Table 9.2). In Africa (omitting Egypt and South Africa) increased area has contributed more than increased yield. By contrast, in India there has been little increase in area and in China the area has decreased, production being raised in both countries by larger yield. It seems probable that these trends will continue. In many African countries poverty and slow economic development may limit the increase in food production.

(4) Estimates of unused land that might be taken into production have been made by FAO, although the potential yields and the sustainability of production are not known. This area of land, assuming average yields, will become insufficient to meet the food requirements of the projected population of developing countries if calorie intake is increased and the trend towards the increased consumption of animal products continues (see Section 9.4). Where it is available and cheap more land will be used, but in most countries, and probably all developing ones, higher yields will be needed sooner or later. As a corollary, the less land that is used, the greater the protection of natural ecosystems and the less will be the area of land at risk of degradation.

(5) Annual yields per unit of land area can be increased by larger harvests per crop and by growing more than one crop per year. Appropriate techniques depend on the local physical, biological and economic conditions and especially on an incentive for the farmer. Insufficient or unreliable rainfall, and drought in particular, will

however limit production in several parts of the developing world, making periodic food shortages inevitable.

(6) Uncertainties in the future include (i) the populations of individual countries in the next 25–50 years, which will depend mainly on the rate of fall of birth rates (which cannot be predicted with any certainty); (ii) effects of climate change, which at present lack precision for individual countries; (iii) the extent of support for agriculture by the state, international organizations and non-governmental organizations; and (iv) the exchange rate between countries, which affects trade and thereby affects decisions about whether to aim for self-sufficiency in food production or import food against exports.

(7) There are strong indications that most developing countries have the potential to provide sufficient food for their people if water is available, the land is properly managed, inputs are used efficiently and crop varieties with higher yield potential are developed. However, shortages can be expected in countries subject to droughts. The farmer is the key figure, but it usually requires all four essentials listed in Table 11.1 for production to be increased.

(8) The extra production resulting from the Green Revolution helped to feed the increased population of the second half of the twentieth century. It is predicted that in some countries populations will continue to increase until the middle of this century and beyond. It is therefore necessary for increased production to be sustainable. The history of land degradation (see Chapter 5) shows that sustainability should not be assumed. Land should be surveyed, risks assessed and any protective measures put in place before it is brought into cultivation. Soils should be monitored to detect signs of erosion, acidification, organic matter and nutrient depletion and, where relevant, salinization.

(9) Under-pinning agricultural development are economic requirements. They include investment in the infrastructure and technological developments that come from research and the extension of these to farmers. The research should aim to improve our understanding of the long-term effects of farming systems on the environment (and on soil fertility in particular) that might find application to the farmer, and should include testing of innovations by field experiments on research stations and on farmers' fields by farmers themselves. To ensure sustainability of farming systems it will be necessary for some field experiments to be

continued for several years. These requirements depend on there being a base of general economic development.

(10) Finally, since the beginnings of agriculture about 10 000 years ago it has evolved to suit local environmental conditions. When soils became unproductive farmers moved on or let the land rest under a long fallow before using it again. In the future food production will depend increasingly on raising and sustaining annual yields.

We now know how to make soils more productive and how to keep them productive. The more we understand about soil properties and processes in a given environment, and apply what we know, the more certain it becomes that the land will support the greater agricultural output which will be required by the increased population of the twenty-first century.

References

Adams, R.McC. 1981. *Heartland of Cities*. University of Chicago Press, Chicago,   **223**
Illinois.

Adriano, D.C., Chlopecka, A. and Kaplan, D.I. 1998. Role of soil chemistry in soil remediation and ecosystem conservation. In: *Soil Chemistry and Ecosystem Health* (ed. P.M. Huang), pp. 361–386. SSSA Special Publication No. 52. Soil Science Society of America, Madison, Wisconsin.

Agnew, C.T. 1995. Desertification, drought and development in the Sahel. In: *People and Environment in Africa* (ed. T. Binns), pp. 137–149. Wiley, Chichester.

Alewell, C., Manderscheid, B., Meesenburg, H. and Bittersohl, J. 2000. Is acidification still an ecological threat? *Nature, London* **407**, 856–857.

Alexandratos, N. (ed.) 1995. *World Agriculture: Towards 2010*. FAO, Rome and Wiley, Chichester.

Allen, P.A. 1997. *Earth Surface Processes*. Blackwell Science, Oxford.

Alloway, B.J. (ed.) 1995. *Heavy Metals in Soils*, 2nd edition. Blackie Academic and Professional, Glasgow.

Alloway, B.J. and Ayres, D.C. 1997. *Chemical Principles of Environmental Pollution*, 2nd edition. Blackie Academic and Professional, London.

American Society of Agronomy 1995. *Climate Change and Agriculture: Analysis of Potential International Impacts*. ASA Special Publication No. 59. American Society of Agronomy, Madison, Wisconsin.

An Zhimin 1989. Prehistoric agriculture in China. In: *Foraging and Farming: The Evolution of Plant Exploitation* (eds. D.R. Harris and G.C. Hillman), pp. 643–649. Unwin Hyman, London.

Anderson, B. 1957. *A Survey of Soils in the Kongwa and Nachingwea Districts of Tanganyika*. University of Reading, Reading.

Anonymous 1997. *Precision Agriculture: Spatial and Temporal Variability of Environmental Quality*. CIBA Foundation Symposium No. 210. Wiley, Chichester.

Artzy, M. and Hillel, D. 1988. A defense of the theory of progressive soil salinization in ancient southern Mesopotamia. *Geoarchaeology* **3**, 235–238.

Assink, J.W. and van den Brink, W.J. (eds.) 1986. *Contaminated Soil*. Martinus Nijhoff Publishers, Dordrecht.

Baggs, E.M., Rees, R.M., Smith, K.A. and Vinten, A.J.A 2000. Nitrous oxide emission from soils after incorporating crop residues. *Soil Use and Management* **16**, 82–87.

Baker, C.T. 1984. Frogs and farmers: the Green Revolution in India, and its murky past. In: *Understanding Green Revolutions* (eds. T.P. Bayliss-Smith and S. Wanmali), pp. 37–52. Cambridge University Press, Cambridge.

Baldwin, K.D.S. 1957. *The Niger Agricultural Project. An Experiment in African Development.* Basil Blackwell, Oxford.

Barber, S.A. 1995. *Soil Nutrient Bioavailability: A Mechanistic Approach*, 2nd edition. Wiley, New York.

Barbier, E.B. 1997. The economic determinants of land degradation in developing countries. *Philosophical Transactions of the Royal Society of London* B352, 891–899.

Barker, G. 1985. *Prehistoric Farming in Europe.* Cambridge University Press, Cambridge.

Bayliss-Smith, T. 1996. People–plant interactions in the New Guinea highlands: agricultural heartland or horticultural backwater? In: *The Origins and Spread of Agriculture and Pastoralism in Eurasia* (ed. D.R. Harris), pp. 499–523. University College Press, London.

Beattie, A. and Ehrlich, P.R. 2001. *Wild Solutions: How Biodiversity is Money in the Bank.* Yale University Press, New Haven, Connecticut.

Bell, B. 1971. The dark ages in ancient history I. The first dark age in Egypt. *American Journal of Archaeology* 75, 1–26.

Bell, B. 1975. Climate and the history of Egypt: The Middle Kingdom. *American Journal of Archaeology* 79, 223–269.

Bell, M. and Boardman, J. (eds.) 1992. *Past and Present Soil Erosion: Archaeological and Geographical Perspectives.* Oxbow Books, Oxford.

Bell, S. and Morse, S. 1999. *Sustainability Indicators: Measuring the Immeasurable?* Earthscan Publications Ltd, London.

Binns, T. (ed.) 1995. *People and Environment in Africa.* Wiley, Chichester.

Birch, H.F. 1960. Nitrification in soils after different periods of dryness. *Plant and Soil* 12, 81–96.

Blum, W.E.H. and Santelises, A.A. 1994. A concept of sustainability and resilience based on soil functions: the role of the International Society of Soil Science in promoting sustainable land use. In: *Soil Resilience and Sustainable Land Use* (eds. D.J. Greenland and I. Szabolcs), pp. 535–542. CAB International, Wallingford.

Blumler, M.A. 1996. Ecology, evolutionary theory and agricultural origins. In: *The Origins and Spread of Agriculture and Pastoralism in Eurasia* (ed. D.R. Harris), pp. 25–50. University College Press, London.

Boardman, J., Foster, I.D.L. and Dearing, J.A. (eds.) 1990. *Soil Erosion on Agricultural Land.* Wiley, Chichester.

Boddey, R.M., de Oliveira, O.C., Urquiaga, S. *et al.* 1995. Biological nitrogen fixation associated with sugar cane and rice: contributions and prospects for improvement. *Plant and Soil* 174, 195–209.

Bolin, B., Döös, B.R. and Jäger, J. (eds.) 1986. *The Greenhouse Effect: Climate Change and Ecosystems.* Wiley, Chichester.

Boserup, E. 1981. *Population and Technological Change: A Study of Long-Term Trends.* Chicago University Press, Chicago, Illinois.

Boserup, E. 1985. The impact of scarcity and plenty on development. In: *Hunger and History* (eds. R.I. Rotberg and T.K. Rabb), pp. 185–209. Cambridge University Press, Cambridge.

Boswinkle, E. 1961. Residual effects of phosphorus fertilizers in Kenya. *Empire Journal of Experimental Agriculture* 29, 136–142.

Bouwman, A.F. (ed.) 1990. *Soils and the Greenhouse Effect.* Wiley, Chichester.

Bowman, A.K. and Rogan, E. (eds.) 1999. *Agriculture in Egypt from Pharaonic to Modern Times.* Proceedings of the British Academy No. 96. Oxford University Press, Oxford.

Brady, N.C. and Weil, R.R. 1999. *The Nature and Properties of Soils*, 12th edition. Prentice-Hall International, London.

Bray, F. 1984. *Science and Civilization in China* (series edited by J. Needham), Vol. 6, *Biology and Biological Technology, Part II. Agriculture.* Cambridge University Press, Cambridge.

Bray, F. 1986. *The Rice Economies: Technology and Development in Asian Societies.* Basil Blackwell, Oxford.

Brown, J.R. (ed.) 1987. *Soil Testing: Sampling, Correlation, Calibration, and Interpretation.* SSSA Special Publication No. 21. Soil Science Society of America, Madison, Wisconsin.

Browne, C.A. 1944. *A Source Book of Agricultural Chemistry.* Chronica Botanica Co., Waltham, Massachusetts.

Bunting, A.H., Dennett, M.D., Elston, J. and Speed, C.B. 1982. Climate and crop distribution. In: *Food, Nutrition and Climate* (eds. K. Blaxter and L. Fowden), pp. 43–74. Allied Science Publishers, London.

Buol, S.W., Hole, F.D., McCracken, R.J. and Southard, R.J. 1997. *Soil Genesis and Classification*, 4th edition. Iowa State University Press, Ames, Iowa.

Buresh, R.J., Sanchez, P.A. and Calhoun, F. (eds.) 1997. *Replenishing Soil Fertility in Africa.* SSSA Special Publication No. 51. Soil Science Society of America, Madison, Wisconsin.

Buringh, P. 1960. *Soils and Soil Conditions in Iraq.* Ministry of Agriculture, Iraq.

Buringh, P. and Dudal, R. 1987. Agricultural land use in space and time. In: *Land Transformation in Agriculture* (eds. M.G. Wolman and F.G.A. Fournier), pp. 9–43. SCOPE No. 32. Wiley, Chichester.

Butzer, K.W. 1976. *Early Hydraulic Civilizations in Egypt.* University of Chicago Press, Chicago, Illinois.

Butzer, K.W. 1983. Long-term flood variation and political discontinuities in Pharaonic Egypt. In: *From Hunters to Farmers* (eds. J.D. Clark and S.A. Brandt), pp. 102–112. University of California Press, Berkeley, California.

Byerlee, D. and Eicher, C.K. (eds.) 1997. *Africa's Emerging Maize Revolution.* Lynne Rienner Pub., Inc., Boulder, Colorado.

Callaway, M.B. and Francis, C.A. (eds.) 1993. *Crop Improvement for Sustainable Agriculture.* University of Nebraska Press, Lincoln, Nebraska.

Cameron, K.C. and Wild, A. 1984. Potential aquifer pollution from nitrate leaching following the plowing of temporary grassland. *Journal of Environmental Quality* **13**, 274–278.

Carter, M.R. (ed.) 1993. *Soil Sampling and Methods of Analysis.* Lewis Publishers, Boca Raton, Florida.

Carter, M.R., Gregorich, E.G., Anderson, D.W., Doran, J.W., Janzen, H.H. and Pierce, F.J. 1997. Concepts of soil quality and their significance. In: *Soil Quality for Crop Production and Ecosystem Health* (eds. E.G. Gregorich and M.R. Carter), pp. 1–19. Developments in Soil Science No. 25. Elsevier, Amsterdam.

Catt, J.A. 1986. *Soils and Quaternary Geology. A Handbook for Field Scientists.* Clarendon Press, Oxford.

Chambers, R. 1984. Beyond the Green Revolution: a selective essay. In: *Understanding Green Revolutions* (eds. T.P. Bayliss-Smith and S. Wanmali), pp. 362–379. Cambridge University Press, Cambridge.

Chambers, R., Saxena, N.C. and Shah, T. 1989. *To the Hands of the Poor: Water and Trees.* Intermediate Technology Publications, London.

Chang, C., Cho, C.M. and Janzen, H.H. 1998. Nitrous oxide emission from long-term manured soils. *Soil Science Society of America Journal* **62**, 677–682.

Chang, T.T. 1989. Domestication and spread of the cultivated rices. In: *Foraging and Farming: The Evolution of Plant Exploitation* (eds. D.R. Harris and G.C. Hillman), pp. 408–417. Unwin Hyman, London.

Chappell, A., Warren, A., Oliver, M.A. and Charlton, M. 1998. The utility of ^{137}Cs for measuring soil redistribution rates in southwest Niger. *Geoderma* **81**, 313–337.

Civil, M. 1994. *The Farmers' Instructions: A Sumerian Agricultural Manual.* Aula Orientalis-Supplementa. Editorial AUSA, Barcelona.

Cleary, S. 1989. *Renewing the Earth: Development for a Sustainable Future: An Economic Perspective.* Catholic Fund for Overseas Development, London.

Cohen, J.E. 1995. *How Many People can the Earth Support?* Norton, New York.

Cole, V. 1996. Agricultural options for mitigation of greenhouse gas emissions. In: *Climate Change 1995. Impacts, Adaptions and Mitigation of Climate Change: Scientific-Technical Analysis* (eds. R.T. Watson, M.C. Zinyowera and R.H. Moss), pp. 745–771. Cambridge University Press, Cambridge.

Conway, G. and Toenniessen, G. 1999. Feeding the world in the twenty-first century. *Nature, London* **402** Supplement C55–58.

Conway, G.R. 1999. *The Doubly Green Revolution: Food for All in the 21st Century.* Penguin Books, London and Cornell University Press, Ithaca, New York.

Cooke, G.W. 1967. *The Control of Soil Fertility.* Crosby Lockwood, London.

Cooke, G.W. 1982. *Fertilizing for Maximum Yield.* Granada, London.

Cooke, G.W. 1988. The development and application of modern knowledge of soils. In: *Russell's Soil Conditions and Plant Growth* (ed. A. Wild), pp. 22–29. Longman, Harlow.

Cooper, P.J.M., Gregory, P.J., Tully, D. and Harris, H.C. 1987. Improving water use efficiency of annual crops in the rainfed farming systems of West Asia and North Africa. *Experimental Agriculture* **23**, 113–158.

Cooper, P.J.M., Leakey, R.R.B., Rao, M.R. and Reynolds, L. 1996. Agroforestry and the mitigation of land degradation in the humid and sub-humid tropics of Africa. *Experimental Agriculture* **32**, 235–290.

Cotterell, A. (ed.) 1980. *The Penguin Encyclopedia of Ancient Civilizations.* Penguin Books, London.

Cowan, C.W. and Watson, P.J. (eds.) 1992. *The Origins of Agriculture: An International Perspective.* Smithsonian Institute Press, Washington, DC.

Craig, G.M. (ed.) 1991. *The Agriculture of the Sudan.* Oxford University Press, Oxford.

Crawford, D.J. 1971. *Kerkeosiris. An Egyptian Village in the Ptolemaic Period.* Cambridge University Press, Cambridge.

Crowley, D.E. and Rengel, Z. 1999. Biology and chemistry of nutrient availability in the rhizosphere. In: *Mineral Nutrition of Crops* (ed. Z. Rengel), pp. 1–40. The Haworth Press, New York.

Crowther, F. 1934. Studies in growth analysis of the cotton plant under irrigation in the Sudan. I. The effects of different combinations of nitrogen applications and water supply. *Annals of Botany* **48**, 877–913.

Davidson, N. and Galloway, R. (eds.) 1991. *Productive Use of Saline Land.* Proceedings of a Workshop held at Perth, Western Australia, 10–14 May 1991. Proceedings No. 42. ACIAR, Canberra.

De Haan, F.A.M. and Visser-Reyneveld, M.I. (eds.) 1996. *Soil Pollution and Soil Protection.* International Training Centre, Wageningen Agricultural University, Wageningen.

Dennell, R.W. 1992. The origins of agriculture in Mesoamerica and central America. In: *The Origins of Agriculture: An International Perspective* (eds. C.W. Cowan and P.J. Watson), pp. 71–100. Smithsonian Institute Press, Washington, DC.

Dhawan, B.D. 1988. *Irrigation in India's Agricultural Development. Productivity, Stability, Equity.* Sage Publications, New Delhi.

Doran, J.W., Coleman, D.C., Bezdicek, D.F. and Stewart, B.A. (eds.) 1994. *Defining Soil Quality for a Sustainable Environment.* SSSA Special Publication No. 35. Soil Science Society of America, Madison, Wisconsin.

Doran, J.W. and Safley, M. 1997. Defining and assessing soil health and sustainable productivity. In: *Biological Indicators of Soil Health* (eds. C. Pankhurst, B.M. Doube and V.V.S.R. Gupta), pp. 1–28. CAB International, Wallingford.

Doran, J.W., Sarrantonio, M. and Liebig, M.A. 1996. Soil health and sustainability. *Advances in Agronomy* **56**, 1–54.

Drower, M.S. 1954. Water-supply, irrigation and agriculture. In: *A History of Technology* (eds. C. Singer, E.J. Holmyard and A.R. Hall), pp. 500–507. Clarendon Press, Oxford.

Dyke, G.V. 1964. Broadbalk. *Report of Rothamsted Experimental Station for 1963*, pp. 174–181.

Edwards, C.A. and Bohlen, P.J. 1996. *Biology and Ecology of Earthworms*, 3rd edition. Chapman and Hall, London.

Eicher, C.K. and Kupfuma, B. 1997. Zimbabwe's emerging maize revolution. In: *Africa's Emerging Maize Revolution* (eds. D. Byerlee and C.K. Eicher), pp. 25–43. Lynne Rienner Pub., Inc., Boulder, Colorado.

Ernle, Lord (Prothero, R.E.) 1961. *English Farming Past and Present*, 6th edition. Heinemann, London.

Eswaran, H. 1994. Soil resilience and sustainable land management in the context of AGENDA 21. In: *Soil Resilience and Sustainable Land Use* (eds. D.J. Greenland and I. Szabolcs), pp. 21–39. CAB International, Wallingford.

Evans, H.J. and Barber, L.E. 1977. Biological nitrogen fixation for food and fibre production. *Science* **197**, 332–339.

Evans, L.T. 1997. Adapting and improving crops: the endless task. *Philosophical Transactions of the Royal Society of London* **B352**, 901–906.

Evans, L.T. 1998. *Feeding the Ten Billion: Plants and Population Growth.* Cambridge University Press, Cambridge.

Fairbanks, R.G. 1989. A 17,000 year glacio-eustatic sea-level record: influence of glacial melting rates on the Younger Dryas event and deep ocean circulation. *Nature, London* **342**, 637–642.

Falkenmark, M. 1997. Meeting water requirements of an expanding world population. *Philosophical Transactions of the Royal Society of London* **B352**, 929–936.

Falkenmark, M. and Lindh, G. 1974. How can we cope with the water resource situation in the year 2015? *Ambio* **3**, 114–122.

FAO 1978–1981. *Reports of the Agro-Ecological Zones Project.* World Soil Resources Report No. 48, Vol. 1–4. Rome. (See Alexandratos, 1995)

FAO 1995. *Irrigation in Africa in Figures.* Water Reports No. 7. FAO, Rome.

FAO 1999. *Yearbook Fertilizer* **49**, 15. FAO, Rome.

FAO–UNESCO 1971–1981. *FAO–UNESCO Soil Map of the World 1:5 000 000*, Vols. 1–10. UNESCO, Paris; revised legend 1988, FAO, Rome.

Fellows, R.J., Ainsworth, C.C., Driver, C.J. and Cataldo, D.A. 1998. Dynamics and transformations in soils and ecosystem health. In: *Soil Chemistry and Ecosystem Health* (ed. P.M. Huang), pp. 85–132. SSSA Special Publication No. 52. Soil Science Society of America, Madison, Wisconsin.

Fischer, G. and Heilig, G.K. 1997. Population momentum and the demand on land and water resources. *Philosophical Transactions of the Royal Society of London* **B352**, 869–889.

Fischer, G., Shah, M., van Velthuizen, H. and Nachtergaele, F.O. 2001. *Global Agro-Ecological Assessment for Agriculture in the 21st Century.* International Institute for Applied Systems Analysis, Laxenburg.

Floate, M.J.S. 1978. Changes in soil pools. In: *Cycling of Mineral Nutrients in Agricultural Ecosystems* (ed. M.J. Frissel), pp. 292–295. Elsevier, Amsterdam.

Folland, C.K., Karl, T. and Vinnikov, K.Ya. 1990. Observed climate variations and change. In: *Climate Change* (eds. J.T. Houghton, G.J. Jenkins and J.J. Ephraums), pp. 195–238. Cambridge University Press, Cambridge.

Foster, G.R. 1988. Modeling soil erosion and sediment yield. In: *Soil Erosion Research Methods* (ed. R. Lal), pp. 97–117. Soil and Water Conservation Society, Ankeny, Iowa.

Foster, G.R. 1990. Process-based modelling of soil by water on agricultural land. In: *Soil Erosion on Agricultural Land* (eds. J. Boardman, I.D.L. Foster and J.A. Dearing), pp. 429–445. Wiley, Chichester.

Frissel, M.J. (ed.) 1978. *Cycling of Mineral Nutrients in Agricultural Ecosystems*. Elsevier, Amsterdam.

Fussell, G.E. 1965. *Farming Technique from Prehistoric to Modern Times*. Pergamon Press, Oxford.

Gaitskell, A. 1959. *Gezira, a Story of Development in the Sudan*. Faber and Faber, London.

Gardner, W.K., Barber, D.A. and Parbery, D.G. 1983. The acquisition of phosphorus by *Lupinus albus* L. III. The probable mechanism by which phosphorus movement in the soil-root interface is enhanced. *Plant and Soil* **70**, 107–124.

Garnaut, R., Cai, F. and Huang, Y. 1996. A turning point in China's agricultural development. In: *The Third Revolution in the Chinese Countryside* (eds. R. Garnaut, G. Shutian and M. Guonan), pp. 185–198. Cambridge University Press, Cambridge.

Garnaut, R. and Guonan, M. 1996. The third revolution. In: *The Third Revolution in the Chinese Countryside* (eds. R. Garnaut, G. Shutian and M. Guonan), pp. 1–9. Cambridge University Press, Cambridge.

Garnaut, R., Shutian, G. and Guonan, M. (eds.) 1996. *The Third Revolution in the Chinese Countryside*. Cambridge University Press, Cambridge.

GEO-2000 1999. *Global Environment Outlook 2000*. UNEP, Earthscan Publications Ltd, London.

Giardina, C.P. and Ryan, M.G. 2000. Evidence that decomposition rates of organic carbon in mineral soils do not vary with temperature. *Nature, London* **404**, 858–861.

Giller, K.E., Cadisch, G., Ehaliotis, C., Adams, E., Sakala, W.D. and Mafongoya, P.L. 1997. Building soil nitrogen capital in Africa. In: *Replenishing Soil Fertility in Africa* (eds. R.J. Buresh, P.A. Sanchez and F. Calhoun), pp. 151–192. SSSA Special Publication No. 51. Soil Science Society of America, Madison, Wisconsin.

Gleick, P.H. (ed.) 1993. *Water in Crisis: A Guide to the World's Fresh Water Resources*. Oxford University Press, Oxford.

Glover, I.C. and Higham, C.F.W. 1996. New evidence for early rice cultivation in south, Southeast and East Asia. In: *The Origins and Spread of Agriculture and Pastoralism in Eurasia* (ed. D.R. Harris), pp. 413–441. University College Press, London.

Goedert, W.J. 1983. Management of the cerrado soils of Brazil: a review. *Journal of Soil Science* **34**, 405–428.

Goldsworthy, P.R. 1967a. Responses of cereals to fertilizers in Northern Nigeria. I. Sorghum. *Experimental Agriculture* **3**, 29–40.

Goldsworthy, P.R. 1967b. Responses of cereals to fertilizers in Northern Nigeria. II. Maize. *Experimental Agriculture* **3**, 263–273.

Goldsworthy, P.R. and Heathcote, R.G. 1963. Fertilizer trials with groundnuts in northern Nigeria. *Empire Journal of Experimental Agriculture* **31**, 351–366.

Goudie, A. 1995. *The Changing Earth.* Blackwell, Oxford.

Goulding, K.W.T. 2000. Nitrate leaching from arable and horticultural land. *Soil Use and Management* **16**, 145–151.

Goulding, K.W.T., Poulton, P.R., Webster, C.P. and Howe, M.T. 2000. Nitrate leaching from the Broadbalk Wheat Experiment, Rothamsted, UK, as influenced by fertilizer and manure inputs and the weather. *Soil Use and Management* **16**, 244–250.

Greenland, D.J. 1981. *Characterization of Soils in Relation to their Classification and Management for Crop Production. Examples from Some Areas of the Humid Tropics.* Clarendon Press, Oxford.

Greenland, D.J. 1997. *The Sustainability of Rice Farming.* CAB International, Wallingford.

Greenland, D.J. and Murray-Rust, D.H. 1986. Irrigation demand in humid areas. *Philosophical Transactions of the Royal Society of London* **A316**, 275–294.

Greenland, D.J. and Szabolcs, I. (eds.) 1994. *Soil Resilience and Sustainable Land Use.* CAB International, Wallingford.

Greenland, D.J., Wild, A. and Adams, D. 1992. Organic matter dynamics in soils of the tropics–from myth to reality. In: *Myths and Science of Soils in the Tropics* (eds. R. Lal and P.A. Sanchez), pp. 17–39. Soil Science Society of America, Madison, Wisconsin.

Greenwood, M. 1951. Fertilizer trials with groundnuts in Northern Nigeria. *Empire Journal of Experimental Agriculture* **19**, 225–241.

Gregorich, E.G. and Carter, M.R. (eds.) 1997. *Soil Quality for Crop Production and Ecosystem Health.* Elsevier, Amsterdam.

Gregory, P.J. 1988a. Growth and functioning of plant roots. In: *Russell's Soil Conditions and Plant Growth* (ed. A. Wild), pp. 113–167. Longman, Harlow.

Gregory, P.J. 1988b. Water and crop growth. In: *Russell's Soil Conditions and Plant Growth* (ed. A. Wild), pp. 338–377. Longman, Harlow.

Gregory, P.J., Simmonds, L.P. and Warren, G. 1997. Interactions between plant nutrients, water and carbon dioxide as factors limiting crop yields. *Philosophical Transactions of the Royal Society of London* **B352**, 987–996.

Grigg, D. 1987. The industrial revolution and land transformation. In: *Land Transformation in Agriculture* (eds. M.G. Wolman and F.G.A. Fournier), pp. 79–109. SCOPE No. 32. Wiley, Chichester.

Grigg, D. 1993. *The World Food Problem*, 2nd edition. Blackwell, Oxford.

Grigg, D.B. 1974. *The Agricultural Systems of the World: An Evolutionary Approach.* Cambridge University Press, Cambridge.

Halstead, P. 1990. Quantifying Sumerian agriculture – some seeds of doubt and hope. *Bulletin on Sumerian Agriculture* **V**, 187–195.

Harlan, J.R. 1989a. Wild-grass harvesting in the Sahara and Sub-Sahara of Africa. In: *Foraging and Farming: The Evolution of Plant Exploitation* (eds. D.R. Harris and G.C. Hillman), pp. 120–135. Unwin Hyman, London.

Harlan, J.R. 1989b. The tropical African cereals. In: *Foraging and Farming: The Evolution of Plant Exploitation* (eds. D.R. Harris and G.C. Hillman), pp. 335–343. Unwin Hyman, London.

Harley, J.L. and Smith, S.E. 1983. *Mycorrhizal Symbiosis.* Academic Press, London.

Harris, D.R. 1996. Introduction: themes and concepts in the study of early agriculture. In: *The Origins and Spread of Agriculture and Pastoralism in Eurasia* (ed. D.R. Harris), pp. 1–9. University College Press, London.

Harris, H.C. 1995. Long-term trials on soil and crop management at ICARDA. In: *Soil Management: Experimental Basis for Sustainability and Environmental Quality* (eds. R. Lal and B.A. Stewart), pp. 447–469. CRC Press, Lewis Publishers, Boca Raton, Florida.

Harris, P.J. 1988a. The microbial population of the soil. In: *Russell's Soil Conditions and Plant Growth* (ed. A. Wild), pp. 449–471. Longman, Harlow.

Harris, P.J. 1988b. Microbial transformations of nitrogen. In: *Russell's Soil Conditions and Plant Growth* (ed. A. Wild), pp. 608–651. Longman, Harlow.

Harwood, R.R. 1990. A history of sustainable agriculture. In: *Sustainable Agricultural Systems* (eds. C.A. Edwards, R. Lal, P. Madden, R.H. Miller and G. House), pp. 3–19. Soil and Water Conservation Society, Ankeny, Iowa.

Hassan, P.A. 1983. Environment and subsistence in Predynastic Egypt. In: *From Hunters to Farmers* (eds. J.D. Clark and S.A. Brandt), pp. 57–64. University of California Press, Berkeley, California.

Hastenrath, S. 1991. *Climate Dynamics of the Tropics*. Kluwer Academic, Dordrecht.

Havlin, J.L. and Jacobsen, J.S. 1994. (eds.) *Soil Testing: Prospects for Improving Nutrient Recommendations*. SSSA Special Publication No. 40. Soil Science Society of America, Madison, Wisconsin.

Hawkes, J.G. 1989. The domestication of roots and tubers in the American Tropics. In: *Foraging and Farming: The Evolution of Plant Exploitation* (eds. D.R. Harris and G.C. Hillman), pp. 481–503. Unwin Hyman, London.

Hayes, K.F. and Traina, S.J. 1998. Metal ion speciation and its significance in ecosystem health. In: *Soil Chemistry and Ecosystem Health* (ed. P.M. Huang), pp. 45–84. SSSA Special Publication No. 52. Soil Science Society of America, Madison, Wisconsin.

Hayward, M.D., Bosemark, N.O. and Romagosa, I. (eds.) 1993. *Plant Breeding: Principles and Prospects*. Chapman and Hall, London.

Heisey, P.W. and Mwangi, W. 1997. Fertilizer use and maize production. In: *Africa's Emerging Maize Revolution* (eds. D. Byerlee and C.K. Eicher), pp. 193–211. Lynne Rienner pub., Inc., Boulder, Colorado.

Higgs, E.S. and Jarman, M.R. 1972. The origins of animal and plant husbandry. In: *Papers in Economic Prehistory* (ed. E.S. Higgs), pp. 3–13. Cambridge University Press, Cambridge.

Hillel, D. 1980a. *Fundamentals of Soil Physics*. Academic Press, San Diego, California.

Hillel, D. 1980b. *Applications of Soil Physics*. Academic Press, San Diego, California.

Hillel, D. 1994. *Rivers of Eden: The Struggle for Water and the Quest for Peace in the Middle East*. Oxford University Press, Oxford.

Hillel, D.J. 1991. *Out of the Earth: Civilization and the Life of the Soil*. The Free Press, New York.

Hillman, G. 1996. Late Pleistocene changes in wild-plant foods available to hunter-gatherers of the northern Fertile Crescent: possible preludes to cereal cultivation. In: *The Origins and Spread of Agriculture and Pastoralism in Eurasia* (ed. D.R. Harris), pp. 159–203. University College Press, London.

HMSO 1996. *Sustainable Use of Soil*. Royal Commission on Environmental Pollution, 19th Report. HMSO, London.

Hole, F. 1996. The context of caprine domestication in the Zagros region. In: *The Origins and Spread of Agriculture and Pastoralism in Eurasia* (ed. D.R. Harris), pp. 263–281. University College Press, London.

Hood, T.M. and Jones, J.B., Jr (eds.) 1997. *Soil and Plant Analysis in Sustainable Agriculture and Environment*. Dekker, New York.

Hornung, M. and Skeffington, R.A. (eds.) 1993. *Critical Loads: Concept and Applications*. Institute of Terrestrial Ecology Symposium No. 28. HMSO, London.

Houghton, J. 1997. *Global Warming: The Complete Briefing*, 2nd edition. Cambridge University Press, Cambridge.

Howells, G. 1995. *Acid Rain and Acid Waters*, 2nd edition. Ellis Horwood, New York.

Huang, J. and Rozelle, S. 1994. Environmental stress yields in China. *American Journal of Agricultural Economics* **77**, 853–864.

Huang, P.M. (ed.) 1998. *Soil Chemistry and Ecosystem Health.* SSSA Special Publication No. 52. Soil Science Society of America, Madison, Wisconsin.

Hudson, N. 1995. *Soil Conservation*, 2nd edition. Batsford, London.

Hyams, E. 1952. *Soil and Civilization*. Thames and Hudson, London.

Hyden, G., Kates, R.W. and Turner, B.L., II 1993. Beyond intensification. In: *Population Growth and Agricultural Change in Africa* (eds. B.L. Turner II, G. Hyden and R.W. Kates), pp. 401–439. University Press of Florida, Gainesville, Florida.

ICARDA 1985. *Annual Report for 1984*, pp. 12–17. International Center for Agricultural Research in the Dry Areas, Aleppo.

IPCC 2001a. *Climate Change 2001: The Scientific Basis.* Cambridge University Press, Cambridge.

IPCC 2001b. *Climate Change 2001: Impacts, Adaptation, and Vulnerability.* Cambridge University Press, Cambridge.

Isager, S. and Skydsgaard, J.E. 1992. *Ancient Greek Agriculture: An Introduction.* Routledge, London.

Jacks, G.V. and Whyte, R.O. 1939. *The Rape of the Earth: A World Survey of Soil Erosion.* Faber and Faber, London.

Jackson, I.J. 1989. *Climate, Water and Agriculture in the Tropics*, 2nd edition. Longman, Harlow.

Jacobsen, Th. 1982. *Salinity and Irrigation Agriculture in Antiquity. Diyala Basin Archaeological Projects: Report on Essential Results 1957-8.* Bibliotheca Mesopotamia No. 14. Udena Publications, Malibu, California.

Jacobsen, Th. and Adams, R.McC. 1958. Salt and silt in ancient Mesopotamian agriculture. *Science* **128**, 1251–1258.

James, D.W., Hanks, R.J. and Jurinak, J.J. 1982. *Modern Irrigated Soils.* Wiley-Interscience, New York.

Jarvis, S.C. 2000. Progress in studies of nitrate leaching from grassland soils. *Soil Use and Management* **16**, 152–156.

Jenkins, A. 1999. End of the acid reign? *Nature, London* **501**, 537–538.

Jenkinson, D.S. 1988. Soil organic matter and its dynamics. In: *Russell's Soil Conditions and Plant Growth* (ed. A. Wild), pp. 564–607. Longman, Harlow.

Jenkinson, D.S. 1990. The turnover of organic carbon and nitrogen in soil. *Philosophical Transactions of the Royal Society of London* **B329**, 361–368.

Jenkinson, D.S., Adams, D.E. and Wild, A. 1991. Model estimates of CO_2 emissions from soil in response to global warming. *Nature, London* **351**, 304–306.

Jenny, H. 1941. *Factors of Soil Formation: A System of Quantitative Pedology.* McGraw-Hill, New York.

Jenny, H. 1962. Model of a rising nitrogen profile in Nile valley alluvium and its agronomic and pedogenic implications. *Soil Science Society of America Proceedings* **26**, 588–591.

Johnson, D.W. and Lindberg, S.E. (eds.) 1992. *Atmospheric Deposition and Forest Nutrient Cycling.* Springer-Verlag, New York.

Jones, M.J. 1973. The organic matter content of the savanna soils of West Africa. *Journal of Soil Science* **24**, 42–53.

Jones, M.J. and Wahbi, A. 1992. Site-factor influence on barley response to fertilizer in on-farm trials in northern Syria: descriptive and predictive models. *Experimental Agriculture* **28**, 63–87.

Juo, A.S.R. and Lal, R. 1977. The effect of fallow and continuous cultivation on the chemical and physical properties of an Alfisol in Western Nigeria. *Plant and Soil* **47**, 567–584.

Kalirajan, K.P. and Wu, Y. 1999. *Productivity and Growth in Chinese Agriculture*. Macmillan, Basingstoke.

Kang, B.T., Donkoh, F. and Moody, K. 1977. Soil fertility management investigations on benchmark soils in the humid low altitude tropics of West Africa. Investigations on Egbeda soil series. *Agronomy Journal* **69**, 651–657.

Kang, B.T. and Fox, R.L. 1981. Management of the soils for continuous production: controlling the nutrient status. In: *Characterization of Soils in Relation to their Classification and Management for Crop Production: Examples from Some Areas of the Humid Tropics* (ed. D.J. Greenland), pp. 202–213. Clarendon Press, Oxford.

Karlen, D.L., Mausbach, M.J., Doran, J.W., Cline, R.G., Harris, R.F. and Schumann, G.E. 1997. Soil quality: a concept definition and framework for evaluation. *Soil Science Society of America Journal* **61**, 4–10.

Kay, M. 1986. *Surface Irrigation: Systems and Practice*. Cranfield Press, Cranfield.

Keating, B.A., Wafula, B.M. and Watiki, J.M. 1992. Development of a modelling capability for maize in semi-arid eastern Kenya. In: *A Search for Sustainable Dryland Cropping in Semi-Arid Eastern Kenya* (ed. M.E. Probert), pp. 26–33. ACIAR, Canberra.

Kemp, B.J. 1989. *Ancient Egypt: Anatomy of a Civilization*. Routledge, London.

Killham, K. 1994. *Soil Ecology*. Cambridge University Press, Cambridge.

Kinjo, T. and Pratt, P.F. 1971. Nitrate adsorption: I. In some acid soils of Mexico and South America. *Soil Science Society of America Proceedings* **35**, 722–725.

Kirkby, J., O'Keefe, P. and Timberlake, L. (eds.) 1995. *The Earthscan Reader in Sustainable Development*. Earthscan Publications Ltd, London.

Kirkby, M.J. 1980. Modelling water erosion processes. In: *Soil Erosion* (eds. M.J. Kirkby and R.P.C. Morgan), pp. 183–216. Wiley, Chichester.

Kirkby, M.J. and Morgan, R.P.C. (eds.) 1980. *Soil Erosion*. Wiley, Chichester.

Kolata, A.L. 1986. The agricultural foundations of the Tiwanaku State: a view from the heartland. *American Antiquity* **51**, 748–762.

Ladizinsky, G. 1989. Origin and domestication of the Southwest Asian grain legumes. In: *Foraging and Farming: The Evolution of Plant Exploitation* (eds. D.R. Harris and G.C. Hillman), pp. 374–389. Unwin Hyman, London.

Laegreid, M., Bøckman, O.C. and Kaarstad, O. 1999. *Agriculture, Fertilizers and the Environment*. CAB International, Wallingford.

Lal, R. (ed.) 1988. *Soil Erosion Research Methods*. Soil and Water Conservation Society, Ankeny, Iowa.

Lal, R. 1989a. Agroforestry systems and soil surface management of a tropical alfisol: IV Effects on soil physical and mechanical properties. *Agroforestry Systems* **8**, 197–215. (See also earlier papers)

Lal, R. 1989b. Conservation tillage for sustainable agriculture: tropics versus temperate environments. *Advances in Agronomy* **42**, 85–197.

Lal, R. (ed.) 1993. *World Soil Erosion and Conservation*. Cambridge University Press, Cambridge.

Lal, R. 1994. Sustainable land use systems and soil resilience. In: *Soil Resilience and Sustainable Land Use* (eds. D.J. Greenland and I. Szabolcs), pp. 41–67. CAB International, Wallingford.

Lal, R. 1995. Technological options for sustainable management of alfisols and ultisols in Nigeria. In: *Soil Management: Experimental Basis for Sustainability and Environmental Quality* (eds. R. Lal and B.A. Stewart), pp. 123–134. CRC Press, Lewis Publishers, Boca Raton, Florida.

Lal, R. 1997. Degradation and resilience of soils. *Philosophical Transactions of the Royal Society of London* **B352**, 997–1010.

Lal, R. and Greenland, D.J. (eds.) 1979. *Soil Physical Properties and Crop Production in the Tropics*. Wiley, Chichester.

Lal, R., Kimple, J.M. and Stewart, B.A. (eds.) 1999. *Global Climate Change and Tropical Ecosystems*. Advances in Soil Science. CRC Press, Boca Raton, Florida.

Lal, R. and Pierce, F.J. (eds.) 1991. *Soil Management for Sustainability*. Soil and Water Conservation Society, Ankeny, Iowa.

Lal, R. and Stewart, B.A. 1995. *Soil Management: Experimental Basis for Sustainability and Environmental Quality*. CRC Press, Lewis Publishers, Boca Raton, Florida.

Lamb, H.H. 1977. *Climate Present, Past and Future*, Vol. 2, *Climatic History and the Future*. Methuen, London.

Lamb, H.H. 1995. *Climate, History and the Modern World*, 2nd edition. Routledge, London.

Landon, J.R. (ed.) 1991. *Booker Tropical Soil Manual*. Longman, Harlow.

Landsberg, H.E. (Editor in Chief) 1985–1995. *World Survey of Climatology*, Vols. **1–16**. Elsevier, Amsterdam.

Laryea, K.B., Anders, M.M. and Pathak, P. 1995. Long-term experiments on Alfisols and Vertisols in the semiarid tropics. In: *Soil Management: Experimental Basis for Sustainability and Environmental Quality* (eds. R. Lal and B.A. Stewart), pp. 267–292. CRC Press, Lewis Publishers, Boca Raton, Florida.

Latham, A.J.H. 1998. *Rice: The Primary Commodity*. Routledge, London.

Le Mare, P.H. 1953. Responses of fertilizers in areas of Tanganyika farmed by the Overseas Food Corporation. *East African Agriculture Journal* **19**, 39–40.

Le Mare, P.H. 1972. A long term experiment on soil fertility and cotton yield in Tanzania. *Experimental Agriculture* **8**, 299–310.

Lee, R.B. and Daly, R. (eds.) 1999. *The Cambridge Encyclopaedia of Hunters and Gatherers*. Cambridge University Press, Cambridge.

Lees, G.M. and Falcon, N.L. 1952. The geographical history of the Mesopotamian plains. *Geographical Journal* **118**, 24–39.

Legge, A.H. and Krupa, S.V. (eds.) 1990. *Acidic Deposition: Sulphur and Nitrogen Oxides*. Lewis Publishers, Chelsea, Michigan.

Leigh, R.A. and Johnston, A.E. (eds.) 1994. *Long-Term Experiments in Agricultural and Ecological Sciences*. CAB International, Wallingford.

Lewis, N. 1983. *Life in Egypt under Roman Rule*. Clarendon Press, Oxford.

Likens, C.E., Bormann, F.H., Pierce, R.S., Eaton, J.S. and Johnson, N.M. 1977. *Biogeochemistry of a Forested Ecosystem*. Springer-Verlag, New York.

Lin, J.Y. 1996. Success in early reform: setting the stages. In: *The Third Revolution in the Chinese Countryside* (eds. R. Garnaut, G. Shutian and M. Guonan), pp. 13–26. Cambridge University Press, Cambridge.

Lobato, E. 1980. *Adubacao fosfatada emsolos sob vegetacao de cerrado*. EMBRAPA Centro de Pesquisa Agropecuaria dos Cerrados, Planaltina-DF, Brazil. (From Goedert, 1983)

Loch, J.P.G. 1996. Behaviour and fate of organic contaminants in soil and groundwater. In: *Soil Pollution and Soil Protection* (eds. F.A.M. de Haan and M.I. Visser-Reyneveld), pp. 181–199. International Training Centre, Agricultural University, Wageningen.

Long, M., Entekhabi, D. and Nicholson, S.E. 2000. Interannual variability in rainfall, water vapour flux, and vertical motion over West Africa. *Journal of Climatology* **13**, 3827–3841.

Loughran, R.J., Campbell, B.L. and Elliott, G.L. 1990. The calculation of net soil loss using caesium-137. In: *Soil Erosion on Agricultural Land* (eds. J. Boardman, I.D.L. Foster and J.A. Dearing), pp. 119–126. Wiley, Chichester.

Lowrance, R.R., Todd, R.L., Asmussen, L.E. and Leonard, R.A. (eds.) 1983. *Nutrient Cycling in Agricultural Ecosystems*. University of Georgia College of

Agricultural Experiment Station Special Publication No. 23. University of Georgia, Athens, Georgia.

Lundgren, B. 1982. Introduction. *Agroforestry Systems* 1, 1–6.

Lutz, W., Sanderson, W. and Scherbov, S. 2001. The end of world population growth. *Nature, London* 412, 543–545.

Macilwain, C. 1999. Access issues may determine whether agri-biotech will help the world's poor. *Nature, London* 402, 341–345.

Malthus, T.R. 1798. *An Essay on the Principle of Population.* The first edition with introduction and bibliography edited by E.A. Wrigley and D. Souden, 1986. William Pickering, London.

Marschner, H. 1995. *Mineral Nutrition of Higher Plants,* 2nd edition. Academic Press, London.

Marschner, H. 1998. Soil–root interface: biological and biochemical processes. In: *Soil Chemistry and Ecosystem Health* (ed. P.M. Huang), pp. 191–231. SSSA Special Publication 52. Soil Science Society of America, Madison, Wisconsin.

Marshall, T.J., Holmes, J.W. and Rose, C.W. 1996. *Soil Physics,* 3rd edition. Cambridge University Press, Cambridge.

Mason, B.J. 1992. *Acid Rain: Its Causes and its Effects on Inland Waters.* Clarendon Press, Oxford.

McBride, M.B. 1994. *Environmental Chemistry of Soils.* Oxford University Press, Oxford.

McCaffrey, S.C. 1993. Water, politics and international law. In: *Water in Crisis: A Guide to the World's Fresh Water Resources* (ed. P.H. Gleick), pp. 92–104. Oxford University Press, Oxford.

McCown, R.L. and Keating, B.A. 1992. Looking forward: finding a path for sustainable farm development. In: *A Search for Sustainable Dryland Cropping in Semi-Arid Eastern Kenya* (ed. M.E. Probert), pp. 126–132. ACIAR, Canberra.

McDonald, A. and Kay, D. 1988. *Water Resources: Issues and Strategies.* Longman, Harlow.

McDowell, L.R. 1992. *Minerals in Animals and Human Nutrition.* Academic Press, San Diego, California.

McGregor, G.R. and Nieuwolt, G. 1998. *Tropical Climatology: An Introduction to the Climates of Low Latitudes,* 2nd edition. Wiley, Chichester.

McLaughlin, M.J., Smolders, E. and Merckx, R. 1998. Soil–root interface: physicochemical processes. In: *Soil Chemistry and Ecosystem Health* (ed. P.M. Huang), pp. 233–277. Soil Science Society of America, Madison, Wisconsin.

Mitchell, J.K. and Bubenzer, G.D. 1980. Soil loss estimation. In: *Soil Erosion* (eds. M.J. Kirkby and R.F.C. Morgan), pp. 17–62. Wiley, Chichester.

Monteith, J.L. 1975. *Principles of Environmental Physics.* Arnold, London.

Monteith, J.L. and Ingram, J.S.I. 1998. Climatic variation and crop growth. In: *Crop Productivity and Sustainability: Shaping the Future* (eds. V.L. Chopra, R.B. Singh and A. Varma), pp. 57–70. Proceedings of the 2nd International Crop Science Congress. Science Publishers, Enfield, New Hampshire.

Morgan, R.P.C. 1995. *Soil Erosion and Conservation,* 2nd edition. Longman, Harlow.

Mortimore, M. 1989. *Adapting to Drought: Farmers, Famines and Desertification in West Africa.* Cambridge University Press, Cambridge.

Mortimore, M. 1993. The intensification of peri-urban agriculture: the Kano close-settled zone, 1964–1986. In: *Population Growth and Agricultural Change in Africa* (eds. B.L. Turner II, G. Hyden and R.W. Kates), pp. 358–400. University Press of Florida, Gainesville, Florida.

Moseley, M.E. 1992. *The Incas and their Ancestors. The Archaeology of Peru.* Thames and Hudson, London.

Mueller-Harvey, I., Juo, A.S.R. and Wild, A. 1985. Soil organic C, N, S and P after forest clearance in Nigeria: mineralization rates and spatial variability. *Journal of Soil Science* **36**, 585–591.

Mueller-Harvey, I., Juo, A.S.R. and Wild, A. 1989. Mineralization of nutrients after forest clearance and their uptake during cropping. In: *Mineral Nutrients in Tropical Forest and Savanna Ecosystems* (ed. J. Proctor), pp. 315–324. British Ecological Society Special Publication. Blackwell, Oxford.

Murty, V.V.N. and Takeuchi, K. 1996. *Land and Water Development for Agriculture in the Asia-Pacific Region.* Science Publishers, Lebanon, New Hampshire.

Mutchler, C.K., Murphree, C.E. and McGregor, K.C. 1988. Laboratory and field plots for soil erosion studies. In: *Soil Erosion Research Methods* (ed. R. Lal), pp. 9–36. Soil and Water Conservation Society, Ankeny, Iowa.

Nair, P.K.R. 1993. *An Introduction to Agroforestry.* Kluwer Academic, Dordrecht.

National Research Council 1993a. *Sustainable Agriculture and the Environment in the Humid Tropics.* National Academy Press, Washington, DC.

National Research Council 1993b. *Soil and Water Quality. An Agenda for Agriculture.* National Academy Press, Washington, DC.

Needham, J. 1971. *Science and Civilization in China*, Vol. 4, Part III. Cambridge University Press, Cambridge.

Newman, J. 1988. The soil fauna other than protozoa. In: *Russell's Soil Conditions and Plant Growth* (ed. A. Wild), pp. 500–525. Longman, Harlow.

Nicholson, S.E. 1989. Long-term changes in African rainfall. *Weather* **44**, 46–56.

Nicholson, S.E. 1993. An overview of African rainfall fluctuations of the last decade. *Journal of Climatology* **6**, 1463–1466.

Nilsson, J. and Grennfelt, P. (eds.) 1988. *Critical Loads for Sulphur and Nitrogen.* Report 1988:15. Nordic Council of Ministers, Copenhagen.

Nir, D. and Finkel, H.J. 1982. Water requirements of crops and irrigation rates. In: *CRC Handbook of Irrigation Technology*, Vol. 1 (ed. H.J. Finkel), pp. 61–77. CRC Press, Boca Raton, Florida.

Nortcliff, S. 1988. Soil formation and characteristics of soil profiles. In: *Russell's Soil Conditions and Plant Growth* (ed. A. Wild), pp. 168–212. Longman, Harlow.

Nye, P.H. 1953. A survey of the value of fertilizers to the food-farming areas of the Gold Coast II. The granitic soils of the far north. *Empire Journal of Experimental Agriculture* **21**, 262–274.

Nye, P.H. 1954. A survey of the value of fertilizers to the food-farming areas of the Gold Coast III. The Voltaian sandstone region and the southern maize areas. *Empire Journal of Experimental Agriculture* **22**, 42–54.

Nye, P.H. and Greenland, D.J. 1960. *The Soil Under Shifting Cultivation.* Commonwealth Bureau of Soils Technical Communication No. 51. Harpenden.

Oldeman, L.R. 1994. The global extent of soil degradation. In: *Soil Resilience and Sustainable Land Use* (eds. D.J. Greenland and I. Szabolcs), pp. 99–118. CAB International, Wallingford.

Oldeman, L.R., Hakkeling, R.T.A. and Sombroek, W.G. 1991. *World Map of the Status of Human-Induced Soil Degradation: An Explanatory Note*, 2nd edition. International Soil Reference and Information Centre, Wageningen.

Oliver, M.A. 1997. Soil and human health: a review. *European Journal of Soil Science* **48**, 573–592.

O'Neill, B.C., MacKellar, F.L. and Lutz, W. 2001. *Population and Climate Change.* Cambridge University Press, Cambridge.

Overton, M. 1996. *Agricultural Revolution in England: The Transformation of the Agrarian Economy 1500–1850.* Cambridge University Press, Cambridge.

Pankhurst, C., Doube, B.M. and Gupta, V.V.S.R. (eds.) 1997. *Biological Indicators of Soil Health*. CAB International, Wallingford.

Parsons, J.W. and Tinsley, J. 1975. Nitrogenous substances. In: *Soil Components*, Vol. I (ed. J.E. Gieseking), pp. 263–304. Springer-Verlag, New York.

Partridge, M. 1973. *Farm Tools through the Ages*. Oxprey, Reading.

Paul, E.A., Paustian, K., Elliott, E.T. and Cole, C.V. 1996. *Soil Organic Matter in Temperate Agroecosystems: Long-Term Experiments in North America*. CRC Press, Boca Raton, New York.

Pearsall, D.M. 1992. The origins of plant cultivation in South America. In: *The Origins of Agriculture: An International Perspective* (eds. C.W. Cowan and P.J. Watson), pp. 173–205. Smithsonian Institute Press, Washington, DC.

Pereira, H.C. 1973. *Land Use and Water Resources in Temperate and Tropical Climates*. Cambridge University Press, Cambridge.

Perkins, D.H. 1969. *Agricultural Development in China 1368–1968*. Edinburgh University Press, Edinburgh.

Peyre de Fabrègues, B. 1992. Observation on the ebb and flow of native grass species in the area of the Ekrafane Ranch, Sahel. In: *Desertified Grasslands: Their Biology and Management* (ed. G.P. Chapman), pp. 37–46. Linnean Society Symposium Series No. 13. Academic Press, London.

Pierce, F.J. and Sadler, E.J. (eds.) 1997. *The State of Site Specific Management for Agriculture*. American Society of Agronomy, Madison, Wisconsin.

Pieri, C. 1995. Long-term soil management experiments in semi-arid francophone Africa. In: *Soil Management: Experimental Basis for Sustainability and Environmental Quality* (eds. R. Lal and B.A. Stewart), pp. 225–266. CRC Press, Lewis Publishers, Boca Raton, Florida.

Pieri, C.J.M.G. 1992. *Fertility of Soils: A Future for Farming in the West African Savannah* (translated from the French by P. Gething). Springer-Verlag, Berlin.

Pierzynski, G.M., Sims, J.T. and Vance, G.F. 2000. *Soils and Environmental Quality*, 2nd edition. CRC Press, Boca Raton, Florida.

Pimental, D. (ed.) 1993. *World Soil Erosion and Conservation*. Cambridge University Press, Cambridge.

Pimental, D.C., Harvey, C. and Resosudarmo, P. 1995. Environmental and economic costs of soil erosion and conservation benefits. *Science* **267**, 1117–1123.

Pimm, S.L. and Raven, P. 2000. Extinction by numbers. *Nature, London* **403**, 843–845.

Pingali, P.L., Hossain, M. and Gerpacio, R.V. 1997. *Asian Rice Bowls: The Returning Crisis?* CAB International, Wallingford.

Platteau, J.P. 1992. *Land Reform and Social Adjustment in sub-Saharan Agriculture: Controversies and Guidelines*. FAO Economic and Social Development Paper No. 107. FAO, Rome.

Ploey, J. de and Gabriels, D. 1980. Measuring soil loss and experimental studies. In: *Soil Erosion* (eds. M.J. Kirkby and R.P.C. Morgan), pp. 63–108. Wiley, Chichester.

Postel, S. 1993. Water and agriculture. In: *Water in Crisis: A Guide to the World's Fresh Water Resources* (ed. P.H. Gleick), pp. 56–66. Oxford University Press, Oxford.

Postel, S.L., Dailey, G.C. and Ehrlich, P.R. 1996. Human appropriation of renewable fresh water. *Science* **271**, 785–788.

Postgate, J.N. 1990. A middle Tigris village. *Bulletin on Sumerian Agriculture* V, 65–74.

Postgate, J.N. 1994. *Early Mesopotamia*. Routledge, London.

Potts, W.T.W. and McWilliams, P.G. 1989. The effects of hydrogen and aluminium ions on fish gills. In: *Acid Toxicity and Aquatic Animals* (eds. R. Morris, E.W. Taylor, D.J.A. Brown and J.A. Brown), pp. 201–220. Cambridge University Press, Cambridge.

Powell, M.A. 1985. Salt, seed and yields in Sumerian agriculture. A critique of the theory of progressive salinization. *Zeitschrift für Assyriologie* **75**, 7–38.

Powlson, D.S., Smith, P. and Smith, J.U. (eds.) 1996. *Evaluation of Soil Organic Matter Models using Existing Long-Term Datasets*. Springer-Verlag, Berlin.

Price, T.D. 1996. The first farmers of southern Scandinavia. In: *The Origins and Spread of Agriculture and Pastoralism in Eurasia* (ed. D.R. Harris), pp. 346–362. University College Press, London.

Quiñones, M.A., Borlaug, N.E. and Dowswell, C.R. 1997. A fertilizer-based green revolution for Africa. In: *Replenishing Soil Fertility in Africa* (eds. R.J. Buresh, P.A. Sanchez and F. Calhoun), pp. 81–95. SSSA Special Publication No. 51. Soil Science Society of America, Madison, Wisconsin.

Qureshi, R.H., Aslam, M. and Rafiq, M. 1991. Expansion in the use of forage halophytes in Pakistan. In: *Productive Use of Saline Land* (eds. N. Davidson and R.G. Galloway), pp. 12–16. Proceedings No. 42. ACIAR, Canberra.

Raglan, J. and Lal, R. (eds.) 1993. *Technologies for Sustainable Agriculture in the Tropics*. ASA Special Publication No. 56. American Society of Agronomy, Madison, Wisconsin.

Redman, C.L. 1978. *The Rise of Civilization*. Freeman, San Francisco, California.

Renard, K.G., Foster, K.G., Weesies, G.A. and Porter, J.P. 1997. *Predicting Soil Erosion by Water: A Guide to Conservation Planning with the Revised Universal Soil Loss Equation (RUSLE)*. USDA Agricultural Handbook No. 703. United States Department of Agriculture, Washington, DC.

Rengel, Z. (ed.) 1998. *Nutrient Use in Crop Production*. The Haworth Press, New York.

Rengel, Z. (ed.) 1999. *Mineral Nutrition of Crops: Fundamental Mechanisms and Implications*. The Haworth Press, New York.

Reuss, J.O. and Johnson, D.W. 1986. *Acid Deposition and the Acidification of Soils and Waters*. Springer-Verlag, New York.

Richardson, S.J. and Smith, J. 1977. Peat wastage in the East Anglian Fens. *Journal of Soil Science* **28**, 485–489.

Rindos, D. 1984. *The Origins of Agriculture: An Evolutionary Perspective*. Academic Press, New York.

Rissler, J. and Mellon, M. 1996. *The Ecological Risks of Engineered Crops*. The MIT Press, Cambridge, Massachusetts.

Roberts, N. 1998. *The Holocene: An Environmental History*, 2nd edition. Blackwell, Oxford.

Rounsevell, M.D.A. and Loveland, P.J. (eds.) 1994. *Soil Responses to Climate Change*. NATO ASI Series: Global Environmental Change, Vol. 23. Springer-Verlag, Berlin.

Rowell, D.L. 1988. Soil acidity and alkalinity. In: *Russell's Soil Conditions and Plant Growth* (ed. A. Wild), pp. 844–898. Longman, Harlow.

Rowell, D.L. 1994. *Soil Science: Methods and Applications*. Longman, Harlow.

Russell, E.W. 1968. The place of fertilizers in food crop economy of tropical Africa. *Proceedings of the Fertilizer Society* **101**, London.

Ruthenberg, R. 1980. *Farming Systems in the Tropics*, 3rd edition. Clarendon Press, Oxford.

Said, R. 1993. *The River Nile: Geology, Hydrology and Utilization*. Pergamon Press, Oxford.

Sanchez, P.A. 1976. *Properties and Management of Soils in the Tropics*. Wiley-Interscience, New York.

Sanchez, P.A., Buresh, R.J. and Leakey, R.R.B. 1997. Trees, soils and food security. *Philosophical Transactions of the Royal Society of London* **B352**, 949–961.

Sanlaville, P. 1992. Sciences de la terre et archéologie: l'evolution de la Basse-Mésopotamie a l'Holocéne. *Memoire de la Société Géologique de France*, N.S. **160**, 11–18.

Scharpenseel, H.W., Schomaker, M. and Ayoub, A. (eds.) 1990. *Soils on a Warmer Earth*. Springer-Verlag, Berlin.

Schulin, R., Desaules, A., Webster, R. and Steiger, B. von (eds.) 1993. *Soil Monitoring. Early Detection and Surveying of Soil Contamination and Degradation*. Birkhäuser Verlag, Basel.

Schulze, E.-D. and Freer-Smith, P.H. 1991. An evaluation of forest decline based on field observations focused on Norway spruce, *Picea abies*. *Proceedings of the Royal Society of Edinburgh* **97B**, 155–168.

Seto, K.C., Kaufmann, R.K. and Woodcock, C.E. 2000. Landsat reveals China's farmland reserves, but they're vanishing fast. *Nature* **406**, 121.

Shah, M., Banerji, D., Vijayshankar, P.S. and Ambaster, P. 1998. *India's Drylands: Tribal Societies and Development through Environmental Regeneration*. Oxford University Press, Oxford.

Sharer, R.J. 1994. *The Ancient Maya*, 5th edition. Stanford University Press, Stanford, California.

Shiklomanov, I.A. 1993. World fresh water resources. In: *Water in Crisis: A Guide to the World's Fresh Water Resources* (ed. P.H. Gleick), pp. 13–24. Oxford University Press, Oxford.

Simiyu, S.C., Gichangi, E.M., Simpson, J.R. and Jones, R.K. 1992. Rehabilitation of degraded grazing lands using the Kitumani pitting technique. In: *A Search for Strategies for Sustainable Dryland Cropping in Semi-Arid Eastern Kenya* (ed. M.E. Probert), pp. 83–87. ACIAR, Canberra.

Simmons, I.G. 1987. Transformation of the land in pre-industrial time. In: *Land Transformation in Agriculture* (eds. M.G. Wolman and F.G.A. Fournier), pp. 45–77. SCOPE No. 32. Wiley, Chichester.

Singh, S. 1997. *Taming the Waters: The Political Economy of Large Dams in India*. Oxford University Press, Oxford.

Singleton, P.W., Bohlool, B.B. and Nakao, P.L. 1992. Legume response to rhizobial inoculation in the tropics: myths and realities. In: *Myths and Science of Soils in the Tropics* (eds. R. Lal and P.A. Sanchez), pp. 135–155. SSSA Special Publication No. 29. Soil Science Society of America, Madison, Wisconsin.

Sivakumar, M.V.K. and Wills, J.B. (eds.) 1995. *Combating Land Degradation in Sub-Saharan Africa*. International Crop Research Institute for the Semi-Arid Tropics, Patancheru 502324, Andhra Pradesh.

Skidmore, E.L. 1988. Wind erosion. In: *Soil Erosion Research Methods* (ed. R. Lal), pp. 203–233. Soil and Water Conservation Society, Ankeny, Iowa.

Skinner, R.J. and Todd, A.D. 1988. Twenty-five years of monitoring pH and nutrient status of soils in England and Wales. *Soil Use and Management* **14**, 162–169.

Skipper, H.D. and Turco, R.F. (eds.) 1995. *Bioremediation: Science and Applications*. SSSA Special Publication No. 43. Soil Science Society of America, Madison, Wisconsin.

Slicher van Bath, B.H. 1963. *The Agrarian History of Western Europe A.D. 500–1850*. Arnold, London.

Smaling, E.M.A., Nandwa, S.M. and Janssen, B.H. 1997. Soil fertility in Africa is at stake. In: *Replenishing Soil Fertility in Africa* (eds. R.J. Buresh, P.A. Sanchez and F. Calhoun), pp. 47–61. SSSA Special Publication No. 51. Soil Science Society of America, Madison, Wisconsin.

Smartt, J. and Simmonds, N.W. (eds.) 1995. *Evolution of Crop Plants*, 2nd edition. Longman, Harlow.

Smith, B.D. 1992. Prehistoric plant husbandry in eastern North America. In: *The Origins of Agriculture: An International Perspective* (eds. C.W. Cowan and P.J. Watson), pp. 101–119. Smithsonian Institute Press, Washington, DC.

Smith, K.A., McTaggart, I.P. and Tsuruta, H. 1997. Emissions of N_2O and NO associated with nitrogen fertilization in intensive agriculture, and the potential for mitigation. *Soil Use and Management* **13**, 296–304.

Smith, R.E. and Knisel, W.G. 1985. Summary of methodology in the CREAMS2 model. In: *Proceedings of Natural Resources Modeling Symposium, Pingree Park, Colorado* (ed. D.G. Decourcey). ARS 30, 33–66. USDA, Washington, DC. (From Hudson, 1995)

Smith, S.E. and Read, D.J. 1997. *Mycorrhizal Symbiosis*. Academic Press, San Diego, California.

Smyth, A.J. and Dumanski, J. 1993. *FESLM: An International Framework for Evaluating Sustainable Land Management*. World Soil Resources Report No. 73. FAO, Rome.

Smyth, T.J. and Cassel, D.K. 1995. Synthesis of long-term soil management research on ultisols and oxisols in the Amazon. In: *Soil Management: Experimental Basis for Sustainability and Environmental Quality* (eds. R. Lal and B.A. Stewart), pp. 13–60. CRC Press, Lewis Publishers, Boca Raton, Florida.

Soane, B.D. and Ouwerkerk, C. (eds.) 1994. *Soil Compaction in World Agriculture*. Elsevier, Amsterdam.

Soil Survey Staff 1975. *Soil Taxonomy: A Basic System of Soil Classification for Making and Interpreting Soil Surveys*. USDA Agricultural Handbook No. 436. United States Department of Agriculture, Washington, DC.

Sprent, J.I. and Sprent, P. 1990. *Nitrogen Fixing Organisms. Pure and Applied Aspects*. Chapman and Hall, London.

Stafford, J.V. (ed.) 1997, 1999. *Precision Agriculture*, Vols. I and II. BIOS Scientific Publishers Ltd, Oxford.

Stahl, A.B. 1984. A history and critique of investigations into early African agriculture. In: *From Hunters to Farmers* (eds. J.D. Clark and S.A. Brandt), pp. 9–21. University of California Press, Berkeley, California.

Stanhill, G. 1986. Irrigation in arid lands. *Philosophical Transactions of the Royal Society of London* **A316**, 261–273.

Stanley, D.J. and Warne, A.G. 1993a. Nile Delta: recent geological evolution and human impact. *Science* **260**, 628–634.

Stanley, D.J. and Warne, A.G. 1993b. Sea level and initiation of Predynastic culture in the Nile Valley. *Nature, London* **363**, 435–438.

Stevenson, F.J. and Cole, M.A. 1999. *Cycles of Soil. Carbon, Nitrogen, Phosphorus, Sulfur and Micronutrients*, 2nd edition. Wiley, New York.

Stewart, B.A. and Nielsen, D.R. (eds.) 1990. *Irrigation of Agricultural Crops*. American Society of Agronomy, Madison, Wisconsin.

Stoddard, J.L., Jeffries, D.S., Lükeville, A. *et al.* 1999. Regional trends in aquatic recovery from acidification in North America and Europe. *Nature, London* **401**, 575–578.

Sumner, M.E. (ed.) 2000. *Handbook of Soil Science*. CRC Press, Boca Raton, Florida.

Syers, J.K. 1997. Managing soils for long-term productivity. *Philosophical Transactions of the Royal Society of London* **B352**, 1011–1021.

Syers, J.K. and Rimmer, D.L. (eds.) 1994. *Soil Science and Sustainable Land Management in the Tropics*. CAB International, Wallingford.

Tapia, E.M. de 1992. The origins of agriculture in Mesoamerica and Central America. In: *The Origins of Agriculture: An International Perspective* (eds. C.W. Cowan and P.J. Watson), pp. 143–171. Smithsonian Institute Press, Washington, DC.

Te-Tzu-Chang 1976. The rice cultures. *Philosophical Transactions of the Royal Society of London* **B275**, 143–157.

Thomas, D.S.G. and Middleton, N.J. 1994. *Desertification: Exploding the Myth.* Wiley, Chichester.

Tiffen, M., Mortimore, M. and Gichuki, F. 1994. *More People, Less Erosion: Environmental Recovery in Kenya.* Wiley, Chichester.

Tinker, P.B. 1997. The environmental implications of intensified land use in developing countries. *Philosophical Transactions of the Royal Society of London* **B352**, 1023–1033.

Tinker, P.B. and Nye, P.H. 2000. *Solute Movement in the Rhizosphere.* Oxford University Press, Oxford.

Tothill, J.D. (ed.) 1948. *Agriculture in the Sudan.* Oxford University Press, Oxford.

Trewavas, A. 1999. Much food, many problems. *Nature, London* **402**, 231–232.

Trigger, B.G., Kemp, B.J., O'Connor, D. and Lloyd, A.B. 1983. *Ancient Egypt: A Social History.* Cambridge University Press, Cambridge.

Troeh, F.R., Hobbs, J.A. and Donahue, R.L. 1999. *Soil and Water Conservation: Productivity and Environmental Protection,* 3rd edition. Prentice-Hall, Inc., Englewood Cliffs, New Jersey.

Tucker, C.J., Dregne, H.E. and Newcomb, W.W. 1991. Expansion and contraction of the Sahara Desert from 1980 to 1990. *Science* **253**, 299–301.

Turner, B.L. and Haygarth, P.M. 2001. Phosphorus solubilization in rewetted soils. *Nature, London* **411**, 258.

Umali, D.L. 1993. *Irrigation-Induced Salinity.* World Bank Technical Paper No. 215. World Bank, Washington, DC.

United Nations 1999. *World Population Prospects. The 1998 Revision.* United Nations, New York.

USDA 1974. Summer fallow in the central Great Plains. In: *Summer Fallow in the Western United States.* USDA Conservation Research Report No. 17. United States Department of Agriculture, Washington, DC.

USDA 1996. *Keys to Soil Taxonomy,* 7th edition. USDA Natural Resources Conservation Service, Washington, DC.

Van Breemen, N., van Grinsven, J.J.M. and de Vries, W. 1996. Effects of atmospheric deposition on soil and groundwater. In: *Soil Pollution and Soil Protection* (eds. F.A.M. de Haan and M.I. Visser-Reyneveld), pp. 239–259. International Training Centre, Wageningen Agricultural University, Wageningen.

Vincent, J.R. and Hadi, Y. 1993. Malaysia. In: *Sustainable Agriculture and the Environment in the Humid Tropics* (National Research Counci). National Academy Press, Washington, DC.

Vlek, P.L.G., Kühne, R.F. and Denich, M. 1997. Nutrient resources for crop production in the tropics. *Philosophical Transactions of the Royal Society of London* **B352**, 975–985.

Wahbi, A., Mazid, A. and Jones, M.J. 1994. An example of the farming systems approach: the fertilization of barley in farmer and researcher managed trials in northern Syria. *Experimental Agriculture* **30**, 171–176.

Wallace, J.S. and Batchelor, C.H. 1997. Managing water resources for crop production. *Philosophical Transactions of the Royal Society of London* **B352**, 937–947.

Walling, D.E. 1988. Measuring sediment yield from river basins. In: *Soil Erosion Research Methods* (ed. R. Lal), pp. 39–73. Soil and Water Conservation Society, Ankeny, Iowa.

Walling, D.E. and Quine, T.A. 1990. Use of caesium-137 to investigate patterns and rates of soil erosion on arable fields. In: *Soil Erosion on Agricultural Land* (eds. J. Boardman, I.D.L. Foster and J.A. Dearing), pp. 33–53. Wiley, Chichester.

Wallis, J.A.N. 1997. Brazil: the Cerrados Region. In: *Intensified Systems of Farming in the Tropics and Subtropics*, pp. 85–103. World Bank Discussion Paper No. 364. World Bank, Washington, DC.

Walsh, L.M. and Beaton, J.D. (eds.) 1973. *Soil Testing and Plant Analysis*. Soil Science Society of America, Madison, Wisconsin.

Walter, H. 1985. *Vegetation of the Earth and Ecological Systems of the Geo-Biosphere* (translated from the 5th German edition by O. Muise). Springer-Verlag, Berlin.

Warington, R. 1900. *Lectures on some of the Physical Properties of Soil*. Clarendon Press, Oxford.

Waterlow, J.C. 1998. Needs for food: are we asking too much? In: *Feeding a World Population of More Than Eight Billion People* (eds. J.C. Waterlow, D.G. Armstrong *et al.*), pp. 3–18. Oxford University Press, Oxford.

Watrud, L.S. and Seidler, R.J. 1998. Nontarget ecological effects of plant, microbial, and chemical introductions to terrestrial systems. In: *Soil Chemistry and Ecosystem Health* (ed. P.M. Huang), pp. 313–340. SSSA Special Publication No. 52. Soil Science Society of America, Madison, Wisconsin.

Watson, A.M. 1995. Arab and European agriculture in the Middle Ages: a case of restricted diffusion. In: *Agriculture in the Middle Ages* (ed. D. Sweeney), pp. 62–75. University of Pennsylvania Press, Philadelphia, Pennsylvania.

Webster, R. 1997. Soil resources and their assessment. *Philosophical Transactions of the Royal Society of London* **B352**, 963–973.

Weiss, H., Courty, M.-A. and Wetterstrom, W. 1993. The genesis and collapse of third millennium north Mesopotamian civilization. *Science* **261**, 995–1104.

Wen Dazhong 1993. Soil erosion and conservation in China. In: *World Soil Erosion and Conservation* (ed. D. Pimental), pp. 63–85. Cambridge University Press, Cambridge.

Wenhua, L. (ed.) 2000. *Agro-Ecological Farming Systems in China*. UNESCO, Paris.

White, H. 1970. Fallowing, crop rotation and crop yields in Roman times. *Agricultural History* **44**, 281–290.

White, K.D. 1967. *Agricultural Implements of the Roman World*. Cambridge University Press, Cambridge.

White, R.E. 1997. *Principles and Practice of Soil Science*, 3rd edition. Blackwell Science, Oxford.

Wild, A. (ed.) 1988. *Russell's Soil Conditions and Plant Growth*, 11th edition. Longman, Harlow.

Wild, A. 1993. *Soils and the Environment: An Introduction*. Cambridge University Press, Cambridge.

Wild, A. and Jones, L.H.P. 1988. Mineral nutrition of crop plants. In: *Russell's Soil Conditions and Plant Growth* (ed. A. Wild), pp. 69–112. Longman, Harlow.

Williams, J.F. 1981. Toward a model of land reclamation/resettlement. In: *The Environment: Chinese and American Views* (eds. L.J.C. Ma and A.G. Noble), pp. 73–90. Methuen, London.

Williamson, H.F. 1963. Soils of the Planalto of Brazil. In: *Survey of the Agricultural Potential of the Central Plateau of Brazil*. USAID Contract 12–120. AIA, Rio de Janeiro. (From Goedert, 1983)

Wilson, S.J. and Cooke, R.U. 1980. Wind erosion. In: *Soil Erosion* (eds. M.J. Kirkby and R.P.C. Morgan), pp. 217–251. Wiley, Chichester.

Wischmeier, W.H. and Smith, D.D. 1978. *Predicting Rainfall Erosion Losses*. USDA Agricultural Handbook No. 537 and Supplement 1981. United States Department of Agriculture, Washington, DC.

Wong, M.T.F., Hughes, R. and Rowell, D.L. 1990. Retarded leaching of nitrate in acid soils from the tropics: measurement of the effective anion exchange capacity. *Journal of Soil Science* **41**, 655–663.

Wood, A. 1950. *The Groundnut Affair*. Bodley Head, London.

Woomer, P.L. and Swift, M.J. (eds.) 1994. *The Biological Management of Tropical Soil Fertility*. Wiley, Chichester.

World Commission on Environment and Development 1987. *Our Common Future*. Oxford University Press, Oxford.

Wright, H.E., Jr, Kutzbach, J.E., Webb, T., III, Ruddiman, W.E., Street-Perrott, F.A. and Bartlein, P.J. (eds.) 1993. *Global Climates since the Last Glacial Maximum*. University of Minnesota Press, Minneapolis, Minnesota.

Wrigley, E.A. and Schofield, R.S. 1981. *The Population History of England 1541–1871: A Reconstruction*. Arnold, London.

Xu Guohua 1991. Summary and conclusions: the characteristics and problems of Chinese agriculture and prospects for the future. In: *The Agriculture of China* (eds. Xu Guohua and L.J. Peel), pp. 255–262. Oxford University Press, Oxford.

Young, A. 1997. *Agroforestry for Soil Management*, 2nd edition. CAB International, Wallingford.

Young, A. 1998. *Land Resources Now and for the Future*. Cambridge University Press, Cambridge.

Zimmerer, K.S. 1995. The origins of Andean irrigation. *Nature, London* **378**, 481–483.

Zohary, D. 1996. The mode of domestication of the founder crops of southwest Asian agriculture. In: *The Origins and Spread of Agriculture and Pastoralism in Eurasia* (ed. D.R. Harris), pp. 142–158. University College Press, London.

Index